THE ADRENALINE JUNKIE'S BUCKET LIST

Mountain Rescue Doctor: Wilderness Medicine in
the Extremes of Nature

Backcountry Ski and Snowboard Routes: Oregon

Introducing Your Kids to the Outdoors

Watersports Safety and Emergency First Aid:
A Handbook for Boaters, Anglers, Kayakers,
River Runners, and Surfriders

Emergency Survival: A Pocket Guide

Emergency First Aid: A Pocket Guide

Backcountry Ski Oregon: Classic Descents for
Skiers and Snowboarders, Including
Southwest Washington

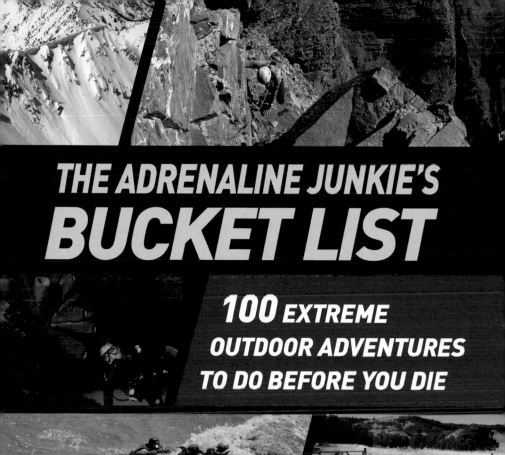

THE ADRENALINE JUNKIE'S
BUCKET LIST

100 EXTREME OUTDOOR ADVENTURES TO DO BEFORE YOU DIE

CHRISTOPHER VAN TILBURG, M.D.

in's Griffin ✹ New York

www.stmartins.com

LIBRARY OF CONGRESS CATALOGING-IN-PUBLICATION PATA

Van Tilburg, Christopher.
The adrenaline junkie's bucket list : 100 extreme outdoor adventures to do before you die / Christopher Van Tilburg.
    p. cm.
  ISBN 978-1-250-02018-5 (trade paperback)
  ISBN 978-1-250-02019-2 (e-book)
  1. Extreme sports. 2. Outdoor recreation. I. Title.
  GV749.7.V36 2013
  796.04'6—dc23

                                          2013003224

St. Martin's Griffin books may be purchased for educational, business, or promotional use. For information on bulk purchases, please contact Macmillan Corporate and Premium Sales Department at 1-800-221-7945 extension 5442 or write specialmarkets@Macmillan.com.

    Book design by Patrice Sheridan
    Maps by Paul J. Pugliese
    First Edition: July 2013
    10 9 8 7 6 5 4 3 2 1

All photos Copyright © Christopher Van Tilburg except the following: David Mackintosh: p. III, 27, 41, 45, 48, 61, 260; Clint Bogard: III, 5, 32, 43, 157; Jen FitzSimons: 52; Caleb Wray Photography: II, III, 56, 59, 64, 71, 94, 97, 180, 187, 192; AJ Wheeler: 69, 141; Big Mountain Adventures www.ridebig.com: 77; World Triathlon Corporation: 29, 99, 101; Andrew McElderry: III, XIV, 99, 109, 112, 121, 143, 163, 235; Clark Bradley Merritt–SoloSports Adventure Holidays: IV, 114, 139; Costa Rica Tourism Board: IV, 119; Sheryl Olson: XI, 5, 125,137, 143, 167, 173, 189; Jennifer Donnelly: 155, 175, 179; Quark Expeditions: V, 165, 223, 227; Viki Tracey: 1, 168; Marc Goddard Bio Bio Expeditions: X, XI, 171, 177, 182, 191, 199; Luanne Freer Everest ER: 141, 171, 183; Ruth Berkowitz: 187, 194, 201, 209, 216, 242; Surf Simply: X, 196; Gergo Szanyi Tour d'Afrique: 197; Totally Tourism New Zealand: 207; John Inglis: 211; Ryan Heath G-Land Surf Camp: 213, 215; Jason Edwards: 218; Michael Hamill: V, 220, 223, 225: Jenni Bergemann: 245, 257; Doug Tompkins, Conservacion Patagonica: 245, 258, 263.

CONTENTS

SOUTH AMERICA   125

EUROPE   145

DISCLAIMER

Adventure sports, outdoor recreation, and wilderness travel are dangerous. It's way safer to watch TV. When you put yourself out there, you could die or become disabled. Or, you might become so addicted to adventure that you sell your house, buy a used car, and quit your corporate job. Either way, neither the author not the publisher accept responsibility for any harm resulting from your pursuit of the adrenaline junkie's bucket list. Instead of a hot tub, boat, or RV, you may end up with a garage full of high-tech surfboards, skis, kayaks, and sharp, pointy objects like crampons, ice axes, and ice screws. You may find yourself traveling into lands so austere that you sometimes wish you were home. In fact, plan on spending many weekends in the same set of clothes, with no chance of a shower. You could also find yourself in grave peril. So be warned.

This book is meant for general information and entertainment only. It is not a substitute for formal education and training; a guide; or knowledge and experience in varied climates, weather conditions, and terrains of the world. Hire a guide, use proper equipment, and stay within your skill level. Have fun, but be safe.

TRUTH IS, I actually almost died.

I, mountain rescue doctor—accustomed to scaling mountains and descending slot canyons to save the lives of hikers, climbers, and skiers—almost died. On *my* mountain, no less: the gargantuan peak that dominates my writings, my work, my adventures, and my life—Oregon's legendary, lethal Mount Hood.

And, of course, I was skiing.

When a person has a near-death experience, he usually reevaluates his life. You might ask: *Am I spending enough time with loved ones? Am I taking all the trips I've longed for? Am I working too hard? Am I in good shape? Do I live well and prosper?*

Not me.

I did no world-shifting reevaluation, nor did I have a grand revelation. I recovered from my accident, and then followed through with pre-accident travel plans: I embarked on a medical mission to Haiti, a family ski trip to Canada, and a physician-education trip to Peru. When a family ski trip to Chile started brewing, I burned vacation days, and some of my savings, to join in. After all, I had almost died. Adventure travel and outdoor sports are a part of my soul—and I've never been one to wait for "someday" to seek out adventure. *Someday* is yesterday. Today and tomorrow are for me.

As a kid, I traveled extensively with my parents around the world, and by the time I finished college and medical school adventuring was an essential part of my life. Sometimes, during my surgical rotation, I'd skip noon conference to go for a run on the ravines of Seattle. Staying in shape, in any way possible, is a fundamental component of the adrenaline junkie's life. Later, I took the slow boat to my education: I lived in Europe for a year; spent summers wind-surfing and tending bar in the mountain-sport town of Hood River, Oregon; skied in Canada and Europe; windsurfed and surfed the Baja; and made a 4-month circumnavigation of the globe—all patched in and around college, medical school, and residency. Eventually, I began writing books on outdoor sports and adventure travel, alongside my career in wilderness, emergency, and travel medicine.

Now, I wear many hats. I'm a father, author, doctor, writer, and educator. But the persona that runs most deeply in my bones, the one that drives me more than anything else, is the sport and travel junkie. Indeed, it's a daily obsession to run, bike, ski, climb, surf, or sail. On my lunch break you won't find me sitting, but running or mountain biking the single-track dirt trail a mile from my clinic. At any given time, I have a half-dozen trips in various stages of planning, at least 2 of them overseas. My daughters have swum in the Vermilion Sea of Baja, snorkeled the South Pacific, and skied in the Andes. I have traveled as a guide, physician, and edu-cator in more than 50 countries. But it's not without hard work, focus, and sacrifice.

After publishing *Mountain Rescue Doctor: Wilderness Medicine in the Extremes of Nature* (St. Martin's, 2007) and my accident, I was on the hunt for another project. I went to work on 5 still-unpub-lished manuscripts. The book I eventually published was a revised edition of a tattered 1998 niche guidebook, *Backcountry Ski and Snowboard Routes: Oregon*. Guidebooks provide little money and demand lots of hard work, but the research is pure, unfiltered ad-venture.

In revising that book, I dug out my log of all my great ski trips in the Pacific Northwest, as well as the yet-to-do list. The latter ranged from dainty trails like the beginner Glade Trail on Mount Hood to big mountain lines like the formidable Glacier Peak in the North Cascades of Washington. Amid the book's revision, and en route home from the family ski trip to Portillo, Chile, it hit me. I needed another list! Not just a ski mountaineering list, but one that encompassed the whole world and all my adventures. So I made one, right there, in the airport.

And therein lies the story behind what you are now holding: *The Adrenaline Junkie's Bucket List*. These are the best trips that I've collected from 4½ decades of living the true adventuring life. It's my list, and I haven't finished it yet, but feel free to cross off a few and add your own.

Adventure travel is not unlike that of a writer. Months of planning, hard work, and diligence are sometimes coupled with immense, thrilling, unbelievable joy and adrenaline; other times, rain, snow, family duties, lost luggage, or delayed flights yielding massive frustration. One thing is certain: If you're an adventurer, you need to go adventure. You *have to* make it happen.

If you grabbed this book, you may be a lifelong, obsessed junkie like me, or, *au contraire*, you may just be breaking out of the work-a-day mold. So peruse these trips, dog-ear a handful of your favorites, and then pick one. Block off time, burn some savings, and book a ticket. Forget the boat, hot tub, new car, and RV. Forget the big-screen home theater. Forget the fancy dinner and a show. Make your next dinner out at a pub in Whistler, British Columbia; a street-side café in Chamonix in the French Alps; or a back-road bar in Queenstown, New Zealand.

Go now. Don't wait. Don't push pause. You won't be sorry.

Christopher Van Tilburg, M.D.
Chamonix, France
March 2012

THE SCOOP ON THIS BOOK

IMAGINE KAYAKING the churning whitewater of Africa's Zambezi River or surfing Fiji's legendary Cloudbreak. Envision trekking New Zealand's famed Milford Track through the lush, green fjords or trail running and mountain biking Copper Canyon, Mexico. When was the last time you felt the wind whip your face on the slopes, or the spray off the rapids shower your arms? What are you waiting for? To recall Warren Miller, an icon of adventure skiing, "If you don't do it this year, you'll be one year older when you do."

With hundreds of tours, outfitters, and guides available, it's hard to sort out which dream trip to book. That's why I've put together 100 outdoor adventures of a lifetime, the quintessential *bucket list* for adrenaline junkies, athletes, outdoor enthusiasts, adventure travelers, and thrill seekers. These are the most fabulous voyages on earth. Many you will recognize. A few are obscure. Some will surprise you. And a handful are near and dear to me. Whatever the case, they are all mouthwatering adventures.

This book covers the full spectrum of water and mountain sports, on all seven continents, for all skill levels—from beginner to expert. You don't have to be an uber-fit, uber-weathly professional athlete to jump on these trips. Most are perfectly feasible for the average adventure traveler with 2 weeks to spare. For instance, crossing the South Pole on skis takes months of preparation and hardship. As an alternative, I describe a week of backcountry skiing and wildlife viewing in Antarctica. Instead focusing on singular activities, like "swimming with sharks," I give you spots to dive shipwrecks and reefs all over the Caribbean. I selected these trips for fabulous scenery, unique geography, a *scosh* of cultural heritage, and ample ópportunities for sport and activity.

If water is your nirvana, peruse the best diving, snorkeling, sea kayaking, surfing, windsurfing, kitesurfing, and sailing trips. For mountain junkies, pick from rock climbing, traditional mountaineering, skiing, and snowboarding. If you prefer a simpler tour, there are plenty of trail runs, mountain bike rides, hikes, and treks to jack your heart rate into the triple digits.

On all of these trips, you will be in motion. I do highlight the occasional market, museum, or city tour—culture transitions through urban jungles are a fascinating component of adventure travel. But for the most part, these trips keep you on the move.

Some are centered on plentiful locations, focal points for a multitude of activities like the Galápagos, Costa Rica, Chamonix, Whistler, or Queenstown. Others focus on very specific goals like climbing summits, running marathons, rock or ice climbing, and finishing triathlons.

Most of these trips can be done in a few weeks. Let's face it, we don't all have the ability to take 1 month or 2 off to kayak in Greece or sail the Caribbean. Most of us are not professional skiers or river guides. Not many of us can take 3 months off to traverse a continent, climb a Himalayan peak, or circumnavigate a country. I did, however, include a few longer "dream" trips in this volume. Maybe you are between jobs, receive a severance check, or have taken a sabbatical. The Seven Summits are classic. Long-distance hikes are epic. Transcontinental cycling, some of the most grueling trips on this list, are worthy of a dream.

Then there's the question of skill level. Be assured that all of these trips are viable if you are proficient at the sport described. You don't have to be a world-class athlete to climb El Cap, surf Fiji, or ski the Haute Route, but you do have to be proficient at climbing, surfing, or skiing respectively, so most of these trips are not recommended for absolute beginners. For others, like kayaking Tofino, surfing Costa Rica, diving the Caribbean, or trekking any of the numerous trails, you can take lessons, hire a guide, and head out in safe conditions.

So, should you go guided? That's one of the adrenaline junkie's big planning quandaries. Many of the more complicated trips are simply best done with a guide. For some, like hiking the Inca Trail or climbing Mount Kilimanjaro, guides are required. But for most, if you are an experienced adventure traveler and you have the time, patience, and skill to plan, you can do many of these on your own. Planning is part of the fun, as long as you are diligent and flexible. You also need to have sound wilderness and survival skills. So if you can't navigate every section of the Haute Route, the ski tour from France to Switzerland, in a whiteout or high avalanche danger, you ought to think seriously about hiring a guide. A guided trip can hit all the best highlights, ensure maximum success, ease planning, and increase safety. Guides are usually well-connected with locals, and knowledgeable about sports. And they're almost always personable— it's part of their job. So think about a guide. It may cost a bit more, but it may also be the best road to success, safety, and satisfaction.

That brings me to volunteerism. I grew up in a culture of volunteering, both in my community and around the world. I have traveled to both Ecuador and Haiti on medical relief missions and have stayed in the homes of kind strangers-turned friends around the world. Adventure travel can be a great way to couple outdoor activity with the chance to help people all over the world. Volunteering is, in fact, a key part of our existence as adventurers. I've listed a few opportunities to augment your travel with a touch of altruism, such as teaching, providing medical relief, building homes, working in national parks, aiding conservation, and assisting with scientific research.

I'm also a big advocate of education. So in the "Toolbox" section, I spell out the vital components of an adrenaline junkie's schooling. Don't hesitate to take a class! It will only boost your skill level and teach you how to be a safer adventurer.

So how exactly does this book work? For each adventure, I've described basic information about the trip and activity. I've included key components in *Don't Miss*, and basic travel and guide information in *Logistics* and *Best Time*. You'll certainly want to gather more specific details from guidebooks, the Internet, resort materials, and regional guides. I added in Web links for one or two guides. If you are short on time or tacking an expedition onto a business or family trip, check out the **Pit Stop** section. If you have the luxury of *mucho* time and *cashola,* check out **Extended Play**. In **Travel Smart**, I put in a few key reminders for sport or region specific safety. It's not totally comprehensive, but these are good reminders. Finally, and this is my most important instruction, peruse the trips, find one, and book it. Go, do, now. Don't wait for tomorrow.

WORLD TRAVEL is rarely simple and smooth. Often, it's downright hard work. It's that hard work that drives some travelers. The uncertainty and surprise detours can be part of the adventure. Others, who have saved vacation time and money for a trip, usually want their plans to fall in line. I'm in the latter camp. I don't really thrive when my flight is delayed, when I'm stuck in an airport, when I need to find a rental car or hotel at the last minute, or when I'm lugging bags of ski or surf equipment across town.

When I was a young traveler, flexibility was pounded into my brain. Now, when toting my family and friends around the world, I leave less to chance. So here is cheat sheet on preparing for your grand adventure. For travel in your home country, or even your home continent, you may not need everything on this list.

PASSPORT AND VISAS

Before you go, make sure you have a valid passport and that the expiration is dated at least 6 months beyond your time of return. Always carry a photocopy of the data page in your pack in case you lose your passport. If you are a solo parent traveling with a child, make sure you have a notarized permission note from the non-traveling parent, whether you are married or not. You should also check to see if you need a visa or entrance permit for the country to which you are traveling. Some visas or tourist cards can be obtained at the airport when you land, but others you need to secure months before you travel. Educate yourself about these details well in advance.

MONEY

Nowadays, you need 3 types of funds: cash, a debit card, and a credit card. Traveler's checks are largely a thing of the past and personal checks are pretty much useless overseas. Cash is usually easy to exchange for local currency at the airport when you arrive, although you can also change money before you leave home. Consider taking a wad of small bills for taxis, tips, and trinkets—the vendors in many countries accept U.S. dollars. If you are traveling to a country where credit cards are not dependable, bring enough cash for daily expenses and emergencies. I stash at least $500 in emergency funds for a 2-week trip overseas.

I also carry a primary credit card with a low credit limit for hotels, tickets, and meals. That way if it's stolen, thieves can only charge up to a few thousand dollars. And you can get a cash advance from your credit card in a crisis. Sometimes I carry a back-up credit card with a larger balance for emergencies. In many cities around the world, debit cards can be used at ATMs, but I usually don't bring mine because credit cards are more secure.

GUIDEBOOKS

There are guidebooks available for almost every spot on the globe. Some are geared toward swanky hotels, bustling cities, and cultural attractions, while others focus on budget travel. I gravitate to the largest guidebook publisher, Lonely Planet (www.lonelyplanet.com), which focuses largely on budget travel and has a large sports section. Moon travel guides (www.moon.com) and Rough Guides (www.roughguides.com) are also geared toward active, budget travel. Guidebooks are useful for general planning, understanding cultural background, and scoping out hotels and restaurants. For grand trips, check out my favorite global guidebooks in Appendix B.

ESSENTIAL SKILLS

The adrenaline junkie needs some essential skills for navigating these adventures. Check the "Toolbox" section for a full list of key components to safe travel, but the following are a few vital points:

    a. Know how to spend the unexpected night outdoors in case you get lost, or experience foul weather or injury.

b. Learn to navigate with a map, compass, and GPS.

c. Study gear-repair basics. Know how to change a flat tire on a bike, repair a raft, and fix a broken ski pole, paddle, and ski binding.

d. Learn body-repair basics. Take a CPR and first aid course via the American Heart Association (www.heart.org) or American Red Cross (www.redcross.org). Learn how to make a basic splint, bandage a wound, and dress blisters.

e. Take precautions to prevent injury. Educate yourself about fending off weather-related injuries like frostbite, hypothermia, heat exhaustion, heatstroke, and altitude sickness. Guard against sunburn and pesky insects.

f. Know how to navigate the cities, airports, and train stations of the world without standing out like a tourist.

STAY IN SHAPE

Adrenaline-infused sports require you to stay in shape. Fitness is a key component for safe and successful adventures. We all know that, but how do we make time for staying in shape? You need cardiovascular, strength, flexibility, and endurance fitness. I try to bike, run, and walk every day, or at least attempt to do so every day. I often squeeze a run or ride in during lunch or after work. Many days I loathe changing into my running clothes when it's raining and I'm tight on time, but I've never regretted it once my shoes hit the trail.

Get rain gear. I live in the Pacific Northwest and liquid sunshine is rarely an excuse to miss a run. Bike commute. Swim at your local pool on your lunch break. Join a gym. Get an indoor bike trainer. Or join a local biking or running team. Group workouts are both a great motivation and fun.

In addition to the daily regimen, try to get in at least 1 or 2 long workouts in every week: a long trail run, a burly bike ride, an extended hike at a brisk pace, or a high-intensity ski tour.

However you make it happen, you don't want to jump on these trips without being ready. And don't forget to check in with your doc before starting or changing a workout routine.

THE TRAVEL CLINIC VISIT

For overseas travel, there's a good chance you'll need shots to cover you for hepatitis, typhoid, rabies, and even yellow fever. In some countries, yellow fever protection is required for entrance. It's also a good idea to discuss malaria medication and emergency antibiotics for travelers' diarrhea and other infections. Some vaccines require a series, so visit a clinic at least 3 months before your trip. Before you go, peruse the CDC travel Web site (www.cdc.gov/travel).

INSURANCE

Insurance seems like a waste of money—until you really need it. For travel and sport, some policies are essential, and others are optional. Buying insurance is a risk/benefit consideration that you need to weigh, but it can save you money in an emergency.

First, check to see if your regular health insurance covers you for overseas travel. If not, you may be able to get a supplemental policy.

Second, consider travel insurance. Depending on the policy, it can cover you for trip cancellation (pay attention to restrictions), overseas healthcare, emergency evacuation, search and rescue, and lost luggage. You may need to get an extra rider for adventure sports like climbing and skiing. Travel insurance is usually relatively inexpensive compared to the cost of a guided trip and airfare.

In addition to travel insurance, you may need separate rescue insurance for some activities and locales, such as climbing the Himalayas or skiing and climbing in some areas of Europe. In some places, the European Alps in particular, if you need to be rescued by helicopter or search and rescue personnel, you may have to provide either proof of insurance or a credit card at the scene of your injury. Rescue personnel may not be volunteers, but rather military or private contractors.

Members of the American Alpine Club have limited worldwide rescue coverage (americanalpineclub.org). In Switzerland, you can get a membership to Rega (Swiss Air-Rescue) for $30/year (www .rega.ch), which may waive rescue costs under certain circumstances in the Swiss Alps. In France, you can purchase rescue insurance per day when you purchase a lift ticket.

For medical evacuation, you can buy insurance from companies like International SOS (www.internationalsos.com), which provides medical assistance, evacuation, and security on a global scale.

GETTING HELP ABROAD

Let's hope you never need it. But if you do, it's nice to be prepared. In case you need to exit a country quickly, bring cash, consulate information, and airport transportation info. If you're in an isolated region, like the Canadian backcountry, know how to navigate to the closest populated area and contact help via a radio or cell phone if someone in your group has an injury or the weather turns foul.

Before you travel overseas, visit the State Department Web site (travel.state.gov) to view travel advisories and print out contact information for consulates and embassies. The Web site also provides information on getting help in both medical and nonmedical emergencies.

Contact International Association for Medical Assistance to Travellers (www.iamat.org) for in-country medical facilities. You might also want to check for local bureaus of the American Express or American Automobile Association if you are a member of those organizations.

TELECOMMUNICATION

Gone are the days when we traveled and sent postcards home weekly. Now, we stay connected. It is part of the adrenaline junkie's life: Facebook posts from Indo, digital images from the Andes, text messages from the Alps, phone calls from the Himalayas.

Because I travel frequently, I usually work in airports and on airplanes and need to stay connected. Thus, I take telecommunication devices on most trips.

We can do a lot with a smartphone: check e-mail, text, send images. I often just get an international text plan to send messages home. For e-mails and phones calls, I usually stick with free wireless and Skype. *Hint:* Turn off data roaming and disable the function that pushes e-mails to your phone.

For computing, I take a mini notebook computer, to keep up on e-mails and store images, and to work on writing and consulting projects. A tablet may work, too.

PACKING

Packing for adventure is part of the fun. But it can also be a pain if you don't do it often. I always try to pack light—and I must emphasize, *always*. I can pack for a weeklong trip in carry-on bags, including a sleeping bag. Not only does it save fees, packing light makes it much easier to cart your gear around airports and train stations.

FOOTWEAR

Shoes take up space, so go simple. After seeing porters climb the entire Inca Trail in sandals made from old tires, Western footwear seems overrated.

I take running shoes on every trip. They are great for cruising the town or for a run or hike. Trail running shoes don't have quite the support of boots, but they are super versatile, take up less space and weight, and are quick to dry. If I go on a substantial trek, I consider an ankle-high lightweight hiker. Lightweight boots are my travel shoe of choice, and I always bring a pair of flip-flops for funky showers, sitting around the campfires, and sunny afternoon strolls. Often I'll need specialty footwear, too, like ski or mountaineering boots (as below).

CLOTHING

Clothing has come a long way since my first trips as a kid when we wore cotton-poly blend and wafflestompers. Nowadays, synthetic quick-drying travel clothing is stylish and durable. I like cotton for travel and synthetic for the trail. Wool/synthetic blend socks are warmer, more durable, and dry more quickly than wool alone.

Outdoor clothing comes in 2 basic flavors: hot and cold. For warm weather, sun and bug protection is the goal. For foul weather, you need both insulation from cold and protection from rain, snow, sleet, and wind.

For shirts, I like casual, button-up collared shirts with a stealth zipper chest pocket to secure my passport, boarding passes, and cell phone when zipping through airports and cities. The zip pockets are also handy on the trail for stashing maps, sunglasses, and sunscreen. Long-sleeve, lightweight shirts are best for insect and sun protection. Having too many pockets, zippers, sleeve buttons, and amulets can make you stand out as a tourist. So go simple. *Hint:* Dress nice for airplanes; if you have a problem, you will be treated better. And avoid the flashy clothes and sunglasses when in transit so you don't stand out as a tourist.

For the sun, bring either a baseball cap with a bandana or a wide brim hat. Full sun hats are nice, but tend to draw attention. Hats are also a great local item to buy.

For pants, zip-off legs on convertible pants are excellent because one item functions as both shorts and pants. But since these aren't readily available in many parts of the world, they can put a target on your back for theft, scamming, or begging. Lightweight nylon pants in earth tones will also do the trick. You can roll them up when fording streams or when the sun comes out in the afternoon. And they fend off both sun and bugs.

CLOTHING FOR WARM WEATHER
Running shoes
Casual or hiking boots
Flip-flops
Cotton travel clothing: pants, button-up shirts, shorts
Cotton travel T shirts and underwear
Synthetic trail pants
Synthetic trail shorts
Synthetic trail T-shirts and underwear
Synthetic/wool-blend socks
Sun hat or cap
Midweight fleece
Lightweight rain jacket
Cocoon travel sack
Toilet kit with travel sizes of everything
Small travel towel
Personal kit as per below

For foul weather, bring layers and don't skimp. You can choose from many fabrics and natural fibers. Synthetics are still less expensive, more durable, easier to wash, and warmer when wet. Down works well in cold, dry climates, because it's light, but when down gets wet it loses all of its insulating properties. Merino wool, a fine, itchless fiber, works well, too, and doesn't retain odors like synthetics. But wool is not durable or light, and it's expensive and slow to dry. When weight and warmth count, take synthetics.

For cold weather trips, I usually wear a base layer, 2 or 3 insulating layers depending on what I'm doing, and take an outer weatherproof layer to fend off rain, snow, and wind.

For base layer tops I wear either silkweight T-shirts or long-sleeve, ¼-zip shirts; the long sleeve is warmer and the zip neck allows for better ventilation when you heat up. For bottoms, I take silkweight boxers, long underwear, or both. For an insulating layer, I like the light, compact midweight fleece, preferably one with a zipper chest pocket (for a phone and sunscreen) and a hood for an emergency hat.

If I go anywhere cold and/or damp, I take a puffy (a high-loft, nylon-encased jacket or vest with synthetic or down insulation). Choose one with PrimaLoft, the synthetic insulating fiber that's woven in sheets and is both warm and compressible. For cold temps, nothing beats the warmth, lightness, and compressibility of down, such as a down parka or down sweater. Either make an awesome pillow or emergency blanket in cold mountain huts or transcontinental airplane flights. Down works as long as it doesn't get wet.

I also rarely travel without a hardshell jacket, except for the tropics. For international trips I like low-key colors, except when I'm ski-mountaineering for visibility in foul weather.

CLOTHING FOR FOUL WEATHER
Running shoes
Trail or casual boots
Synthetic/wool-blend socks
Cotton travel clothing: pants and button-up shirts
Cotton travel T-shirts and boxers
Synthetic underwear
Synthetic long underwear tops and bottoms
Synthetic trail or mountain pants
1 or 2 light- or midweight fleece sweaters; 1 with a hood
Puffy PrimaLoft vest or jacket if cold and wet; down parka, if
    cold and dry

Lightweight nylon Gore-tex jacket and pants
Fleece hat
Lightweight gloves
Warm bulky gloves
Neck gaiter
Sleeping bag and pad
Toilet kit with travel sizes of everything
Small travel towel
Personal kit as noted below

ESSENTIALS

Take some kind of personal kit that combines first aid, survival, and personal items. The specific contents of this kit will depend on each trip. The list below shows the kit I take almost everywhere. I'll add additional gear for particular trips. On a ski mountaineering trip to Europe, I take ski-repair gear. I always take antibiotics, and, when in the tropics, malaria medicines. On big backcountry expeditions, I'll take a full medical and survival kit.

PERSONAL KIT
Small first aid kit

    First aid tape is most important (I like Johnson & Johnson waterproof tape)*

    Self-adhering elastic bandage like Coban or Co-Flex*

    Blister bandage like moleskin or Compeed pads*

    Wound closure strips with benzoin glue (aka butterfly bandages)

    Oral rehydration electrolytes packet

    Gloves and pocket CPR mask

Medicines

    Ibuprofen and Tylenol*

    Immodium*

    Pepto-Bismol*

    Diphenhydramine*

    Prescription medicine, as recommended by your doctor.

Miscellaneous

    Headlight with batteries like the Petzl Tikka*

    Map, compass, and GPS

Chemical heat packs*

Perlon cord for making an emergency shelter, clothesline, or gear tie-downs

Whistle

Multi-tool, usually something small like a SwissTool or a Leatherman Juice

Duct tape

Safety pins

Plastic cable ties for tying luggage zippers or gear repairs

Polyurethane straps for repairs and strapping gear onto a pack

Tarp

Personal

Hand sanitizer*

Travel wipes (like wet wipes)*

Sunscreen, at least SPF 25*

Insect repellent*

Water purification tablets, chlorine, or iodine*

Water bottle, 1 rigid and 1 collapsible (usually 1 liter each)*

Small notebook with pen

Silk or cotton travel sheet or mummy liner

Electronics

Mini notebook with charger

Cell phone with charger*

Digital camera with spare battery and memory card*

GPS receiver

Altimeter, barometer, compass watch*

Plug converter*

---

* A small kit with just these essentials can be useful.

SAFE TRAVEL is essential. And it's not that difficult. A few precautions, no matter where you are, will keep you healthy and happy, and above all, SAFE.

ACCIDENTS

No, it's not malaria or dengue fever or the Ebola virus. Motor vehicle accidents are the most likely cause of injury and death when traveling abroad. Riding an overfilled bus on a single-lane road through rural Haiti or Ecuador can be part of the adventure. But you should always exercise basic precautions. Wear a seatbelt, drive cautiously, and choose taxi drivers wisely. If you rent a motorized scooter, wear a helmet. If you have kids, bring car seats if appropriate.

SOL PATROL

The sun can be damaging, both long-term and short. One bad sunburn can ruin a trip, but worse, one bad sunburn can dramatically increase your risk of skin cancer. Always wear sunscreen that is hypoallergenic and protects against ultraviolet A and B rays. Thick cream stays on longer than sprays. Use SPF 15 at minimum (but there is no clear benefit to an SPF above 50). Most people don't apply enough sunscreen (SPF is measured at 2.2mg/cm^2 which is about half of what most people apply) so lather it on, thickly and frequently, at least every 2 hours when in direct sun.

Nowadays, sun-protective clothing, rated by Ultraviolet Protection Factor (UPF), is ubiquitous in travel stores and online suppliers. In recent years, UPF ratings are frequently included on all manner of outdoor clothing. Something with a UPF 30 rating blocks approximately 97 percent of UV light. Whether it's rated or not, all clothing acts as a physical block to sun's rays. A basic cotton T-shirt offers an SPF of 8 to 10. Clothing is superior to sunscreen because protection doesn't wear off.

And don't forget a wide-brim hat and sunglasses!

BUGS OFF

Dengue, malaria, and yellow fever! Oh, my! Insects are, for the most part, harmless. In many cultures these critters are dinner delicacies! But the bane of adventure travel is the ubiquitous and malicious mosquito. Mosquitoes carry the protozoa malaria and viruses such as dengue fever and yellow fever. Fortunately, if you follow these military-tested guidelines, you can reduce your chance of getting bitten to less than 0.1 percent and the risk of infection to almost nil.

Before you embark, visit a travel-medicine clinic and see if your destination poses a high risk of malaria or yellow fever. Consider a yellow fever vaccine, which is good for ten years; it is required to visit some countries. Proof of immunization is required to get in or out of a few countries and airlines may not let you board without proof, such as a certified yellow fever vaccination certificate. There are several medicines you can take to prevent malaria. It kills the microbe in your blood if you get infected. Unfortunately, there are no pills or vaccines for dengue fever, carried by day-biting mosquitoes.

For bug protection, wear long-sleeve shirts and long pants, especially during dawn and dusk. Before you leave home, spray clothing with permethrin, an effective insect and tick repellent derived from the chrysanthemum plant. Light cotton works best for hot desert or coastal climates; otherwise use nylon travel shirts and pants in the jungle and mountains. Look for insect-proof clothing that has permethrin embedded in the fibers.

Also, take a silk or cotton travel sheet or mummy liner. You can spray a travel-mummy liner with permethrin for added protection. That way, no matter where you sleep, you have your own private bug-proof bedding.

For exposed skin, use CDC-approved DEET (N,N-Diethyl-meta-toluamide) or picaridin insect repellant, especially for areas where clothing doesn't quite reach like the face, neck, wrists, and ankles. DEET combined with permethrin has been shown to be 99.9 percent effective in military troops, so it works! You don't need 100 percent jungle juice, 30 percent DEET is adequate.

Try to avoid the outdoors during dawn and dusk if mosquitoes are thick. Day-biting mosquitoes carry dengue, especially in dark, urban alleys with lots of standing water.

Air-conditioned rooms help ward off critters, too. Mosquito nets that cover beds are essential in the tropics. Check to see if your hotel or lodge has them. If not, bring your own compact kit. If camping, use a bug-proof tent. You can also treat it with permethrin or buy one pretreated.

Finally, when you get home, if you have any flu-like symptoms, especially a fever, check in with your doctor ASAP.

AGUA

Water is a precious commodity when traveling. Finding safe drinking water can be simple or an involved task. Bottled water has long been thought safe, but tests show that even bottled water in developed countries may contain germs. If bottled water is suspect, the safest source for hydration is carbonated water or beverages such as soda.

If you need to purify water, there are many methods. The easiest is chemical disinfection. Iodine or chlorine dioxide tablets are widely available, compact, inexpensive, and kill all germs. They do take up to 4 hours to completely kill germs, so you won't have potable water instantly. *Hint:* A ½ tab of vitamin C takes away the chemical taste of iodine or chlorine. When all else fails, you can use chlorine bleach. Five drops in a liter of water purifies water in 4 hours.

There are a few other options, but they aren't quite as easy.

You can purify with UV Light. SteriPEN is a UV light source that's either battery or solar powered. The disadvantages are its weight and bulk, the need for power, and its inability to purify cloudy water.

Boiling water is an option, too—snow is particularly easy to purify this way if you are already melting snow for drinking water.

Water just needs to be heated to a rolling boil, but this can use up precious cooking fuel.

Mechanical filters are bulky and clog easily in turbid water. They are a reasonable option if you have space and don't want to use chemical treatment. Unless they are impregnated with iodine, they won't neutralize viruses, which are too small to be removed by the 0.4 micron filters. You can also use an inline water-bottle filter. It's the same concept as a filter, but on a personal scale.

The MIOX is another battery-powered option that converts table salt and water to a slurry of oxidants with the push of a button. After you create the slurry, add 2 cc to a 1-liter water bottle.

Whatever you choose, be careful with drinking water.

FOOD: BE CAREFUL WHAT YOU EAT

Local fare can be a great pleasure when traveling, but it can also be disastrous. Foodborne pathogens include all sorts of bacteria such as E. coli, campylobacter, and salmonella, viruses such as hepatitis A, and protozoa such as giardia. You're most likely to get food poisoning at a campsite, street vendor, or restaurants.

Eat these food items ONLY if they are in the following forms:

- Peeled fruits and vegetables
- Cooked eggs
- Pasteurized milk
- Cooked meat (and it should be steaming hot!)

Pepto-Bismol has been reported to prevent traveler's diarrhea. If you do get ill, prompt treatment with Imodium and antibiotics (in some cases) can halt the effects of food poisoning. You'll need to talk to your doctor about antibiotics.

Visit your travel clinic before you embark on a trip. You can get a 2-shot immunization for hepatitis A and a vaccine for typhoid (salmonella), which comes in a single shot or 4 pills.

DEHYDRATION AND HEAT ILLNESS

Once, on a canyoneering trip to southern Utah, I got water intoxication. I was drinking so much water that I diluted my blood without replacing electrolytes. Drastically low on sodium, I became dizzy and nauseated. Drinking more plain water made it worse. The outdoor temperature was 110 degrees Fahrenheit and I felt awful. Luckily, it was the end of a 3-day trip. At a roadside diner at the end of the trail, I gobbled down a grilled cheese, consumed a huge sodium load, and instantly felt better.

Heat illness is a collection of conditions, and there are several forms:

Dehydration can be mild to severe. In a mild case you may experience thirst, dizziness, headaches, dry mouth and eyes, and a decrease in urine production. Moderate to severe symptoms include restlessness, irritability, rapid heart and breathing rate, sunken eyes, dry eyes and mouth, severe thirst, and confusion.

Heat exhaustion is a general term for feeling bad when your core temperature rises. It's quite common in dry, desert environments and in the tropics, especially on open beaches where the sun scorches. Symptoms may include flushed skin, rapid heart rate, headache, nausea, confusion, weakness, and cramps. It's often coupled with dehydration. Acclimatization helps, so it's helpful to spend 3 or 4 days in the heat prior to embarking on a trip.

Heat stroke is a medical emergency and it's important to recognize the symptoms. It's basically an extension of heat exhaustion and is defined by a core temperature higher than 104 degrees Fahrenheit (40 degrees C) and mental-status changes. These changes may include confusion, lack of memory, slurred speech, staggered gait, blurred vision, severe dizziness, and nausea. So if someone is acting, speaking, or walking funny, get help ASAP.

Water intoxication is a condition that stems from drinking too much water without replacing electrolytes, namely sodium. When your sodium level gets too low, you may experience confusion, dizziness, and nausea. It happens commonly among desert hikers in the Grand Canyon and in endurance events and races like century bike rides, marathons, ultramarathons, and triathlons.

Fortunately, the fix for all of these conditions is the same. Stop, rest, seek shade, and start sipping an electrolyte drink. Fanning and misting helps. Salty snacks can, too. If you have heat stroke, you need to seek help right away.

Not sure what to drink? Electrolyte solution is the best to rehydrate quickly. They come prepackaged as oral rehydration salts. Otherwise, water, half-strength juice, or half-strength sports drink all work well. Or you can make your own drink: The World Health Organization formula is 1 liter water, 1 teaspoon salt (5 g), and 1 cup rice cereal (50 g).

Hint: Monitor your urine. If it is copious and clear, you're hydrated. If it's scant and dark, you're not drinking enough.

BRRR: HYPOTHERMIA AND FROSTBITE

Everyone has a different threshold for cold. How quickly one cools is variable and depends on your metabolism, clothing, sweat production, activity level, and food intake. Hopefully, by the time you're out adventuring you'll know how your body reacts to the cold.

There are several ways your body loses heat. Evaporation and exhaling breath expels some heat. Convection—when the wind blows against skin—and conduction—when you come into contact with cold matter—accounts for heat loss. By far the biggest heat loss is radiation, when your body expels heat directly into the environment.

Hypothermia occurs when your body drops to a dangerously low core temperature. Mild hypothermia usually results in shivering and nothing more. Moderate to severe hypothermia has serious effects such as confusion, poor judgment, lack of coordination, and cessation of shivering.

Frostbite, on the other hand, is when skin actually freezes. It usually occurs on exposed nose and ears, as well as on fingers and toes. Often, damage is irreversible. The skin is usually pale, white, cold, and numb.

Luckily, with quality clothing, proper hydration, and adequate nutrition, cold illness can be prevented. Here are some tips:

- Wear proper clothing. Synthetic tends to be warmest when wet. I like down for cold, dry climates. Otherwise, fleece and bulky synthetic insulation like PrimaLoft work in cold, wet climes
- Replace wet socks, gloves, and clothing
- Wear a hat and bacalava to cover all exposed skin, especially if it's windy

- Wear goggles and a helmet or a jacket with a hood
- Mittens are warmer than gloves
- Make sure boots are not too tight so feet can get adequate circulation
- If you stop and rest, insulate your body from the cold ground by using a pad or your pack
- Drink lukewarm sugar fluids! It's the calories that help you warm up, not the hot water
- Keep active; motion generates heat
- Seek shelter
- Heat packs help alleviate hypothermia when placed in the groin area, underarms, or on the chest; to prevent frostbite, place in gloves and boots

CLIMB HIGH, SLEEP LOW: ACUTE MOUNTAIN SICKNESS

Up on the mountain, you start to feel a slow-burning headache. First nagging, then pounding, and finally piercing. You're short of breath and sluggish. You never feel this way. You can't be suffering from altitude illness? You're only at 9,500 feet (3,000 m) and you're in great shape. Is it the altitude? Possibly.

Acute mountain sickness (AMS), also called altitude illness, results from low oxygen pressure, which causes low oxygen content in the blood, called hypoxia. With hypoxia, not enough oxygen is being delivered to the brain and muscles. Altitude can affect anyone venturing over 8,000 feet (2,500 m), even fit athletes. The *sine qua non* symptom is a headache coupled with nausea, poor appetite, lassitude, and/or fatigue. To compensate for hypoxia, you start breathing harder in an attempt to take in oxygen, so you become short of breath to boot.

Poor coordination and confusion are doubly dangerous; they can signal high altitude cerebral edema (HACE), when the brain swells. Difficulty breathing can mark its equally treacherous twin, high altitude pulmonary edema (HAPE), when fluid fills the lung.

When a headache hits on a trek, take a break, chomp an energy bar, and guzzle water. Sometimes it's difficult to differentiate AMS from fatigue, dehydration, and sun exposure. Try ibuprofen. If the headache passes, it may be okay to continue ascent. If symptoms persist: head down. Sometimes, a quick jaunt down to lower altitude resolves the symptoms and you can finish the day's route. Remember: Confusion, poor coordination, and severe shortness of breath are critical warning signs of more severe illness.

A key in preventing any of these ailments is proper nutrition, adequate hydration, good fitness, rest, slow ascent, and sleeping elevation. Hence the climbers' mantra: "Climb high, sleep low." Spend your first night below 8,000 feet (2,500 m). Then change sleeping elevation by no more than 1,500 to 2,000 feet (500 to 600 m) each night, even if you top out at a higher point during the day.

Before you go trekking above 8,000 feet (2,500 m), ask your doctor about a preventive medicine called acetazolamide (Diamox), which is safe and effective, even for kids.

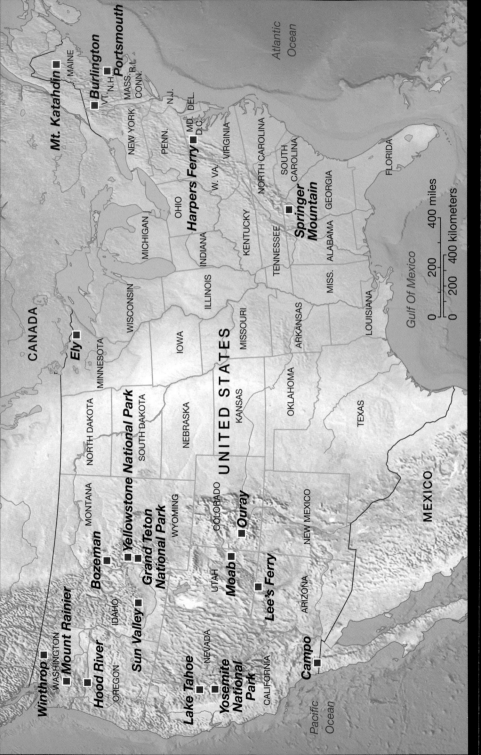

MAINLAND UNITED STATES

HEREIN LIES the beginning of your journey through the 100 best outdoor adventures of a lifetime. The United States is a vast and varied country: from the dry slickrock deserts of the Southwest, to the dank, humid swamps of the Southeast; big mountain ranges out East taper to equally picturesque New England mountains, rocky seacoasts, and hardwood forests. Scattered across the country, in every state, are fabulous hiking trails, wicked-fast mountain bike rides, and raging rivers awaiting your raft or kayak.

The United States has nearly 110 million acres of wilderness playground managed by the National Park Service, National Forest Service, Bureau of Land Management, and the Fish and Wildlife Service. These areas range from the gigantic Wrangell-St. Elias in Alaska to the tiny Thaddeus Kosciuszko in Pennsylvania. And that doesn't include state, tribal, and county parks. What's more, any adrenaline-fused athlete knows you don't necessarily need to be off the beaten track to move, sweat and rev your heart rate; you can run, ride, or hike anywhere, even city rail trails or bike-pedestrian pathways.

Indeed, many of these classic trips are located in the West, but you'll find a smattering of epic adventures in the East and South as well. And, if you don't live near one of these locales, use it as a springboard for ideas. If you can't rock climb El Cap, go for some fabulous vertical stone in Virginia's New River Gorge or New York's Shawgunks. If you can't paddle the Boundary Waters, seek solace on the Florida or Maine Coast—on anywhere in between.

So where to start? Well I always say the best time for a trip of a lifetime is right now. If you're a cyclist, ride the whole shebang—

coast to coast. Whether you are a rafter, kayaker, or a river novice, pushing off at Lee's Ferry and embarking on a descent of the Grand Canyon tops just about everyone's list. And sure, if you have the gumption, climb Denali.

Or, if you're like me, squeeze in some achievements which don't require a huge wad of cashola or a giant chunk of time. Run your first marathon, finish a full-length triathlon, jump into a cyclocross race, try road-bike racing, and . . . *gulp* . . . run an ultramarathon, even if you clock in a 12-plus minute-per-mile pace.

Finally, don't rule out going somewhere for the landscape, and making the activity secondary; enjoy cycling and hiking the fall colors of New England or summer canoe or kayak through the Boundary Waters.

Go, do, now. Don't wait. Work is overrated!

WHITEWATER RAFT THE COLORADO RIVER: DOWN THE GRAND CANYON (ARIZONA)

The best adventure of all time? Possibly. Although I hesitate to say it's a trip of a lifetime because you'll meet people who run this river time and again. It's that fantastic.

Dubbed as one of the seven natural wonders of the world, the Grand Canyon is one of the true marvels of nature. At 277 miles (446 km) long, 18 miles (29 km) wide, and 6,000 feet (1,820 m) deep, it's so enormous that it can be seen from space. And there's no better way to see it than running the gigantic, churning whitewater of the Colorado River. Rafting and kayaking down the gullet is the best way to truly, deeply experience the wonders of the deep, multilayer rock carved by the ancient waters.

Embark at Lee's Ferry (aka River Mile 1), and then descend into 40 layers of a 2 billion-year-old Paleozoic rock of multicolored earth tones, from crimson and vermillion to espresso and shoe-polish black.

The river will roll you over hundreds of named rapids, from class 1 to 10, with eye-popping, throat-gulping spray like Sheer Wall, Nankoweap, and the "gems" section including Ruby, Emerald, Sapphire, Crystal, Turquoise, and Agate. If you are experienced or have a guide, run the famed Lava Falls, the most difficult, and treacherous, rapid on the river.

Don't Miss. Havasupai Falls is a spectacular waterfall and plunge pool located within the Havasupai Indian Reservation, the name meaning Blue Water People. Check out the 125-foot Deer Creek Falls and make the hike up Nankoweap Trail in the footsteps of John Wesley Powell's exploration in 1882. You'll find epic, jaw-dropping vistas and mysterious granaries of historic cliff-dwelling Pueblo people. Before you go, read Wallace Stegner's *Beyond the Hundredth Meridian: John Wesley Powell and the Second Opening of the West.*

Logistics. Fly into Flagstaff, AZ, and take a van shuttle to Lee's Ferry. To experience the entire canyon, you'll need 12 to 18 days. Book a guided trip and show up at Lee's Ferry with a waterproof duffel. Everything else is covered: food, toilets (you have to pack out solid waste), life vests, helmets, boats, and a professional river guide. Alternatively, you can reserve a permit via a lottery, bring your own gear, and plan your own trip, for roughly half the cost. Keep in mind 18 days of prepackaged, presorted food for a 21-day trip for 16 people is 1,000 meals! Details are available at the Grand Canyon National Park (www.nps.gov/grca/planyourvisit/whitewaterrafting .htm), where you can link to outfitters and guides, including ones like Canyon REO (www.canyonreo.com) or OARS (www.oars.com) for guides, rental gear, and shuttles.

Best Time. Whitewater runs year-round, but the main season is from April to October. Try the shoulder months, April and October, to avoid scorching daytime temps and motorcraft.

Pit Stop. Don't have time for the whole shebang? You can easily raft half the canyon. Phantom Ranch, River Mile 88, is a ½-day hike to or from the South Rim Visitor Center. There, you can depart from or join a trip in progress.

Extended Play. You can take up to 25 days on the river, which allows loads of layover time to hike and explore the North and South Rims. Most people end at River Mile 225, Diamond Creek.

But a few extend the trip all the way to River Mile 296, the South Cove on Lake Mead. Alternatively, before or after your tour, trek rim to rim via the Bright Angel Trail, a 44-mile (71 km) round-trip, and one of the most classic hikes in the world.

Travel Smart. If you decide to tackle the big whitewater, arm yourself with excellent swimming, rowing, and paddling skills. Always wear a personal flotation device and helmet. If you do this on your own, you should be an expert river runner. For the less-than-expert or total novice, book a commercial trip with a guide, who will be worth the extra bucks in safety, logistics, and natural-history info. Don't forget sunscreen, sun-protective clothing, and a warm sleeping bag and tent, as the desert can get cool (and even snow) at night. Because extrication and communication is difficult, consider a satellite phone or radio that can reach river rangers and aircraft.

2. RUN THE QUINTESSENTIAL ULTRAMARATHON: WESTERN STATES 100 (CALIFORNIA)

World Triathlon Corporation

If you're a runner, you probably broke out into a cold sweat just reading this title. Your feet, legs, and back now hurt. You're hungry and thirsty. You feel pain, suffering, and agony.

Indeed, the Western States 100, or more properly the Western States Endurance Run, is the quintessential ultramarathon, the one all others are measured by. Yes, you can do a shorter ultra, defined as any run that exceeds the marathon distance of 26.2 miles. Typically, ultras are 31 miles (50 km). But this granddaddy clocks in at triple that; it's a full century in miles (161 km).

If that's not enough, did I mention it's also uphill? The race starts at Squaw Valley Ski Resort near Lake Tahoe, California, ascends a cumulative of 18,090 feet (5,500 m) and descends 22,970 feet (7,000 m). Runners limp in to Auburn, California, somewhere before the 30-hour time limit.

The WS100 started as a horseback trail ride in 1955. In 1974, after his horse became lame 29 miles (47 km) into the jaunt, Gordy Ainsleigh ran the course in under 24 hours. The first official run in 1977 had 14 participants. Now 369 runners join in the pain every year, the maximum number allowed by the U.S. Forest Service.

And so you don't slack, keep these stats in mind. In 1994 Ann Transon ran the race in 17 hours and 37 minutes and in 2010 Geoff Roes completed it in 15 hours and 7 minutes.

Don't Miss. Finishers get a belt buckle, whoo-hoo! Finish in under 24 hours, and you haul home silver. Finish in under 30, bronze. No matter the metal, an old-West buckle, like the ones the original trail riders wore, is the goal.

Best Time. The WS100 is held the last full weekend in June, starting at 5 a.m. But you need to start planning (and training) at least a year in advance, because you have to qualify with a shorter ultra first. Then you'll enter a lottery in December, the year before. So start planning . . . and running. (Then go run some more).

Logistics. Fly into Reno, Nevada. It's just a short drive up to Squaw Valley. You'll want to schedule in a few days on the front end to acclimatize. Get the details from Western States 100 (www.ws100 .com).

Pit Stop. If the 100 miles and 38,000-foot elevation change is a bit over the top for you, try another ultra. Pick one of the shorter, standard 30-mile (50 km) or 50-mile (81 km) ultras. You can probably find one a few hours, or an easy weekend trip, from wherever you live.

Extended Play. If you haul home a WS100 belt buckle, kick back in the Lake Tahoe Sierra Nevadas. Spin out your legs on a road bike by cycling the pavement loop around the lake; it's only 72 miles (116 km). And if you get addicted? Do the Grand Slam of ultramarathons, including the Vermont 100 (www.vermont100.com), Utah's Wasatch Front 100 (www.wasatch100.com), and Colorado's Leadville Trail 100 (www.leadvilleraceseries.com). Want a little inspiration? Read Dean Karnazes's *Ultramarathon Man: Confessions of an All-Night Runner* or run the 100-mile (161 km) Mont Blanc Ultra, all the way around the legendary Alp.

Travel Smart. This is no ordinary run, nor is it an ordinary ultra—if there is such a thing. The biggest issue is lack of proper pre-race training. The most common problems on the course are blisters, which can be debilitating, and dehydration, which can be deadly. You'll also be at risk for hypothermia, heat exhaustion, hyponatremia (low sodium), hypoglycemia, renal failure (from dehydration), and . . . did I mention blisters? The WS100 Terrible Three problems are preexisting injury, insufficient training mileage, and ibuprofen-masked injury. So make sure you train hard, keep your body healthy, and remain cognizant of all the aches and pains. You'll also encounter rugged terrain, potentially hazardous wildlife, poison oak, and extreme altitude. There are aid stations with mandatory medical checks, but they are scattered throughout the course. Much of the run takes place in the mountain wilderness, so self-sufficiency is key. Most ultrarunners carry a small hydration pack with food, water, and emergency gear. Tired yet?

3. WINDSURF AND KITESURF THE COLUMBIA GORGE (OREGON AND WASHINGTON)

Top-shelf for high-knots, burly-wave, white-knuckle wind sports. The benchmark that all others are measured by.

The Columbia Gorge is a geologic adventure-sports master-piece. Start the geologic wonder with a 90-mile-long stretch of a 1,200-mile-long (1,900 km) river. Then carve around 4,000-foot (1,200 m) basalt walls made from ancient mud and lava flows. Then toss in a little weather disturbance to keep it interesting. Cool, moist, marine air drifts from the Pacific Ocean into western Oregon and Washington. Scorching, dry desert air on the east side of the states rises. The air is sucked through this giant geologic wind tunnel, via the Venturi effect, which accelerates the westerly flow up to 40 knots.

This is *The Gorge*, known for its fabled *nuclear* westerlies, named after the decommissioned Hanford Nuclear Power Plant up-river. Unlike Maui's gentle trade winds and big ocean waves, the Gorge is the premier destination for high-wind windsurfing and kitesurfing, and it's the global focal point of those industries.

Come here, and ride the wind if you dare.

Don't Miss. Oregon is famous for its microbrews, and there's no shortage in the Hood. You'll find summer-weight Session Lager at Full Sail Brewing, and powerful hoppy IPAs at Double Mountain in quaint, boutique-spackled downtown Hood River, Oregon. Or check out a nice brown ale at Walking Man in Stevenson, Washington, near novice-friendly Kite Beach. Off the beaten path is new kid on the river, White Salmon's Everybody's that creates their own brew with great food, such as their killer sweet potato burrito. Not a hophead? You'll find 3-dozen wineries in one of the PNW's newest federally designated appellations (www.columbiagorgewine.com), many of which have tasting rooms right in downtown Hood River.

Logistics. Fly into Portland, Oregon, rent a car, and spend a week in Hood River, Oregon, epicenter of the Gorge. Stay at the high-end Columbia Gorge Hotel (www.columbiagorgehotel.com). Over 100 years old, the hotel rests on the cliff above the 208-foot Wah Gwin Gwin Falls. Or go cheaper and camp in a van down by the river—I'm not disclosing all the secret spots!

Best Time. In June through August, the wind scene is in full swing. In spring and fall, you'll find fewer crowds, steady wind, and epic mountain biking and kayaking.

Pit Stop. If you don't have much time, learn to kitesurf with Kite The Gorge (kitethegorge.com) or Hood River Waterplay (www.hoodriverwaterplay.com). Both schools take you to the west of Wells Island, away from the crowds, where you can learn in waist-deep water.

Extended Play. If windsurfing and kitesurfing isn't enough, or if you hit a spell of no wind, not to worry. Try standup paddling on the glassy, windless days. Rent a mountain bike from Dirty Fingers

Bicycles (dirtyfingersbikes.com) and ride the famed Lewis River Trail in Gifford Pinchot National Forest. Go kayaking—Hood River is world renowned for dropping in the spectacular creeks. You'll see the Little White Salmon River in almost any kayak film. You can ski on Mount Hood year-round (www.timberlinelodge.com) or climb and ski the trifecta of volcanoes: legendary Mount Hood, less-traveled Mount Adams, and fuming Mount St. Helens. Need to come down from your buzz? Take a mellow hike to one of the spectacular waterfalls that pop out of the andesite basalt between Hood River and Portland, Oregon.

Travel Smart. It's one thing to be in the water and it's another to be in the water and loaded with gear. Use a wetsuit, consider a flotation device and helmet when learning, and take a lesson. There's no specific rescue service on the river: If you get in trouble, wave down another river rider, or swim to shore. Big bulky barges are particular to this riverine system. They haul grain, sawdust, and salmon up and down the river, and they can't stop or slow down. If you get into trouble in the Gorge, call 911. The Crag Rats, the oldest mountain rescue unit in the country, may respond (www.cragrats.org).

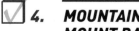

4. MOUNTAIN TRIATHLON: RIDE, RUN, AND CLIMB MOUNT RAINIER (WASHINGTON)

As adventure seekers, we tend to get caught up in the glitz of high-tech gear and extreme sports. Sometimes, however, you have to revert back to the basics, the classics. I mean running, cycling, and climbing. But here's the trick. They're all rolled into one—on a mountain. It's what I call a Mountain Triathlon. You don't have to complete this feat on Mount Rainier, but this place is particularly special.

Mount Rainier National Park is one of the most scenic areas of the country: gigantic glaciers; crystalline lakes; lush, old-growth forests of western red cedar, mountain hemlock, and Douglas fir. If that isn't enough, the wildflowers—Indian paintbrush, purple lupine, stark-white daisy—create eye-popping fields of intense color.

So what's the gig? Easy. Just head up, around, and around again.

Part one: Ride the RAMROD, short for Ride Around Mount Rainier in One Day. It's a 155-mile (250 km) road-bike ride. The official RAMROD is the last Thursday in July every year and you have to enter the lottery in February through the Redmond Cycling Club (www.redmondcyclingclub.org), or just ride it with a buddy, a jersey full of food, and $20 for supplies along the way.

Part two: Hike the Wonderland Trail. Built in 1915, it's arguably one of the most sought-after hikes in the world. It circumnavigates the peak in 93 miles (150 km). You'll read about people taking 10 to 14 days, but if you're like me and hoard your vacation, plan a fast-packing tour in 4 days with ultralight gear. Or, if can get a team to support you, you can trail run/speed hike--it's been done, more than once—in under 2 days.

Part three: Climb to the top of the 14,411-foot (4,392 m) peak. It's a gargantuan climb, requiring crevasse avoidance and glacier navigation skills, but it's one of the most spectacular and difficult feats you'll ever accomplish in 24 hours. You can ascend the shortest route, which is also the most crowded, Disappointment Cleaver. Or take the slightly longer, safer Emmons-Winthrop Route. Once you reach the summit, add a bonus and ski down the Nisqually Glacier, Fuhrer Finger, and Turtle snowfield. Some years you can make a 10,000-foot ski descent to the Nisqually River Bridge.

Don't Miss. Check out the lodge and climbing history museum at Longmire and the historic Paradise Inn. Get details at Mount Rainier National Park (www.nps.gov/mora).

Logistics. Fly into Sea-Tac in Seattle. The best place to coordinate airport shuttles and guide services is Ashford-based Rainier Mountaineering (www.rmiguides.com). Whittaker Mountaineering in Ashford (www.whittakermountaineering.com) has gear rental. Whittaker's Motel and Historic Bunkhouse offers cheap lodging and food (whittakersbunkhouse.com). Go to www.nps.gov/mora for detailed info on climbing and hiking permits in Mount Rainier National Park. You'll need to sign up for a permit in March for the Wonderland Trail, or you can take your chances for last minute space.

Hint: You can send a resupply box with food to one of the ranger stations.

Best Time. This adventure is all about snow conditions. For the RAMROD, go June through October; just make sure snow is melted off road. The Wonderland isn't usually snow free until August. Climbing season runs all year, but July through September offers the best chance of good weather unless you're skiing; then choose May or June.

Pit Stop. If you can't do all 3, pick 1 and go for it. Although the hike and ride are spectacular, there's nothing like reaching the summit of the iconoclastic peak.

Extended Play. If you go for all 3, give yourself 2 weeks, including rest days. The hardest to achieve, with weather and snow conditions, is the summit climb: I've done the climb in 24 hours, but on average it takes 3 days with a guide. The RAMROD takes 1 day. If you are a glutton, climb and ski as many Cascade Volcanoes as you can. They start at Lassen Peak in California and stretch all the way to Garibaldi in British Columbia. The big 3 next to Mount Rainier include Hood, Adams, and St. Helens; find comprehensive info on Amar Andalkar's Ski Mountaineering and Climbing Site (www.skimountaineer.com). Or climb, bike, and circumnavigate Oregon's legendary 11,250-foot (3,429 m) Mount Hood: the Timberline Trail is *only* 43 miles (69 km) and the road bike circumnavigation is *only* 100 miles (161 km).

Travel Smart. If you try to pull off the trifecta in one trip, build in rest days. For climbing, foul weather and falls are big risks. Altitude illness, hypothermia, and frostbite can occur throughout the year. You'll need a full set of glacier travel gear and a repertoire of mountain-safety skills including avalanche and crevasse rescue skills. For long-distance fastpacking or mountain running, be prepared for blisters, mosquitoes, and intense sun. Also, it gets cold at night, even in August, so bring warm gear, including a sleeping bag and tent. And this is the grand Pacific Northwest; rain, snow, and wind can sweep in at anytime. Be prepared.

5.   *RUN AN ALL-NIGHT RELAY*

If you've never done a long-distance relay run, you could be in for the best or most challenging time of your sporting life (or both). Your group dynamics may be difficult; your 2 a.m. race pace may be marred by the tiny headlamp lighting your way; and your night-shift driving the team van will certainly be in the dark when your muscles are tight and cramping, your belly empty, and your head pounding from dehydration. What fun!

All the same, running an all-night relay is a pretty cool feat and with great friends and a relaxed attitude (you will not PR your 10K pace here), it is a blast.

One of the longest-running and most famed all-night relays is Hood to Coast (www.hoodtocoast.com), which begins at Oregon's Timberline Lodge on Mount Hood at 6,000 feet (1,829 m) and finishes at the Pacific Ocean in Seaside. With some 20,000 participants, the 200-mile (322 km) route is split between 12 people, each running 3 legs. This was the brainchild of Bob Foote, who started the shebang in 1982. He was at the time president of the Oregon Road Runners Club and ran the course with a mere 8 teams. It grew to the maximum 1,050 teams.

But you don't have to travel to Oregon. Check out one of the Ragnar Relay Series events (www.ragnarrelay.com). These races are held all over the United States in places such as Cape Cod, Chicago, Wisconsin/Minnesota, and in the New York Adirondacks. Or for spectacular scenery, check out the Reno-Tahoe Odyssey, which circumnavigates Lake Tahoe over 178 miles (286 km) of Sierra Nevada mountain beauty (renotahoeodyssey.com).

Don't Miss. Watch the *Hood to Coast* movie, which follows 4 quirky teams on their journey to run the famed race (www .hoodtocoastmovie.com). Run this relay with the best of friends—probably the only way you can tolerate foul-smelling flatus, feet, and armpits for 24 hours in the same vehicle.

Logistics. Get your team, pick a race, and start organizing. Most races only allow 2 vans, and have preset transition points.

Best Time. Most races are in summer when the weather is nice enough to run all night. The Hood to Coast is late August.

Pit Stop. You can probably find shorter relays, but you'll want to do the whole shebang: 12 people, 2 vans, 200 miles (322 km).

Extended Play. If you get addicted to the fun and pain, check out the entire series of Ragnar Races and pick a different locale every year. Or, if you are burly like Dean Karnazes (www .ultramarathonman.com) do the Hood to Coast, solo.

Travel Smart. Despite how loopy you'll get in a van full of endorphin-infused friends, you'll have to pay attention to your body. You'll be running a race pace and then jump in a van for 6 hours. You'll then run again, and jump back into the van again. Warm up before running, stretch after, and make sure you eat and hydrate. Pasta and potatoes are good—or anything easy to digest. When you take your turn behind the wheel at 3 a.m., after running, drive carefully.

6.   *24 HOURS OF PEDALING: MOUNTAIN BIKE ALL NIGHT*

If fat-tire pedaling is more your gig than road-running a relay, don't fear. A 24-hour mountain bike race may be the most fun—and the most pain—you'll ever experience with a group of crazy mountain pedalers. The team relays are wild, adrenaline-fused, foggy-brained craziness.

There are races all over like 24 Hours of Adrenalin in Idyllwild, California (www .24hoursofadrenalin. com), the BURN 24

Hour Challenge in Wilkesboro, North Carolina (www.burn24hour
.com), and the 24 Hours of Moab in the famed red-rock canyon
country of southwest Utah (www.grannygear.com).

Pick a race, get a crew of MTB-buddies, and have a ball.

Don't Miss. Check out the film *24 Solo* (www.24-solo.com)
or one of the most epic, outdoor films of all time, *Roam* (www
.thecollectivefilm.com/roam).

Logistics. Surf the Net for a race near you. Pack up your crew in
a van, tune your bikes, and head to the race. Plan on setting up
camp at the race venue so you have a place to sleep when you're pals
are pedaling.

Best Time. Most races take place during summer.

Pit Stop. If you can't make a 24-hour race work, pick a shorter
relay. There are lots of 6-hour, 2-person relay races. Or just enter a
race solo. You can pick one of the disciplines of mountain bike racing according to your persuasion: cross-country, downhill, dual
slalom, short track, or Super D. A great race is the famed Sea Otter
Classic in Monterey, California (www.seaotterclassic.com).

Extended Play. For a serious a test of endurance, enter a 24-hour
race solo. You'll have to get racing down to a science: rest, eat, hydrate. Or pick a 100-mile (161 km) mountain bike race like
Michigan's Lumberjack 100 (www.lumberjack100.com).

Travel Smart. Make sure your bike is tuned. As soon as you finish a lap, you'll have to eat, drink, and rest. And don't forget to
stretch. If you jump off your bike and get supine, you'll cramp up
right away.

This is the most fun you'll ever have in an hour. And be warned. This is highly addictive. You'll find yourself shaving your legs and longing for mud and rain. So if you've never ridden in a Cyclo-Cross race, or only vaguely know what this sport entails, you've been warned.

You will get addicted.

You will need to buy a new bike.

Your bike components will get trashed, and you will have to make weekly jaunts to your local wrench (aka bike mechanic).

You will become obsessed.

What is it? Cyclo-Cross is an old sport that started when road bike racers in Europe outfitted their bikes for rain and mud to ride in the off-season. A CCX bike looks like a road bike, but is stronger. The tires are knobbier, the brakes are beefier, and the frame is more durable. The races are 1 hour or less on a 2-mile track. The track is usually part dirt, mud, gravel, and pavement. Some even weave in and out of buildings. Almost all races have at least one obstacle for which you have to dismount, shoulder your bike, and jump over. At one Halloween race, the obstacle was two humans lying across the track! Another race, it was a flight of stairs.

Anyone can ride a bike in the mud. What's more, this is a sport that's manageable for someone with a job and family. The 45-to 60-minute races require some training, but not the grueling prep of a century ride or ultramarathon run. If you can get in a few rides and 1 run a week, you can be a Cyclo-Cross racer.

These races are also spectator extravaganzas, like a college tailgate parties rife with cheering, cowbells, and heckling (all in good fun). And you'll learn high-tech skills like après-race bathing in mud puddles the color of a double latte. Oh, such fun.

If you get reasonably good at the average Cyclo-Cross, check out the USA Cycling Cyclo-Cross Nationals (www.usacycling.org/cx). The Nationals are in January, at the end of the race season. If you get to that point, forget skiing. You'll be riding your bike in the snow, sleet, and hail.

Don't Miss. If you can, enter a local race. There's no traveling involved, it'll be easy to work into your weekend, and you'll be bolstered by local camaraderie. If you're in the neighborhood, Boulder, Colorado, has the first purpose-built Cyclo-Cross venue, Valmont Bike Park (www.bouldermountainbike.org/valmontbikepark).

Logistics. Almost every state holds Cyclo-Cross races. Find ones close to you at USA Cycling (www.usacycling.org/cx). You'll want to purchase a Cyclo-Cross bike. Luckily they are quite versatile. Add fenders and a handlebar light, and they are great for commuting. Add a rack and panniers, and they'll work for long-distance cycling. Or just use it for a rain bike when you want to leave your carbon roadie in the garage. Hint: Don't spend a bundle on a CCX bike; it'll get trashed.

Best Time. Cyclo-Cross is a fall sport. Races run August through December. The early races are often dry, but come October and November they turn to mud, mud puddles, and mud pits.

Pit Stop. Just want to try? Every race has a beginner category that's usually only 30 minutes long, about 3 laps at 2 miles each. You can just ride a mountain bike or a not-so-nice road bike that's fixed up with cantilever brakes and knobby tires. Lots of kids and families do this sport, so give it a try.

Extended Play. Pick a series if you have one locally. Portland, Oregon, has the largest Cyclo-Cross series in the world, Cross Crusade (www.crosscrusade.com), which runs 8 weekends. But most states and communities have shorter, 4-weekend series. You'll get to know your local racers and have some friendly competition. If you get good, consider a regional or national race.

Travel Smart. Get quality gear and ride cautiously. When you go down, you can go down hard. Races trails are typically a mix of asphalt, dirt, gravel, and mud. In some races, I've ridden in and out of horse barns at fairgrounds, run up flights of stairs, or even made a lap on a velodrome—a circular, paved cycling track. Some races have several hundred people, so if you can, pick a category or race that has smaller groups, such as one with 50 people.

8. ROAD RIDE THE FALL FOLIAGE (NEW ENGLAND)

Almost every state has a picturesque loop, a National Scenic Byway, and an epic long ride favored by the local bike racers. But, sooner or later, you can't pass up the spectacular fall colors of New England.

Depending on your style, such breathtaking landscape ogling and cycling can be mellow, or an adrenaline-fused thrill ride, especially if you group ride at a race pace and sprint up hills.

There's few more spectacular than New England: See the crimson, gold, and tangerine foliage melded with quaint historic towns and warm hospitality. Here are a few of the best chromatic loops in New England:

- Ride the 3-state, a 314-mile (505 km) classic loop from Portland, Maine, through New Hampshire and Massachusetts; the route meanders through Norman Rockwell communities of colonial architecture
- Ride around Burlington, Vermont, a college, ski, and sports town with spectacular climbs in the Green Mountains
- Spin the Kancamagus Highway bisecting the White Mountains of New Hampshire
- Climb Cadillac Mountain in Acadia National Park, Maine
- Circumnavigate Oneida Lake in New York's Finger Lakes
- Spin Nova Scotia's Cape Breton Island

Don't Miss. Portsmouth, New Hampshire, is a college town with quaint shops, and a beautiful waterfront. Calorie load on their famed New England clam chowder, steamer clams, or lobster at Oar House (www.portsmouthoarhouse). Stowe, Vermont, and Lake Placid, New York, are both classic ski and cycle towns. And if you need a city fix, there's always Boston.

Logistics. Boston is an easy jumping-off point. Bike transport will cost a bit if you're flying. If you can't pack a bike yourself, ask your local shop to do it. You'll need to remove the saddle, wheels, and pedals and turn the handlebars to fit in a plastic case (or just ask your local shop for a cardboard bike box). Airlines usually charge $100 each way. Alternatively, bring your clothing kit, pedals, shoes, and helmet and rent a bike.

Best Time. Although the foliage season varies slightly from year to year, October is a good bet for maximum color saturation of the leaves.

Pit Stop. If you don't have a ton of time, drive or fly into Boston, rent a bike, and ride the 11-mile (18 km) Minuteman Bikeway north from Cambridge to Bedford. Or pick one of many bike routes in Beantown, including the Cape Cod Rail Trail. You can hang out in Harvard Square after the ride for a pint of frothy Sam Adams.

Extended Play. Climb Mount Washington at 6,288 feet (1,917 m), the classic New England summit. Surf Montauk, New York, the famed Long Island break. Mountain bike forest trails near Boston at Middlesex Fells, Lynn Woods, and Great Brook Farm State Park. Kayak the spectacular, rocky coastline of Acadia National Park, Maine.

Travel Smart. Logistically, bringing your own bike can be difficult and costly, especially when flying. If you rent, you'll want to bring your own clothing kit (jersey, bib shorts, socks, shoes, and helmet) as well as your pedals. Distracted drivers are the bane of cycling safety. Be careful!

 9.   *COMPETE IN A CYCLING STAGE RACE*

Like running a marathon (see Trip #52) and completing an Ironman-distance triathlon (Trip #30), riding in a stage race is something every adrenaline junkie should do once (and then, of course you'll get addicted). Road bike racing is physically demanding, mentally taxing, and both thrilling and dangerous. Your effort will depend on what class you race and how comfortable you are riding fast in big groups. Often you'll have to ride with your tires and shoulder just a few inches from other racers.

The granddaddy of all is the 21-stage, 3-week Tour de France. You're not likely to jump in that one, but check out the 8-day Amgen Tour of California (www.amgentourofcalifornia.com) or the Bend, Oregon, Cascade Cycling Classic (www.cascade-classic.org), the longest consecutively running stage race in the United States. There are many stage races around the country, and probably even one in your hometown.

Usually a stage race is composed of 3 or 4 gut-wrenching components. Usually there's a longish road race, somewhere around 50 to 100 miles (80 km to 161 km) depending on what class you enter. Then there's a time trial, when riders pedal a short point-to-point course solo against the clock. The criterium, or crit, is a 1- or 2-mile loop, often through city streets, in which riders make as many laps as they can in hour or less. And finally, there's the circuit race, when riders make several laps of a larger loop, usually around 20 miles (32 km) per lap.

The beauty of stage racing is it awards all-around riders. Sprinters, climbers, and endurance cyclists all compete, and hopefully excel, in their disciplines.

Don't Miss. If you enter a race, join your local cycling club to train for camaraderie, inspiration, race info, and the cool-looking matching clothing kit (jersey, shorts, and socks from your local team or shop).

Logistics. You'll need a bike, an entry fee, and scads and scads of time to train. Find a race in your area by asking the wrench (aka bike mechanic) at your local shop or check out USA Cycling (www .usacycling.org). Go pro and get a team kit.

Best Time. Some people love spring races if they can train all winter. Others pick summer so they have time to stack up the training miles in milder weather.

Pit Stop. Pick a 4-race weekend. Usually this is a Friday circuit race or prologue (a short intro to the race). Saturday often brings a morning time trial and evening crit. Sunday is the long road race. Beginners may want to pick a 1-day road race to check out how well you ride in the pelaton (the main pack of riders in a race). If you're a climber, pick a hill climb to test your skills against KOM (aka king of the mountain, best climber in the race). Or, go check out Strava (www.strava.com), upload your Garmin GPS data (www.garmin .com), and compete against local riders in a virtual race.

Extended Play. Pick some early-season single-event rides. Get racing legs with individual crits, hill-climb time trials, or 1-day road races. Then set your sights on a multi-day stage race after you've logged 1,000 miles (1,600 km) of training. Better, ride a stage of one of the Grand Tours: Tour de France (Trip #53), Giro d'Italia, or Vuelta a España. Or head to Belgium for the Spring Classics, a group of races at the world's cycling central.

Travel Smart. Purchase a quality bike and keep it maintained. Wear a helmet and gloves. Keep fluids and nutrition up to par. Log lots of base miles (long, medium-pace rides). Climb hills. And do some race pace sprints. Go on group rides, especially with better riders. Complete a century (100 miles, 160 km) or a double century.

When you feel like you have a solid cycling base as well as some sprint and hill-climbing experience, go for another ride.

Moab, Utah, is one of the most magical places on earth. The red, smooth sandstone (aka red rock or slickrock) of the Colorado Plateau is a marvel. The canyons—jammed with chockstones, arches, quicksand, drywashes, spires, hoodoos, and stacks—are punctuated by the smooth, rust-colored sandstone of the Southwest canyon country. Take all that magical desert scenery and add in some of the best mountain biking in the world and you have one of the most magnificent spots in the world.

Start with the famous, Slickrock Trail, which is right outside of Moab. For longer rides, choose the legendary Porcupine Rim or Poison Spider Mesa trails which meander among rocky cliffs, natural arches, sandy washes, and unworldly views.

Don't Miss. Back of Beyond Books (www.backofbeyondbooks .com) is one of my favorite bookstores on earth for its Edward Abbey collection and its pick of environmental titles, travel guides, and folklore books on the Colorado Plateau. Before you go, read 2 of Abbey's most famous environmental treatises *Desert Solitaire: A Season in the Wilderness* and *The Monkey Wrench Gang.*

Logistics. Fly into Salt Lake City and drive 5 hours to Moab. You can rent bikes and load up on local info at Poison Spider

Bicycles (poisonspiderbicycles.com). Stay in town at a cheap motel, camp along the Colorado River, or, for upscale accommodations, check out the Pack Creek Ranch (www.packcreekranch.com).

Best Time. Spring and fall have great riding weather; though don't be surprised if you find a snow dusting in March. Summer brings stifling heat and loads of national park motorists—go elsewhere for water sports.

Pit Stop. Zip down from Salt Lake City for a long weekend. The 5-hour drive you can easily get in 3 days' riding.

Extended Play. Moab is truly a multisport town. Try skiing the La Sal Mountains in Spring, which provide the scenic backdrop for Arches National Park (www.fs.usda.gov/manitlasal). Go canyoneering in Canyonlands, Bryce Canyon, and Zion National Parks. Grab a road bike and complete the loop road from Moab through the La Sal foothills, into Castle Valley, and back to town along the Colorado River. Bring lightweight mountain climbing gear and summit 12,482-foot (3,805 m) Mount Tukuhnikivatz. Find a big fat meadow full of snow and snowkite. Raft the Green River. Rock climb the famed Fisher Towers.

Or if you want to keep mountain biking, zip over to the equally spectacular, but less crowded, Fruita, Colorado (www.gofruita .com).

Travel Smart. A good helmet, a hydration pack with lots of water, and repair kits for the bike and body are vital. This is the desert so keep water with you at all times. Consider adding thorn-proof tubes to your tires or use tubeless tires with thorn-proof sealant. Tires can be tricky—wide and soft work better with sand and soft dirt, but sticky, small, well-inflated tires work better on slick sandstone.

Oh, and did I mention bring water?

11. FLOAT THE MIDDLE FORK SALMON RIVER: THE RIVER OF NO RETURN (IDAHO)

Few rivers are more spectacular. Few are more remote. Few are as thrilling and technical.

Also known as "The River of No Return," or, more properly, the Middle Fork of the Salmon River, which rushes through the second largest contiguous wilderness in the lower 48, the Frank Church—River of No Return Wilderness Area. It's among the steepest, deepest canyons in North America.

Kayak or raft through conifer woodlands and swiftwater rapids. Cruise alongside bald eagles, mountain lions, gray wolves, black bears, coyotes, red foxes, wolverines, and bighorn sheep. The River of No Return is famous for fly-fishing steelhead and other trout species, hunting upland birds like the chucker and quail, and shaking through thrilling whitewater.

This wilderness region was created in 1980 by Congress and named after Senator Frank Church—the sponsor of the Wilderness Act of 1964, which protected 9 million acres, and the Wild and Scenic River Act of 1968, which originally protected the Middle Fork Salmon River, the Main Salmon River, and 138 other streams.

Don't Miss. Sun Valley and the neighboring town of Ketchum are arguably America's original ski towns. Ice-skate the rink in Sun Valley, Peggy Fleming's stomping grounds; catch *Sun Valley Serenade* at the theater; ski the smoothest, high-speed-quad-served, fall-line groomers; or trail run and mountain bike some of the best trails of the west (www.sunvalley.com).

Logistics. Fly into Ketchum via Salt Lake City. Nearby Stanley, Idaho, is whitewater central. Bunk at Mountain Village Lodge (www.mountainvillage.com), stop in at McCoy's Tackle Shop (www.mccoystackleshop.com) for fishing gear, and rent a bike or boat at Riverwear (www.riverwear.com). You can launch at either Boundary Creek or Newland Ranch or fly into Indian Creek. Find a guide via the Middle Fork Outfitters Association (www.idahosmiddlefork.com). If you want to raft on your own, you'll need to obtain a permit through the U.S. Forest Service (www.fs.usda.gov/scnf).

Best Time. Late spring through fall you can run the Middle Fork. Choose later for family trips because stream flow is slower and the rapids mellower. Or go before mid-June for huge whitewater. Either way, check river flow and with a ranger before you go.

Pit Stop. If you can't make the full trip, check out a raft or kayak descent in your area. There is whitewater kayaking, touring kayaking, rafting, and canoeing all around the United States. Get out, get wet, and paddle—human- and river-powered boats are way better than motorized ones.

Extended Play. Paddle as many big U.S. rivers as you can, like the remote Owyhee in Oregon, the Green and San Juan rivers in the Southwest, the American River in California, and the New River Gorge in West Virginia, often called the Grand Canyon of the East. Or, go big: paddle down the Grand Canyon (Trip #1).

Travel Smart. You'll need rafting skills and protective gear, including a helmet and a personal-flotation device. You can kayak or use a paddle or an oar raft. If you've never run a river, go with a guide to be safe. This is a remote river and extrication in an emergency can be very difficult.

12. PADDLE A MILLION ACRES: CANOE THE BOUNDARY WATERS (MINNESOTA) AND QUETICO PROVINCIAL PARK (ONTARIO, CANADA)

Let's be clear. Canoeing isn't going to jack your heart rate into the triple digits. But then, neither is fly-fishing (Trip #13). There are a handful of adventures that are so cool, the scenery so magical, the solace so needed, that they are well worth the slower heart rate. They are also great for family vacations. One such trip is the Boundary Waters.

Spend a week paddling the 1.1 million acres and 1,200 navigable waterways of Minnesota's Boundary Waters Canoe Area Wilderness—it's unlike any place on earth. Once this land was the water road of the Voyageurs, French-Canadian fur trappers who hunted with birchbark canoes. You'll come out with a peaceful mind akin to touring Thoreau's Walden Pond or Edward Abbey's sandstone canyons. Just north of the border is equally spectacular Quetico Provincial Park in Ontario. For trips across the border, check out Quetico Provincial Park (www.ontarioparks.com).

Whether you're a spin-cast angler or prefer a fly rod, drop a line for walleye, smallmouth bass, largemouth bass, northern pike, lake trout, crappie, perch, sunfish, and bluegill—all from the solace of a wide-open lake. If that's not enough, keep your eyes peeled for moose, beaver, bobcats, bald eagles, peregrine falcons, Canada lynx, bears, and wolves. The Boundary Waters has one of the largest wolf populations in the Lower 48.

Don't Miss. Paddle by the red-ochre pictograph at Crooked Lake, evidence that adrenaline junkies paddled this lake hundreds of years ago.

Logistics. Start in Ely, Minnesota, where you can rent a canoe and gear. Book guided trips through Wilderness Outfitters (www.wildernessoutfitters.com) or Canadian Waters (www.canadianwaters.com) For a 50-miler (80 km), start off at Moose River North and paddle to Iron and Crooked Lake. Or loop through Little Indian Sioux River then Loon, Slim, North, and Finger Lakes to Lady Boot Bay and Moose River. You'll need a permit to book one of the 2,200 campsites, most of which are boat-in only. Check with Superior National Forest headquarters for permit info (www.fs.usda.gov/superior).

Best Time. Go in August for the best weather or in September to beat the crowds.

Pit Stop. Drop in to Ely for a long weekend; there are several short paddles right from town.

Extended Play. Take the fly-in option. A bush plane can shuttle you, your gear, your buddies, and 2 canoes to Quetico Provincial Park. Get dropped at Lac La Croix, and paddle to Curtain Falls, Rebecca Falls, Warrior Hill and the pictographs on Lac La Croix. Take 10 days to paddle back to Ely.

Travel Smart. Although this is flat-water paddling, carry a personal-flotation device to be safe. Consider a satellite phone for emergencies, pack everything in dry bags, and learn how to right a swamped canoe in case you capsize.

13. FLY-FISH THE GALLATIN RIVER: TIE, CATCH, AND RELEASE (MONTANA)

You can fish just about anywhere in the world. It doesn't have to be a big expedition or production. You can fish from a kayak or a canoe or even a stand-up paddleboard. You can fish in remote lands accessible only by foot or bike. You can fish, quite possibly, right near you home. And, with a compact rod, you can pack it all on a carry-on bag.

Big Sky Country is probably one of the most spectacular and scenic places in the world to cast. And nowhere is better than the Gallatin River or the 90-mile (144 km) stretch from Yellowstone National Park to Three Forks, where the Yellowstone, Jefferson, and Madison rivers create the great Missouri River. From the Yellowstone to Spanish Creek, there's

While at home recovering from your last adventure, learn the art of fly-tying. Sure it's a detail that requires meticulous attention, a calm heart rate, tactile fingers, and probably reading glasses. You can take a fly-tie class at your local fishing shop, find out what fish are biting at your local fishing hole, then start tying. A skill of adventure, fly-tying is a much more useful adrenaline junkie skill than learning about wine or becoming a cigar aficionado. Then take your quiver of home-tied flies and go casting on one of the most beautiful rivers in the world, the Gallatin.

Don't Miss. Read David James Duncan's *The River Why* and Norman Maclean's "A River Runs Through It." Then see both films.

Logistics. Gear up with a good rod and waders. Fly into Bozeman, Montana. Then hire a guide from Gallatin River Guides (www.montanaflyfishing.com). They can take you via drift boat on the Gallatin, Yellowstone, and Madison rivers.

Best Time. One of the great things about fishing is that you can do it year-round. Prime time is June through October on the Gallatin River. Check with a local guide to time your trip around the salmonfly, mayfly, and caddis hatches.

Pit Stop. You can drop in for a long weekend and still fish 3 rivers in 3 days: the Gallatin, Madison, and Yellowstone. Your best bet for a short trip is to aim for the 50-mile (80 km) stretch from Yellowstone National Park to Spanish Creek.

Extended Play. With a compact rod, you can travel the globe to fish. Some of the best spots:

- Wind River Canyon, Wyoming, for brown, rainbow, and cutthroat trout
- Henry's Fork, Idaho, for rainbow trout
- Nakalilok and Bristol Bay, Alaska, for silver salmon
- Umpqua River, Oregon, for famed steelhead trout
- Green River, Utah, for trout
- Au Sable River, Michigan, for trout
- The Florida Keys for the famed bonefish and tarpon
- Upper Delaware River, New York, for rainbow trout

Too close to home? Try these global casting holes:

- Mangrove Cay, Bahamas, for bonefish
- Mataura River, New Zealand for brown trout
- Amazon River, Brazil, for giant peacock bass
- Ponoi River, Russia, for salmon
- Futaleufú River (Patagonia, Argentina) for trout and dorado
- Turneffe Atoll, Belize, for bonefish, permit, tarpon, and barracuda

Travel Smart. Rivers are swift, rocks are slippery. You don't absolutely need waders or felt-sole fishing boots, but they sure do help. If you're fishing from a boat, bring a personal-floatation device. Watch for hooks. Every season in the emergency room I pull fishhooks out of hands—it's not fun for the patients.

14. *BIG-WALL ROCK CLIMB EL CAPITAN (CALIFORNIA)*

Not a climber? You may think this trip isn't for you, but read on . . .

Sure, big-wall rock climbing is the pinnacle of rock climbing. Many people take years to acquire the skills necessary for a big wall.

This kind of climbing combines the intellectual focus of a chess match, the physical strength and agility of scaling a cliff, and the strategy of packing a week's worth of gear and food into a tiny bag to be hauled up that cliff. As big walls go, El Capitan in Yosemite National Park in California is where it's at.

Rock climbing in Yosemite flourished in the 1970s, when rag-tag climbers ascended the granite faces of Yosemite and camped all summer at the famed Camp 4. Yvon Chouinard, Warren Harding, Allen Steck, and Royal Robbins are among the famous pioneers. Now, high-tech gear allows climbing technique and skill to be pushed way beyond the early routes. The route called the Nose was first climbed in 1957 by a team led by Warren Harding using aid climbing: pitons and other steel devices are pounded in the cracks of the rock, a climber ties a rope into the anchors, and then he or she uses the anchors to ascend the wall. Ray Jardine and Bill Price free climbed—which is a style of climbing that uses anchors for safety only, not for ascent—the West Face route in 1979. The first free ascent of the famed Nose route wasn't until 1988 by Todd Skinner and Paul Piana. In 1993, Lynn Hill was the first to free solo (free climbed alone) the Nose, followed up the next year by Dean Potter, who free soloed the Nose in just 1 day. Dean Potter and Sean Leary set the speed record of 2 hours 36 minutes in 2010, a feat that many recreational big-wall climbers take a week to complete.

There are hundreds of routes on El Cap, ranging from free solo climbs to aid routes. The most famous include the North American Wall, the Salathé Wall, and the Muir Wall. But the Nose is the absolute prize.

Don't Miss. Check out the spectacular waterfalls, including Yosemite, Bridalveil, Ribbon, Illilouette, Vernal, Nevada, and Horsetail Falls. Book a night après climb at the Ahwahnee Hotel, constructed in 1925 out of 5,000 tons of stone and 30,000 feet of timber. Refuel on organic, sustainably harvested, locally grown fare like the pan-roasted steelhead trout, and reward yourself at the Grand Brunch on Sunday morning (www.yosemitepark.com/the-ahwahnee.aspx).

Logistics. Fly into Fresno/Yosemite International Airport and drive 1 hour to the park. Base your team out of Camp 4 or find more civilized lodging in the surroundings. Visit the National Park Web site to start planning your trip (www.nps.gov/yose/planyourvisit/climbing.htm). For the best climbs, check out Yosemite Mountaineering School (www.yosemitepark.com/rock-climbing.aspx).

Pit Stop. Don't have time for El Cap? Pick one of several shorter routes on the equally famous Half Dome, which take about 2 to 3 days.

Extended Play. There's a summer's worth—scratch that—a lifetime's worth of climbing in Yosemite in addition to big walls. Knock off majestic spires such as Liberty Cap, Leaning Tower, and Washington Column. Bang around on the crags at sun-soaked, less-crowded Tuolumne Meadows and the long cracks of the Merced River Canyon. Find superb hiking and trail running, such as the half marathon-length Valley Floor Loop or the 16-mile (26 km) John Muir Trail to the top of Half Dome. Shoulder seasons may have enough snow to backcountry and cross-country ski in the high country of Badger Pass, Glacier Point, Mariposa Grove, and Crane Flat. If you have some downtime, set up a slack line—a tightrope between 2 trees, which climbers use to work on balance.

Travel Smart. For big-wall climbing you need a trifecta of good stuff: good gear, good partners, and good sense. Lightening, thunder, and rainstorms are common during climbing season; many parties have been trapped on the wall for days. Make sure you have a weatherproof, big-wall shelter, aka portaledge. Yosemite staffs a sizable rescue team, but they may be delayed due to weather or logistical difficulty. If an injury occurs, or you just can't make the top, make sure you have the skill and equipment needed to rappel off the wall. And before you start, know that you'll need to package your waste and pack it out. Yosemite National Park focuses on low-impact climbing.

15. SKATE SKI THE METHOW VALLEY (WASHINGTON)

It's all about the glide.

Fast, fluid, and graceful. Smooth and elegant. Technically com-plicated and physically taxing. Indeed, skate skiing is a complex technique to master and a demanding full-body workout that in-volves your arms, core, and legs to work in tandem. Skate skiing is guaranteed to both jack your heart rate and build your quads. But be advised: This is not the same as leisure cross-country classic ski-ing (the forward kick-and-glide motion of cruising straight on a trail). Comparing the 2 disciplines of Nordic skiing, skate and clas-sic, is akin to throwing a hockey team and figure skaters together on the ice.

What's more, skate skiing is fabulous cross-training for just about any adrenaline sport. You don't need a lift or even mountains, but you do need a groomed track. Groomed skate tracks are found all over the country, but there is one that is rather special.

The Methow (pronounced "met tao") Valley is nestled in the famed North Cascades of Washington, a mere 28 miles (46 km) from Canada. The Methow River courses between 3 quaint, old

West towns: Twisp, Winthrop and Mazama. This small, bucolic valley has 120 miles (193 km) of groomed Nordic trails. Yup, that's 120 miles—one of the largest network of skate and classic Nordic trails in the United States. You can ski right from your lodge to the local coffee shop and then into the café for lunch. Winthrop is the hub, a rustic gold-mining and fur-trapping town-turned-sports berg. You'll skate so far and wide that after a few days you'll want to take a day off, look for a cozy fire, and relax with a good book.

Don't Miss. If it's open, take a tour of the smokejumper base in Twisp. Book a room at Sun Mountain Lodge. You can stay in the deluxe rooms and enjoy the spa (www.sunmountainlodge.com). When cruising the trails, drop into Wolf Creek Bar & Grill for a Thomson's Custom Meats Old-fashioned Frank or a Big Valley Ranch burger. Also consider a clinic or camp from Methow Valley Nordic Club (www.mvnordic.com) to hone your technique. They also host a lot of fun races, too.

Logistics. Part of the draw for the Methow is that it's hard to get to and expansive, so don't expect to find huge crowds. Fly into Seattle, Portland, or Spokane, and then rent a car, probably a 4-wheel drive if you come in winter. Methow Valley Recreation (www.mvsta.com) is a great 1-stop Web site for finding snow conditions, lodging, and rentals. In Winthrop, rent skate or classic Nordic gear at Winthrop Mountain Sports (www.winthropmountainsports.com) or Methow Cycle & Sport (methowcyclesport.com).

Best Time. Come in winter or early spring. Christmas and New Year's can be magical in this remote little valley, but January and February will be less crowded. But let's face it. With 120 miles (192 km) of trails, it's rarely crowded.

Pit Stop. You can easily come for a long weekend and get so much skate skiing in you'll be dead-dog tired.

Extended Play. If you're a backcountry skier, don't miss cranking turns on the North Cascades Highway. Since it's closed off to cars and unplowed in winter, you'll need a snowmobile to get up the highway in winter or spring. You may be able to drive partway in late spring. For something a bit less intense, try a hut-to-hut trip through the Rendezvous Huts (www.rendezvoushuts.com). Book a full-moon tour if you can. Spend 1 night or 2 in nearby Leavenworth, a Bavarian-themed mountain town with a Nordic, Alpine, and backcountry skiing scene of its own.

Travel Smart. It's winter. It's cold. Weather can change quickly. Take a small pack with food, water, and extra clothing. A small, mountain biking hydration pack is perfect for skate skiing. Bring a map of the valley, a phone for emergencies, and $20 so you can ski to a café for lunch. The valley road can be treacherous during the winter, so drive safely. This isn't the trip to drive all night, wing a couple days of skiing, and blast home. Save that for a summer surf safari.

16. CANYONEER BUCKSKIN GULCH (UTAH)

Once an esoteric sport, canyoneering, aka canyoning, is now a mainstream sport in the outdoor world. You can drop into slot canyons all over the United States and in valleys in France, Switzerland, New Zealand, Costa Rica, and Hawaii.

So first, what the heck is canyoneering? Akin to caving and mountaineering, canyoneering involves descending slot canyons that are too steep and narrow to hike into. They are only accessible by descending on a rope. You'll climb or rappel into canyons, swim across plunge pools, scramble down rock chutes, traipse through streambeds, and climb back out. This is a technical sport that takes you into the wilds that few ever see.

The epicenter of canyoneering in the United States is the American Southwest, particularly the slot canyons of the Colorado Plateau. Although not the most difficult, the most spectacular is probably the entry-level canyon hike of Buckskin Gulch and Paria River, nestled in the remote Paria Canyon-Vermilion Cliffs Wilderness area, in the slick-rock southern Utah desert.

The 24-mile (39 km) descent of the Buckskin and Paria takes 1 to 3 days and requires walking through muddy, cold pools, up and over rock and logjams, floating packs over plunge pools, and using a handline to lower packs and descend log and rock jams. Walk through varnished red-rock amphitheaters along Navajo sandstone arches, and through hanging gardens, percolating springs, and quicksand-laden pools. You may even spy bighorn sheep or deer.

It's a spectacular and wonderful world deep in the red, slick rock sandstone.

Don't Miss. Grand Canyon National Park is right around the corner. If you've never been there, check out either the North Rim or South Rim (www.nps.gov/grca).

Logistics. Fly into Phoenix or Las Vegas. Then make your way to Highway 89 toward Kanab, Utah. Start at the White House, Buckskin, or Wire Pass Trailhead. Take 2 to 3 days to hike the 24 miles (38 km) or 3 to 4 to go all the way to Lee's Ferry Trailhead. Several companies offer shuttle services to get you back to your car. Check them out at the Wilderness Area headquarters (www.blm.gov/az/st/en/arolrsmain/paria). If you want a guide, check out American Canyon Academy (www.canyoneering.net) or the American Canyon Guides Association (www.canyonguides.net).

Best Time. September and October are good bets for mild

weather and temperatures. Summer is hot. Avoid the rainy season; flash floods can be dangerous.

Pit Stop. If you don't have time for the whole shebang, pick a shorter, 1-day canyon descent in Zion National Park: there are many to choose from.

Extended Play. If you have time, spend a week in Zion National Park. There are many canyons that you can descend in 1 to 3 days, including the 1-day technical descent of Pike Creek. For that you'll need a rope, a wetsuit, a waterproof pack, and strong rappelling and swimming skills. Or descend the spectacular 2-day Kolob Canyons, which exits into the Zion Narrows. This one's also quite technical with many plunge pools and some awesome, long rappels.

Travel Smart. Canyons, like caves and mountains, are dangerous. Remember Aron Ralston? The man who was descending Utah's Blue John Canyon, and lost his hand when a chockstone fell on it and trapped him? You may know his story from the movie *127 Hours*. Rappelling on cliffs is one thing. Rappelling through a waterfall or down loose logs or rock jams is another. The hydraulics of plunge pools can suck you down and pin you to the bottom. This sport requires excellent climbing, rappelling, backpacking, and swimming skills. And make sure to watch out for flash floods. For most technical canyons you'll need a wetsuit, a helmet, and a dry bag for gear as well as canyon-specific rappel gear. Because of the narrow, deep slots, radio and phone communication is almost impossible; have an escape plan.

Now, imagine the opposite of canyoneering. It's winter instead of summer. You're surrounded by ice, not rock canyons. Instead of rappelling raging waterfalls, you're climbing up frozen ones.

No, ice climbers are not lunatics. It's perfectly normal to strap on 24 razor-sharp spikes to your feet, carry a couple of knife-edged ice tools, and ascend frozen ice pinnacles. Totally normal. People do it all the time. When it all works, you stick like Velcro. When it doesn't, you'll have a trusted rope, partner, and helmet to fall back on.

The ice-climbing mecca is a one-of-a-kind venue in a Colorado canyon called Ouray.

A few decades ago, Ouray hoteliers Bill Whitt and Gary Wild had an idea to boost their winter occupancy. They already had world-class natural ice climbs like Stone Free and Tangled Up in Blue in the nearby canyons, but they wanted more routes. So they dug out PVC pipe and sprinkler heads, tapped leaks in the city water supply in a nearby canyon, and presto! They created the premier human-made ice park in the world.

Ouray Ice Park is nestled in the spectacular Uncompahgre Gorge and sports over 200 ice and mixed—as in rock, ice, snow—climbing routes. The gravity-fed system run by the city of Ouray is an engineering feat: no pumps, motors, or turbines. Using 7,500 feet (2,286 m) of yellow mine irrigation pipe and 150 showerheads, the system pours out about 200,000 gallons per night. Built by volunteers from donated materials, the park is free, despite a technical and costly operation. The routes run the gamut of skill level, from beginner to expert. Many have fixed anchors and there's even a beginner's and kid's climbing area.

It all adds up to 3 miles (5 km) of vertical frozen water in the form of waterfalls, arêtes, fangs, curtains, pillars, columns, and supersized icicles.

Don't Miss. Check out the Ouray Ice Festival held in January every year (ourayicepark.com/ice-festival). In addition to a climbing exhibition, you can rub elbows with famous guides like Steve House, attend clinics, test gear, or enroll your kid in the free Kid's Climbing College and kick back at a climbing film. Stop in at Ouray Brewery (ouraybrewery.com) for an Alpine Amber, San Juan IPA, or Silvershield Stout.

Logistics. Fly into either Grand Junction or Durango, Colorado, for easiest access. Check out Ouray Ice Park for conditions and guide recommendations (ourayicepark.com). Hire Clint Cook, chief of the official guide operation, the reputable San Juan Mountain Guides (www.ourayclimbing.com). Explore Box Canyon Lodge and Hot Springs (boxcanyonouray.com) a 5-minute walk to the park. You can also dip into Ouray Hot Springs Pool (ourayhotsprings .com), an especially nice treat if you decided to tough it out camping in the back of your pickup.

Best Time. The Ouray Ice park season runs mid-December to late March.

Pit Stop. Hire a guide, rent some gear, and pick one of many beginner routes, like School Room where the ice isn't sheer and you can walk down instead of rappelling.

Extended Play. If you have time, you're only an hour away from some of the most famous, classic ice and mixed climbs in the west, including Bridal Veil Falls, Ames Ice Hose, Stairway to Heaven, and Bird Brain Boulevard.

In late spring, just before the ice park shuts down, create a multisport extravaganza like floating the San Juan or Green rivers or mountain biking in Moab or Fruita (Trip #10).

Travel Smart. Ice climbing involves many sharp pointy tools, a rope, a harness, and loads of technique. Have I mentioned that those tools are sharp! Get yourself some quality gear, go with a guide, pick a beginner route, and take your time. Ice climbing is a technical sport that takes years to master. Wear a helmet to prevent dropping a sharp point into your noggin.

☑ 18. SKI (OR MOUNTAIN BIKE) THE 10TH MOUNTAIN DIVISION HUTS (COLORADO)

Many backcountry skiers and snowboarders have, at least once, loaded up a 50-pound pack and camped in the snow. When I think of snow camping midwinter I think of cold, soggy clothes that never dry; crawling into a tent at 4:30 p.m. when the sky becomes pitch black; and cooking outside when the clouds are spitting snow. Fun? Sure, a blast!

Is a lighter pack more appealing? If you've never experienced a hut trip, you're in for a treat. Hut trips combine pure powder adrenaline with all the comfort of a roof, warm fire, and a light load. (If you want to snow camp, go for it!) You can find huts most places in the world, but Colorado is a different story. To experience the dry powder snow of Colorado, book one of the 10th Mountain Division Huts. Managed by a nonprofit association (www.huts.org), the 30 huts in the Colorado Rockies are stocked with 3 to 20 bunks, wood-heating stoves, propane cooking stoves, solar lights, and usually an outhouse toilet. You just need to bring food, a sleeping bag, and ski gear. If you're of a 2-wheel persuasion, you can bike some of the 350 miles (560 km) of trails that connect the huts in spring and summer.

Originally, many of the huts were used by sheepherders or served as U.S. Forest Service guard stations. The first chain to open for skiers and hikers was in the beautiful, rugged Maroon Bells-Snowmass Wilderness outside of Aspen. The huts were named after the Army's famed 10th Mountain Division, which trained in ski mountaineering and mountain warfare at Mount Rainier, Washington, and Camp Hale, Colorado, during World War II.

Don't Miss. Ski hut to hut between Aspen and Crested Butte through the Maroon Bells-Snowmass Wilderness. This tour uses the Alfred A. Braun Memorial Hut System: namely the Tagert, Green-Wilson, and Friends huts. Read Hal Clifford's *The Falling Season: Inside the Life and Death Drama of Aspen's Mountain Rescue Team*, about his years working with famed technical rescue experts of Aspen Mountain Rescue. (But stay safe! You don't need to end up in a mountain rescue book.)

Logistics. Fly into Denver to start your trip. Choose the 10th Mountain Huts (www.huts.org), the Summit Huts Association (www.summithuts.org), or a number of other private and public huts outside the 10th Mountain system. For guides, check out Aspen Alpine Guides (www.aspenalpine.com), Aspen Expeditions (www.aspenexpeditions.com), Paragon Guides (paragonguides.com), and Crested Butte Mountain Guides (crestedbutteguides.com). For summer mountain biking, check out The World Outdoors (www

.theworldoutdoors.com) and Timberline Bike Tours (www.timber
linebike.com).

Best Time. January through early March for skiing and snowboarding; July for wildflower-packed, single-track mountain biking.

Pit Stop. Head to Aspen, and pop into Markley Hut for 1 night;
it's just a 2.3-mile (3.7 km) ski from the trailhead in the Alfred A.
Braun Memorial Hut System.

Extended Play. Look into the Alpine Club of Canada network in
British Columbia, the humongous peaks of the Purcells, Monashees,
Bugaboos, and Selkirks (Trip #25) or traverse the Haute Route from
Chamonix to Zermatt (Trip #48).

Travel Smart. You don't necessarily need a guide, but one can
be helpful. Winter backcountry can get cold and wet at times. Many
have been caught in storms or gotten lost. Guard against hypothermia, frostbite, acute mountain sickness, fatigue, and dehydration.
In the huts, you may need to purify water. And because you'll be
staying in cramped quarters, remember to use good hand hygiene
(bring hand sanitizer). Be careful when cooking or building a fire in
the huts. Watch out for avalanche hazards: wide-open steep slopes,
cornices, and recent avalanches. You will cross avalanche terrain
skiing to some of these huts.

19. CLIMB THE GRAND TETON: SCALE A CLASSIC (WYOMING)

Grand Teton is a rite of passage, nestled in a bucolic valley near the glitzy mountain town of Jackson, Wyoming. The 13,775 feet (4,199 m) peak is a bold, craggy summit. It's high on a rock and mountain climber's tick lists for its sheer beauty, technical challenge, and accessibility.

Although controversial, the first climbers to summit the peak were likely Nathaniel Langford and James Stevenson in 1872 or William Owen, Franklin Spalding, Frank Peterson, and John Shive in 1898. In 1927, Glenn Exum started one of the oldest and most reputable outfitters in the United States, Exum Mountain Guides in the Tetons. In 1965, Paul Petzoldt started National Outdoor Leadership School. And well before backcountry skiing and ski mountaineering became mainstream, Bill Briggs made the first ski descent in 1971.

The Grand Teton is one of the most sought after mixed climbs in the world and the Upper Exum Ridge Route is perhaps the most popular. It's mostly rated as a Grade II, Class 5.5, which is something a novice climber can complete with some basic instruction and a guide. It's such a beautiful climb, the route is listed in Steve Roper and Allen Steck's tome *Fifty Classic Climbs of North America*.

Don't Miss. You can skip the boutiques and galleries of Jackson, but everyone wants to saddle up at the famed 1937-era Million Dollar Cowboy Bar (www.milliondollarcowboybar.com). Even better, fuel up on elk sliders or Idaho trout at one of the 10 hottest après ski bars in the world, Mangy Moose Saloon (mangymoose.com/saloon), where you can also check out local live music on weekends.

Logistics. Fly into Jackson then stop at Jenny Lake Ranger Station in Grand Teton National Park for permits and last minute info (www.nps.gov/grte). You can ascend in 1 long day. Or take 2 days and bunk at the Exum Hut, perched at the saddle between the Middle and Grand. Hook up with the most famous guide service in the United States, Exum Mountain Guides (www.exumguides.com) or climb with Jackson Hole Mountain Guides (www.jhmg.com), operated by Barry Corbet since 1967.

Best Time. For the best chances of clear weather, pick a week in July through September.

Pit Stop. Zip into Jackson, hire an Exum guide, and make the 2-day climb in a long weekend. If you stay at the Exum hut, you can go super light.

Extended Play. Information on Jackson Hole and the surrounding area is abundant. Yup, you can ski one of the steepest resorts in the world, Jackson Hole (www.jacksonhole.com), or dip into the backcountry for some of the best powder on earth. With Exum, take an avalanche course and go backcountry skiing. During the summer, trail run or mountain bike some of the most beautiful single-track networks in the world at Granite Canyon, Jenny Lake, Death Canyon, and Lupine Meadows. Kayak or raft the Snake River; the section above town is great for the whole family and you'll likely see river otters and bald eagles.

Travel Smart. You'll need a full cadre of climbing gear, including good boots and a helmet. Prepare for mixed climbing: rock, ice, and snow. Foul weather can occur anytime, even in summer; thunderstorms can sneak down the valley. Keep an eye out for lightning, rockfall, avalanches, crevasses, and foul weather. And watch for bears—yikes!

20. CLIMB OR SKI ALL 54 FOURTEENERS (COLORADO)

Okay, this may seem daunting. Colorado has 54 of the world's 547 fourteeners, mountains punching over 14,000 feet (4,267 m). But North American climbers and ski and snowboard mountaineers set lofty goals. Lou Dawson was the first person to ski all 54, a project he started in 1978 and completed in 1991, several of which were first descents. Chris Davenport took it a step further and skied all 54 in 1 year. Although Mount McKinley (Denali) in Alaska is the highest peak in North America and Mount Whitney is the highest in the lower 48, the Colorado peaks are worthy of trip after trip after trip.

The crown is Mount Elbert in the Sawatch Range at 14,428 feet (4,398 m).

Don't Miss. The Maroon Bells Wilderness above the town of Aspen is laden with spectacular wildflower meadows. Hike the Aspen to Crested Butte traverse and bag North Maroon Peak or Maroon Peak en route.

Logistics. Fly into Denver to access Front, Tenmile, and Mosquito ranges. You can use Aspen as a base for Sawatch Range and Elk Mountain. The Sangre de Cristo Range and San Juan Mountains are south of Denver, so use Alamosa and Durango as a base, respectively. Scope out the peaks online (www.14ers.com) or check out Lou Dawson's books, the 2-volume series *Dawson's Guide to Colorado's Fourteeners.*

Best Time. July through September has the best weather for pure climbing, but some of the peaks are navigable in shoulder seasons. If you plan to ski, pick winter or spring. Many of the mountains do have snow through early summer.

Pit Stop. Okay, if you can't do all 54—climb or ski just 1! There are several easier peaks to bag, especially the tallest, Mount Elbert. If you're pressed for time, pick those in the Front Range close to Denver, like Grays Peak, Torreys Peak, and Mount Bierstadt.

Extended Play. Ski all 54. Only a few have done it. Buckle up and be prepared for the long haul, which means your job and home life may suffer the consequences of a ski mountaineer obsession. Next you'll want to ski the Seven Summits . . .

Travel Smart. Some fourteeners are trekking peaks and others require full mixed-climbing gear for rock, ice, and glacier terrain. Even in mild weather, watch out for lightning and sudden thunderstorms. Like anytime you climb above timberline, be on guard for hypothermia, frostbite, dehydration, and acute mountain sickness. Stay cautious on your descents. More injuries occur on the way down—just because you bag the summit doesn't mean you're out of the danger zone.

21. TAKE A LONG WALK: HIKE THE APPALACHIAN TRAIL (GEORGIA TO MAINE)

It's long. It's famous. And for a trekker or hiker, it's the apex of long-distance hiking. If you make it, you'll be in an elite club. It's one of the most famous treks in the world.

The Appalachian Trail, or more simply AT, starts in Springer Mountain, Georgia, and terminates at Maine's Mount Katahdin. The 2,184-mile (3,515 km) trail passes through 14 states, spectacular woodlands, gentle hills, bucolic valleys, gurgling streams, and quaint towns. Without the elevation or snow of its sister, the Pacific Crest Trail (Trip #22), the AT is the place to begin thru-hiking— hiking an entire long-distance trail in 1 trip, as opposed to hiking in sections on multiple trips.

The AT was developed by Benton MacKaye in 1921. It was first thru-hiked in 1936 by Myron Avery. Earl Shaffer did the same in

1948, and then repeated the hike at age 80 in 1998. Now there are over 12,000 recorded completions.

The whole shebang takes 3 to 7 months, depending on how rugged you are. If you're ambitious, trail run the AT (with support), and try to top Jennifer Pharr Davis's 2011 record of 46 days.

Don't Miss. Stop in the Appalachian Trail Conservancy headquarters in Harpers Ferry, West Virginia, roughly the midpoint of the trail (www.appalachiantrail.org).

Logistics. Get maps, guidebooks, and the scoop on shuttles and gear at Appalachian Trail headquarters (www.applachiantrail.org). Crash in 1 of 250 shelters and campsites along the trail and resupply at several points. You can also get information on conditions and using bounce boxes (cartons for shipping gear to post offices along the trail).

Best Time. Most thru-hikers start in Georgia in March or April and finish in September. You can also start in Maine in June and finish in November or December.

Pit Stop. Thru-hiking not for you? Become a section hiker. Try the beautiful Blue Ridge Mountains in Shenandoah National Park in Virginia, the rugged White Mountains' Presidential Traverse in New Hampshire, or day hike Mount Katahdin in Maine. If you want to get creative, do a flip-flop: complete the south half, northbound; then fly to Maine and do the north half, southbound. To beat the weather and fatigue, consider a leap frog (completing sections out of order) or a head start, by hiking the most difficult section in Maine first.

Extended Play. Include the International Appalachian Trail, a 1,900-mile (3,100 km) extension through New Brunswick and Quebec, Canada. Start even further south, and tack on the Pinhoti National Recreation Trail in Alabama and Georgia. If you're a real junkie, knock off the Triple Crown of thru-hiking: the Pacific Crest (Trip #22) and Continental Divide Trails. The latter is still a work in progress.

Travel Smart. You're just hiking, what could go wrong? There's a big list: animals, blisters, poison ivy, and, unfortunately, sometimes violent crime. Black flies, mosquitoes, and ticks can be nasty. Stream crossings are often dangerous. And let's not forget the hot and humid summertime on the Eastern seaboard. Use your brain, be careful, and don't get so set on your itinerary that you push beyond your physical and mental limits. As with any long trip, don't be afraid to quit. You can always try again.

☑ 22. TAKE A LONGER WALK: HIKE THE PACIFIC CREST TRAIL (MEXICO TO CANADA)

More rugged. More remote. Higher elevation. Longer. Burlier.

Much like the Appalachian Trail (Trip #21), the Pacific Crest National Scenic Trail, or PCT, is one long, gnarly hike. It's the granddaddy of all long-distance trails. None is more difficult or ruggedly beautiful.

Originally conceived by Clinton Clarke in 1932, the trail was designated a National Scenic Trail in 1968, but not officially completed until 1993. Tackle the Pacific Crest and you'll be one of a small elite group of ultralight, ultralong backpackers.

The 2,650-mile (4,625 km) PCT winds in and out of the most spectacular terrain in the world: from the low, dry desert of Mexico to the high-alpine, old-growth forests of Canada. The trail traverses the spines of the Laguna, San Jacinto, San Bernardino, San Gabriel, Liebre, Tehachapi, Klamath, and the famed Sierra Nevada Mountains in California, and the Cascade Range in Oregon, Washington, and British Columbia. It pierces 6 of the country's 7 ecozones.

Don't plan on having a hot shower for more than a handful of days. Roughly 300 attempt to thru-hike the trail every year, usually starting in Mexico and heading north. More than half finish.

All I can say is good luck.

Don't Miss. Crater Lake, Oregon's only National Park, is one of the deepest lakes in America. Glacier Peak and the North Cascades in Washington have some 750 permanent snowfields. Northern California's Trinity Alps, Yosemite's Tuolumne Meadows wildflowers, and the John Muir Trail sections are spectacular. The 220-mile-long (354 km) John Muir Trails section is considered one of the world's most beautiful hikes.

Logistics. Yup, it's complicated. Fly to San Diego and hitch a ride to Campo, California, via the San Diego Metropolitan Transit System. Then set on foot to Manning Park, British Columbia, Canada. You'll want to pick an April or May start and plan to trek for 5 to 6 months with an average of 20 miles (32 km) per day. There are nearly 100 resupply depots and general delivery U.S. Post Offices so you can send mail (or better, receive care packages). You'll also want to shuttle items between sections: cold weather and rain gear, extra shoes, and food. Some hikers choose to wear running shoes, and often go through a pair every month. Find trail information, books, and maps through the Pacific Crest Trail Association (www.pcta.org).

Best Time. Hike south to north. Leave Mexico in April to finish in September or October.

Pit Stop. If you only have a few weeks or a month, it'll be hard to decide which section of this beautiful trail to hike. Some of the most spectacular parts are the John Muir Trail in the Sierras and the less-traveled Trinity Alps in California. Jefferson Park and the Three

Sisters Wilderness in Oregon are favorites. The famed towering North Cascades of Washington are also popular.

Extended Play. If you're looking for more, you likely already read about the triple crown of long distance trails: the Appalachian (Trip #21) and the Continental Divide Trails (currently not completed). If you're truly daring, follow Scott Willamson's bootprints and yo-yo (hike round-trip), which he did in 2004 in 197 days.

Travel Smart. Watch for halfway blues around the California/ Oregon border. Keep your pack light, consider running shoes or ultralight hikers and aim for a 30-pound pack. Most PCT hikers keep a shuttling box for food and clothing that they mail from supply post to supply post. Blisters and minor injuries are common, lower extremity sprains and strains can end a trip. Expect snow along the trail, even in midsummer. Remember, don't push it. If you have to bail for health or safety reasons, bail.

✅ 23. RACE ACROSS AMERICA BY BIKE (PACIFIC TO ATLANTIC OCEANS)

Big Mountain Adventures www.ridebig.com

You don't have to race. You can just ride.

Like competing in an Ironman Triathlon (Trip #30) or rafting the Grand Canyon (Trip #1), cycling across the Continental United States is a crowning life achievement for sports enthusiasts and adrenaline junkies alike. It's on everyone's bucket list, but is often a rather elusive goal. The actual riding is not the difficult part. Getting a chunk of time off, lining up places to stay, training, and committing are where it gets tough.

If you're the competitive type, sign up for the most prestigious, long-distance randonneur race. The RAAM, Race Across America (www.raceacrossamerica.org), was first organized in 1982. It blasted from the Santa Monica Pier in Los Angeles to the Empire State Building in New York City. Now riders embark in Oceanside, California, and spin to Annapolis, Maryland. The race takes place every June. Unlike the European Grand Tours—Tour de France, Vuelta a España, and Giro d'Italia—the RAAM isn't a stage race, but one long haul: 3,000 miles (4,828 km), 12 states, 170,000 vertical feet (51,816 m) of climbing. All at once. In about 2 weeks.

But, you don't have to race or crank out the transcontinental ride in 2 weeks. Better to take 6 weeks, go with a few buddies, and crash in friends' houses, a tent, or cheap hotels along the way.

Don't Miss. If you get the chance, and you will, take strangers up on good ol' American hospitality. Good Samaritans may offer to let you camp in their yards. Or sleep on their sofas. Or dine on grits.

Logistics. You'll need to outfit yourself with a touring bike, panniers, and cycle-weight camping gear (read: ultralight and ultra-compact). Choose from several routes that connect the Pacific and Atlantic. The northern route connects the Pacific Northwest with New York. The central route begins in San Francisco, travels through Denver, and ends anywhere in the mid-Atlantic. The southern route starts in Los Angeles and weaves through Texas and then lands in Florida. The TransAmerica Bicycle Trail, established by Adventure Cycling Association (www.adventurecycling.org), connects the charming town of Astoria, Oregon, with Yorktown, Virginia, traveling through the Yellowstone and Grand Teton National Parks.

Best Time. The RAAM runs every June. But you can go anytime during the summer. August has the best weather on the northern Route.

Pit Stop. Pick 1 state, and transect it via 2 wheels. Cycle Oregon, another option in my home state, offers a weeklong supported ride in one interstate area (www.cycleoregon.com). Check with the Adventure Cycling Association (www.adventurecycling.org) for other weeklong, intrastate rides near your home. You can also link to the U.S. Bicycle Route System.

Extended Play. If you really want to go for it, think about the Trans-Canada Route 1. It's arguably more scenic and less-crowded than its U.S. counterparts. Or traverse another continent, like Europe (Trip #54) or Africa (Trip #72). Try to beat Mike Hall's amazing feat—the fastest circumnavigation of the globe by bike. He rode 24,000 miles (38,400 km) on a modified cyclo-cross bike . . . in 92 days!

Travel Smart. Cars are the biggest hazard for cyclers, especially motorists who like to drive while holding their cell phones and a mochachino. Fatigue is another issue. Go light with gear. You'll want a rear rack and panniers, but be careful with front panniers. They can make the bike difficult to handle. Take a repair kit for your bike and first aid essentials for your body. Make sure to carry a credit card and cash for food, lodging, and an emergency ride home.

Go light, did I say that?

CANADA AND ALASKA

WIDE-OPEN PLAINS. Epic, remote mountains. Unspoiled, rugged coastlines. Creeks that transform into raging rivers. The deepest powder on earth.

Canada and Alaska are 2 of the most beautiful and least crowded places on the planet.

With 35 million people spread out over 3.8 million square miles (9.9 million km²) in Canada, you'll find lots of wide-open space in the Great White North. British Columbia alone has mountains and coasts that rank among the most scenic and dramatic in the world. Much like the South Island of New Zealand and Patagonia region of Chile and Argentina, British Columbia is an outdoor adventurer's paradise.

If you haven't been to British Columbia, and you live nearby, put it at the top of your list. If you have access to a plane or boat, you can get way off the beaten path. Even if you don't, these trips will give a great taste of what the region has to offer us adrenaline junkies.

24. SKI OR MOUNTAIN BIKE WHISTLER (BRITISH COLUMBIA)

To adrenaline junkies, the name means big mountain. Big mountain free skiing and snowboarding. Big, free-eride mountain biking trails. Big-wall rock climbing. Indeed, you can do it all at Whistler.

Like the extreme adventure towns of Chamonix, France (Trip #51), and Queenstown, New Zealand (Trip #75), come to Whistler to experience pure mountain culture, the awe of long climbs, and fear of long descents. You'll leave exhausted—physically spent and mentally taxed—and love every moment of it.

With its epic size, Whistler was chosen as the site for the 2010 Olympic Winter Games. Sure the quaint-turned-glitz town is expensive, but this place harbors some of the best adventure lines in the world. The only problem is picking a season and a sport. Unlike some sports towns, you'll have a hard time fitting it all in.

- Rock climb the world-class Stawamus Chief, the second most massive chunk of granite worldwide. The tiny berg of the same name still has a rural, small-town backcountry vibe.
- Ski the highest vertical drop in North America at Whistler Blackcomb Resort and experience the best sidecountry skiing and snowboarding in the world.
- Go helicopter and snowcat (an enclosed-cab tracked snow vehicle) skiing and snowboarding, right from town.

- Explore 80 miles (129 km) of skate and classic cross-country trails.
- Mountain bike the epic trails in the summertime. These are some of the best trails in the world for cross-country riding and lift-access downhill at the Whistler Mountain Bike Park.
- Take a family rafting or kayaking trip on the River of Golden Dreams, which links Alta and Green Lakes.
- Trail run some of the most rugged and scenic mountains around.

Don't Miss. Grab a table and a pint of Irish Smithwicks at the Dubh Linn Gate Pub (www.dubhlinngate.com) right at the gondola terminal (or try the local Powder Mountain Lager) after a long day on the mountain.

Logistics. Fly into Vancouver, British Columbia, and then grab a shuttle or rental car and cruise on the beautiful, newly refurbished Sea to Ski Highway. Once at Whistler, pick one of hundreds of high-end slope-side condos or hotels. Or grab a bunk in the youth hostel on Alta Lake. Hint: Get reduced-price lift tickets at the 7-Eleven in Squamish. The Whistler tourism office has tons of information on lodging and packages (www.whistler.com).

Best Time. Really, there's no bad time to come here. Come in winter for deep powder; in spring for blue-sky skiing and snow-boarding on Blackcomb Glacier; in summer for mountain biking, trail running, rock climbing, and kayaking; and in fall to miss the crowds.

Pit Stop. You don't have to do it all. Come to Whistler for a long ski weekend in the winter or mountain biking trip in the summer. You're guaranteed to arrive in awe and fear and leave utterly exhausted.

Extended Play. You have to do it all. Ski, snowboard, bike, kayak, and climb. If you have more time, climb and ski Mount Garibaldi (www.env.gov.bc.ca/bcparks/explore/parkpgs/garibaldi/), zip out to Vancouver Island to explore the fabulous kayak and surf village of Tofino (Trip #26), or, go surfing at the small berg of Sooke on the southern tip of Vancouver Island. For big mountain back-country skiing, hit remote, rugged Bella Coola (www.bellacoolahe liskiing.com).

Travel Smart. Adventure sports are dangerous. Wear a helmet. Stay within your skill level. Go with a buddy and a guide. Get solid gear. And don't try to keep up with the locals—they will ride, ski, run, and climb you into the ground!

25. SKI AND SNOWBOARD THE CANADIAN ROCKIES: THE POWDER HIGHWAY (BRITISH COLUMBIA)

If you're a serious skier, mention of the Canadian Rockies probably sends a chill down your back.

You won't find this route plastered all over ski magazines. You won't find this on lists of top resorts for best nightlife, best food, or best deluxe condos. You won't find slope-side glitz and glamour. There are no mega resorts or boutiques or ritzy ski villages. *Nada.*

If you come to this place, you will find fresh powder and some of the most rugged, bold, beautiful mountains on earth. Access the white smoke via an old-school, lift-served snowcat and helicopter operations, and by your own power by uphill hiking. Bunk in weathered west-Canadian ski towns full of wonderful, family-run restaurants, bookstores, markets, and motels.

This is the Powder Highway. Here lie the famous deep powder stashes of the Purcell, Selkirk, Monashee, and Bugaboo ranges. The Canadian Rockies have one of the highest concentrations of winter ski and snowboard areas, snowcat and helicopter operators, backcountry lodges, and Nordic clubs in the world.

Stop reading. Go book your trip now.

Begin at the cute lakeside town of Nelson and Whitewater Ski Resort (www.skiwhitewater.com). Then hit Rossland, home to steep and deep Red Mountain (www.redresort.com) and many unearthly backcountry and sidecountry routes just north of town. Drive up to Revelstoke (www.revelstokemountainresort.com) for a few laps. Then go touring on the famed Rogers Pass, nestled at the apex of Glacier National Park on the Trans-Canada Highway (watch out for avalanches). There's many a lift, backcountry line, or snowcat to catch on your way south through Golden, Invermere, and Fernie (www.skifernie.com). For heli-skiing, Canadian Mountain Holidays (www.canadianmountainholidays.com) or Mike Wiegele Heli Skiing (www.wiegele.com) are 2 of the oldest and most reputable companies. Or try snowcat skiing at Island Lake Lodge (www .islandlakecatskiing.com).

Don't Miss. Utilize one of the huts of the Alpine Club of Canada (www.alpineclubofcanada.ca), such as the A. O. Wheeler Hut or Asulkan Cabin in the famed Rogers Pass of Glacier National Park, to ski the epic backcountry. Check out Selkirk Mountain Experience (www.selkirkexperience.com), one of the best outfitters in the area, run out of the Durrand Glacier Chalet and Mt. Moloch Chalet in Revelstoke.

Logistics. Fly into Calgary or Spokane, Washington, or take a local puddle jumper to Cranbrook, Castlegar, Trail, or Kelowna. Shuttles are easy to arrange if you're headed to a resort, or rent a car and drive the loop. Even better, book a backcountry lodge for a week, and then plan to come back every year. Stop at Powder Highway for all of the mountain info you'll need (www.powder highway.com).

Best Time. Come hither in winter, when the sky pukes powder.

Pit Stop. Short on time, fly into Spokane and hit Red Mountain for a long weekend. It's a fabulous resort for the whole family, has steep lift-access, and backcountry powder stashes lie just north of town.

Extended Play. Drive the loop, and pick a backcountry hut to hang out for a week. Hit Whitefish Mountain Resort (skiwhitefish .com) and Glacier National Park in northeast Montana, or tack on a Nordic ski extravaganza in the Methow Valley, Washington (Trip #15).

Travel Smart. Backcountry skiing is not the sort of activity to test out on your own. Go with a guide. The best option is a guided hut trip combined with an avalanche course. Watch out for hypothermia, frostbite, dehydration, and, if you hit the right weather, sunburn. Bring avalanche survival and rescue gear and learn how to use it.

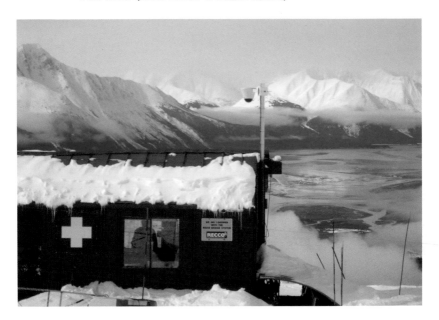

Go ahead. Live the dream.

Quit your corporate job (or finagle a telecommuting position). Trade your 4,000-square-foot hardwood floors, and stainless steel kitchen for a quaint cottage with a ginormous garage and vinyl-floor mudroom. Sell the boat and RV and get a sturdy 4 x 4 with a rooftop cargo box. Then move to a surf or ski town. It doesn't matter where.

And you might have to move first, then figure out how to make a living. I did it and 12 years later, I'm still loving the life. In all of my travels to outdoor towns, I've never met a person who's regretted this kind of move.

There are many small sports town around the world. Just look for a list in any outdoor magazine or blog. You probably have a special spot or 2 on your bucket list. One of mine is Tofino with its raw and rugged beauty; its mountains spilling into the sea; its wild surf; its thick, dank conifer rainforests; and its spongy peat bogs.

Tofino is a fishing village turned surf-and-kayak town on the remote west coast of Vancouver Island. You can surf and paddle all day, trail run through spectacular coastal growth or on pristine beaches, and feast on wild salmon at night. During the winter, climb and descend some of the best backcountry winter skiing routes in the world at Bella Coola.

If surfing and kayaking in a remote, rugged coastal village isn't your gig, pick another town, another country, or another sport. If you aren't a skier or surfer, every state has a cycling, climbing, or paddling town.

Don't Miss. If you make it to Tofino, hike the famed West Coast Trail, the 47-mile (75 km) trail that runs from Bamfield to Port Renfrew. It was built in 1907 to help rescue shipwreck survivors from the Graveyard of the Pacific and now courses along the coast through spectacular, rugged, dank Pacific Rim National Park.

Logistics. Part of the beauty of a place like Tofino is that it's difficult to get to. Fly into Victoria, or take the ferry from Washington or Vancouver, Canada. Then drive to Tofino, with kayaks, surfboard, and bikes in tow.

Best Time. For surfing, kayaking, and fishing, head over in the summer. Better yet, just move there!

Pit Stop. If you can't make it to Tofino, check out Canada's Gulf Islands where you'll find some of the best sea kayaking in the world. You should also scope out the east coast of Nova Scotia, Canada.

Extended Play. Move anywhere you can play more than you work.

Travel Smart. One caution about a place like Tofino, is that it's fairly remote so use caution when surfing, kayaking, trail running, and biking. Waves and currents can be tricky if you aren't used to the surroundings. The water is also cold so bring a full wetsuit with booties and gloves. And bring rain gear. It comes down in buckets.

Why is the Iditarod called the Last Great Race? Let's see. Take a 1,149-mile (1,688 km) course. Plaster it with ice, snow, blizzards, gales, and subzero temps. Weave it through jagged peaks, frozen rivers, thick forests, and miles of flat, harsh tundra. Then add in the cold darkness of an Alaskan March. Oh, and race the Anchorage-to-Nome track with a team of 12 to 16 sled dogs in less than 2 weeks.

Indeed, the famed Iditarod sled-dog race is one of the harshest, most grueling, most difficult competitions in the world.

The Iditarod Trail was first used by Inupiaq and Athabasca American Indians, and was named for either a Holikachuk, an Ingalik, or a Shageluk word for "far distant place," or "clear water." Later, Russian fur traders and Yukon gold miners used the track for shuttling mail and supplies. Eventually the town of Iditarod was abandoned, but the name has stuck to the trail. The first Iditarod took place in 1967. In 1972, Joe Redington codified the race and preserved the historic trail.

The race dogs are beautiful and athletic. Stout Inuit sled dogs bred by the Mahlemut Indians were the original runners, but the dogs used now are generally Alaskan and Siberian Huskies. The dogs burn close to 5,000 calories a day and their lungs have 3 times the capacity of a world-class marathon racer. In 2011, John Baker led a team that finished in 8 days, 19 hours, and 49 minutes, the fastest finish to date.

Don't Miss. The opening ceremony in Anchorage is not to be missed—even if you're not racing.

Logistics. It's complicated. You have to be an experienced musher (dogsled racer) and meet minimum qualifications to participate. Get the full scoop at Iditarod headquarters (iditarod.com).

Best Time. The Iditarod starts the first Saturday in March.

Pit Stop. You can mush dogs for a day without much experience. Head to Anchorage and go dogsled racing or skijoring, in which you wear cross-country skis instead of standing on a sled, for a day (www.ididaride.com). Mush your own team down the spectacular Resurrection River Valley into Exit Glacier during the winter. In the summer, head to Girdwood, take a chopper ride to Punch Bowl Glacier, and mush a team in the bright sun of the Chugach Range.

Extended Play. If you're headed to Anchorage in spring, don't miss a chance to heli-ski with Chugach Powder Guides (www .chugachpowderguides.com); ski or snowboard for a day at the steep, deep, and uncrowded Alyeska Resort (www.alyeskaresort. com); backcountry ski tour up Turnagain Pass; or windsurf the hellacious and tricky tides of Turnagain Arm.

Travel Smart. Alaska is big, bold, and rugged. A friend once took me on a 1-hour Super Cub flight out of Anchorage to see the surroundings. We were equipped with snowshoes, sleeping bags, food, water, and a survival pistol that shot both shotgun shells and bullets (bullets for bear protection, shells to kill small game to eat). You have to be prepared with keen survival skills up in the fortyninth state. Bring excellent gear and be careful.

28. SAIL OR PADDLE THE INSIDE PASSAGE (BRITISH COLUMBIA)

This route is at the top of the list for sailors and kayakers. You won't find the warm-water sailing of the Caribbean (Trip #35), nor the rich and glorious history of the Turquoise Coast (Trip #56). This is a long sail or paddle on a sparsely populated, weather-torn, current-ripped coast where mountains quite literally spill into the sea.

The Inside Passage is marked with rugged, towering coastal mountains that drop straight into the sea. There are deep fjords; hanging glaciers; scattered, uninhabited islands; colonies of bears and bald eagles; and endless forests of old-growth conifers like Douglas fir, cedar, hemlock, and spruce.

The Inside Passage is a waterway that links Anchorage and southeast Alaska to Vancouver, British Columbia. It's traveled by cruise ships, commercial vessels, fishing boats, freighters, and ferries.

You can paddle or sail for several months, or just do portions in separate trips like Jonathan Raban chronicled in the lyrical *Passage to Juneau: A Sea and Its Meanings.*

Don't Miss. Watch icebergs calve from hanging glaciers into the ocean from a sea kayak or boat. There's no better place to do so than Glacier Bay National Park.

Best Time. June through August is ideal for long days and calm weather.

Logistics. If you're kayaking, go one way from Anchorage down to Victoria, or you can just do portions of this trip. Take the Alaska Marine Highway ferry system (www.dot.state.ak.us) or BC Ferries (www.bcferries.com) to transport boats to Anchorage. Then plan on taking a couple of months to paddle home.

Pit Stop. Don't have enough time for the whole shebang? The Inside Passage is still not to be missed. Consider kayaking through Glacier Bay and parts of southeast Alaska, like the quaint town of Sitka. Not a boater? You can cruise southeast Alaska on a budget using the Alaska Marine Highway ferries where you just pitch a tent on deck. Or, *gulp,* take a cruise ship, but plan to hike or bike ride at each port to avoid the kitschy wharfside tourist traps at the docks. I did it, and found spectacular hiking and running trails in Juneau, Ketchikan, and Sitka within walking distance of our dock.

Extended Play. Sail the whole trip over a summer, Anchorage to Seattle. Or bring your skis and poach some big lines in Bella Coola (www.bellacoolaheliskiing.com). Bring a bike like a compact-folding Bike Friday (bikefriday.com) to zip around the towns.

Travel Smart. Be cautious of open water. Use a personal flotation device, carry a marine band radio, and research the local currents. Expect prolonged periods with no help. Be ready to hole up if weather is foul. And bring fishing gear.

Next to Everest and Vinson Massif, Denali is one of the crown jewels of mountaineering. It's also one of the most difficult climbs among the Seven Summits, or the highest peaks of each continent.

Meaning "the High One" in Athabaskan, Denali is the state-recognized name for the peak also known as Mount McKinley, after gold prospector William McKinley. The peak is massive, clocking in at 20,320 feet (6,194 m). Hudson Stuck, Harry Karstens, Walter Harper, and Robert Tatum were the first to conquer the peak in 1913. Now, it's often first on the list for Seven Summit questers.

Jutting out from the rugged Alaska Range, the classic West Buttress route is the primary ascent line. You may read that it's a "nontechnical" climb, which generally means there's no vertical ice or rock. But you'll need glacier travel gear and avalanche safety and slope climbing skills to do this climb safely. You should also know how to ascend fixed ropes and have a high tolerance for bitter cold, raging winds, and extreme altitude. Because Denali is so far north, you often don't need a headlamp; you'll be climbing in the midnight sun.

Start at 7,300 feet (2,300 m) on the Kahiltna Glacier and ski up to advance base camp at 14,000 feet (4,300 m) where a block of

Tillamook cheddar is worth its weight in gold. You'll be lucky if you get good weather. Typically you'll find 60-mile-per-hour (96 km/h) winds and -40 degree-Fahrenheit (-40 C) temperatures, so prepare to be tent-bound for days. You should plan on 3 weeks for the entire expedition.

Don't Miss. Peruse Bradford Washburn's legendary black-and-white images. Washburn first climbed the West Buttress route in 1951 and his images became world renowned. You can find them in *Bradford Washburn: Mountain Photography* or at the University of Fairbanks's Alaska and Polar Regions Collection.

Logistics. Fly into Anchorage and then take a shuttle to the tiny outpost of Talkeetna, a funky sports town and the gateway to Denali National Park. You'll have to sign in, get permits, and do a mandatory safety training. Your last good meal and bunk may likely be at the Talkeetna Roadhouse (www.talkeetnaroadhouse.com), a gathering spot for climbers built in 1917. Order a frontier breakfast: sourdough hotcakes, giant cinnamon roll, thick peppered bacon, piles of scrambled eggs, and a slab of Granny's Chocolate Potato Cake to go. From there take a bush plane to Base Camp at 7,300 feet (2,200 m) on the tongue of the Kahiltna Glacier. Check out Rainier Mountaineering (www.rmiguides.com), Alpine Ascents International (www.alpineascents.com), and International Mountain Guides (www.mountainguides.com). The Denali National Park Web site has a complete list of authorized guides (www.nps.gov/dena).

Best Time. The main climbing season is May through July.

Pit Stop. If you don't have the 3 weeks necessary to climb Denali, shoot for climbing Mount Rainier, a burly mountain that can be conquered in a weekend (Trip #4). It'll give you that big-mountain experience.

Extended Play. If you're looking for more technical climbs, try neighboring Mount Foraker (17,400 ft; 5,304 m), or smaller peaks like Ruth Glacier, Little Switzerland, Kichatna Spires, and the

Ramparts. You can backcountry ski the famed Chugach Range (www.chugachpowderguides.com). Consider volunteering for a monthlong patrol at the 14,000-foot base camp, comprised of doctors and climbers tasked with assisting the National Park Service climbing rangers.

Travel Smart. Okay, it's a big mountain. You'll experience bitter cold, high altitude, and weeks of traveling through glaciers across avalanche-prone slopes. Guard against acute mountain sickness, especially severe complications from high-altitude pulmonary edema and high-altitude cerebral edema, when the lungs and brain fill with fluid respectively. Hypothermia and frostbite are very common. Falling into crevasses or down steep slopes is also possible. It's best to go with a guide. There are medical outposts with a climbing ranger and doctor at 14,000 feet (4,300 m) during the climbing season.

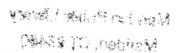

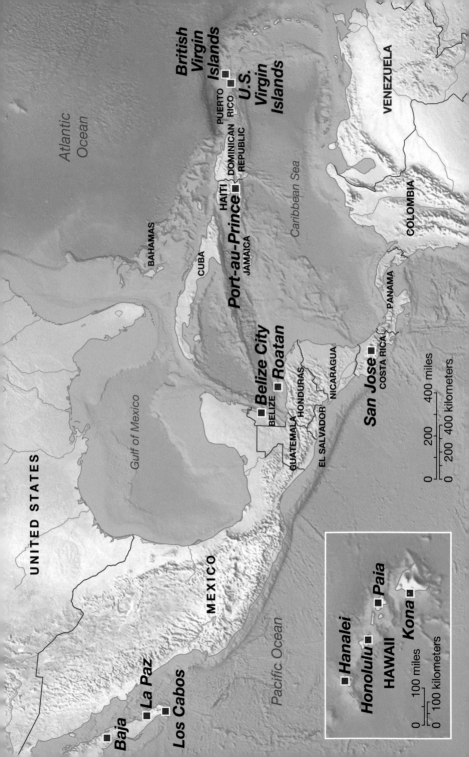

WARM BREEZES, scads of sun, pristine beaches, and perfect, turquoise water. Stick it in a blender and you'll get some of the most fabulous playgrounds in the world. Sure, solitude is rare—many of these sun-drenched locales are popular with tourists and other adventurers. But searching for sun, wind, and waves in the equatorial sunbelt isn't necessarily about going deep into the wild. It's about escaping the cold, clouds, and rain. The tropics dish up some of most spectacular underwater reefs, thrilling whitewater, and cleanest waves on the planet.

When you feel stuck in the dreariness of winter, zip over to Hawaii, explore the islands of the Caribbean, or book a week in Central America—a region rich in multicultural heritage as well as sun and beaches.

Your biggest problem will be picking one sport or one location. These areas are water sports central. Go diving, snorkeling, sailing, surfing, kitesurfing, windsurfing, or, the latest rage, stand up paddling. If water sports aren't your gig, you can find world-class rainforest canyoneering or climb a volcano.

If you're a multisport junkie wanting to rough it a bit, Baja, Mexico, or Costa Rica are great spots. If you're a diver or sailor, definitely go to the Caribbean. Kayakers will want to check out Belize. Costa Rica is where it's at for surfers. If you want to pick a singular trip—especially if you are hauling family—head to Hawaii.

Whatever the case, go there, do it, don't wait.

30. SWIM, RUN, AND RIDE THE IRONMAN TRIATHLON (KONA, HAWAII)

World Triathlon Corporation

Back in 1977 at the Oahu Perimeter Relay, 2 groups of überfit athletes got in a debate. The Mid-Pacific Road Runners and Waikiki Swim Club argued: Who was the fittest? With triathlons popping up all over California, the debate was ultimately settled by a little experiment. The Waikiki Roughwater Swim (2.4 mi/3.9 km), the Around-Oahu Bike Race (115 mi/185 km), and the Honolulu Marathon (26.2 mi/42.2 km) were combined into 1 epic event. A year after inception, the 1978 race spawned an entire culture, and became the gold standard for endurance athletes: the full-length triathlon.

To participate in the Ironman World Championship, now hosted at Kona, you'll need to qualify at another half- or full-length triathlon. There are no wetsuits allowed in the open ocean swim in Kailua Bay. You'll endure a hot and windy ride across the lava fields to Hawi and back. And you'll run a marathon along the Keauhou coast, often in the heat of the day. What fun!

Now Ironman and Half Ironman (also called "70.3" for half the Ironman distance) events take place worldwide. If you can, try the granddaddy at Kona. You don't have to beat the current record holder, Craig Alexander, who blasted through in 8 hours, 3 minutes, and 56 seconds in 2011.

Don't Miss. Where fire meets water. Check out the triple volcanoes. Mauna Kea punches 33,000 feet (10,058 m) from the seafloor. Both Mauna Loa and Kilauea actively ooze molten lava into the sea.

Logistics. Fly into Kona and set up shop. You'll need to arrive the week before to acclimatize, scout the course, and start the check-in process. Get all the info you need at Ironman central (www.iron man.com).

Best Time. The Ironman World Championship at Kona is held once a year in October.

Pit Stop. If you don't have time for Kona, pick any triathlon close to home. You can do a full Ironman, Half Ironman, Olympic (1 mile/1.5 km swim, 24 mile/40 km bike, and 6mile/10 km run), or Sprint triathlon (half of the Olympic distances).

Extended Play. Start with a Half Ironman, then try a full, then go for Kona. Can't make Kona work for your schedule? Surf Ironman central (ironman.com) and pick an international race, like the ones in Kalmar, Sweden; Port Elizabeth, South Africa; Busselton, Australia; or Florianópolis, Brazil.

If you decide to do Kona, enjoy the Big Island, which has 11 of the world's 13 climate zones. It's another multisport paradise. Hike the lava beds and rainforests. Surf, kayak, paddle, and snorkel the uncrowded beaches of Kona Coast. Horseback ride through grassy plains of *paniolo* (cowboy) country.

Travel Smart. You've got to train. A lot. And then train some more. Run, ride, and swim. Plot a reasonable schedule. And then, ride, run, and swim some more. When that's all done, get on your bike for a ride. But always remember, this is an endurance event. Proper hydration and nutrition are essential.

31. SURF AN ELEPHANT OR RHINO: THE NORTH SHORE (OAHU, HAWAII)

Monsters. Giants. Elephants. Rhinos. They're the big, bad burly waves. And you should try to ride one! No place is more prominent in surfing lore than the North Shore. You may find bigger waves around the world, but the North Shore is a pilgrimage every surfer makes, sooner or later. It's one of the most difficult and challenging surfing spots in the world.

Surfing began as a royal sport of ancient Polynesia. When explorer Captain James Cook landed in Hawaii in 1778, he spied Polynesian royalty riding waves on long wood planks crafted from hardwoods like *koa* (Hawaiian mahogany), *ulu* (breadfruit), and *wili-wili* (Hawaiian balsa). Mark Twain wrote about surfing in his 1866 book, *Roughing It,* as did Jack London in his 1907 article, "A Royal Sport: Surfing in Waikiki." But mainstream surf culture truly emerged when Olympic freestyle gold medalist, Duke Kahanamoku, brought it to California. Now surf culture is embedded deep in our lifestyle, from clothing to music.

Surfers come here to surf the trifecta of breaks: Waimea Bay, Sunset Beach, and Ehukai Beach, aka Banzai Pipeline. They are all dangerous, but if you can capture just one clean ride, you will forever be one of the North Shore elite.

Don't Miss. If you can time it, plan a trip during the Triple Crown of Surfing: Reef Hawaiian Pro, O'Neill World Cup of Surfing, and Billabong Pipeline Masters. Watch the best surfers in the world catch the best waves in the world. Looking for local culture? Grab a mixed plate lunch at Lei Lei's Bar & Grill (www.turtlebayresort .com). Mixed plate is a local tradition that started when people of the many cultures on the islands began sharing their lunches.

Logistics. You can fly directly to Honolulu from many West Coast cities. Then negotiate the traffic to the North Shore. The main hotel is Turtle Bay Resort, (www.turtlebayresort.com). You can also book a private condo, house, or hostel.

Best Time. Winter is the best time for big waves—Thanksgiving through February.

Pit Stop. If you don't have several weeks to hone your surf skills, try the user-friendly, tourist-friendly waves of Waikiki. You can stroll out of your hotel, rent a decent surf or stand up paddle board, and catch long rides on clean, small waves (alongside plenty of tourists so you don't feel like a total dork).

Extended Play. Take big-wave surfing one step further and ride Peahi, aka Jaws, Maui's legendary big-wave, deep-water break. You'll need a tow-in board and a partner with a personal watercraft. And you'll have to be ready to pounce because it only breaks a few times a year. The waves down? No problem. Ski or snowboard Oahu's other big elephant, the 13,796-foot-high (4,105 m) Mauna Kea (meaning "white mountain") volcano. There are nearly a dozen backcountry ski and snowboard runs.

Not so into surfing? Hawaii too far? Try one of the many incarnations of board sports at near home, like riverboarding (surfing rapids and standing waves), stand-up paddling (paddling a large surfboard on lakes, rivers, or ocean waves), windsurfing, kitesurfing, or skateboarding.

Travel Smart. Surfing is dangerous, sure. But so is driving a car. Just stay within your skill range. Take surf lessons. Don't jump into Banzai Pipeline your first day. Practice on smaller breaks in Oahu. Oahu has one of the finest water-rescue patrols in the world, but hopefully you won't need their help.

✓ 32. *WINDSURF HO'OKIPA: KITESURF AND STAND-UP PADDLE, TOO (MAUI, HAWAII)*

Take clean waves, add in gentle winds, and then adapt your surfboard for wind power with a sail or kite. Use the power of the wind to harness the power of surf. That's basically how wind and wave sports melded into new kinds of water sports. Ride the wind out, and the waves back in.

What Oahu's North Shore is to surfing, Maui's Ho'okipa is to windsurfing. It's the epicenter of wave sailing.

Nope, this isn't a beginner, intermediate, or advanced break. It's for experts only.

Windsurfing was invented in 1948 when Newman Darby used a universal joint to attach a sail to a plank. In 1968 Jim Drake and Hoyle Schweitzer, an engineer and a surfer, patented the Windsurfer, which utilized a universal joint instead of the fixed mast of a sailboat. Nowadays, the north shore of Maui is a windsurfer's heaven.

Many windsurfers have now moved to kitesurfing. Wide-open Kanaha Beach in Maui is kite central. If you're a windrider, make the journey to Maui.

Don't Miss. The tiny sports town of Paia is base camp for Maui. The Paia Fish Market is one of my favorite culinary spots in the world. Grab a huge, après-sports slab of fresh-grilled ono, mahimahi, ahi, or whatever else came out of the sea that day. Carbo-load with Hawaiian-style potatoes and Cajun rice (www.paiafishmarket.com). For a more romantic affair, Mama's Fish House has a small inn, a great beach for kids and a delicious Polynesian ono marinated in lime and coconut milk (www.mamasfishhouse.com).

Logistics. Fly into Kahului. You can find direct flights from many West Coast cities. There are no big resorts in Paia, quite unlike the West Maui hotel sprawl of Kaanapali. You'll have to book a house, condo, or hostel. Rent a car and ask for a roof rack. You can rent gear at Naish Maui (naishmaui.com) or Maui Windsurf (www.maui-windsurf.com).

Best Time. Fall and spring are the best times for wind and waves (and to escape the dreary clouds at home).

Pit Stop. If you don't have time or skills to conquer Ho'okipa, check out Kanaha Beach Park, very close to the Maui airport. Gentle waves, a calm environment, and open fields of grass make this spot ideal for a quick windsurfing trip. No wind or waves? Don't worry. Rent a stand-up paddleboard; the smallish waves at Lahaina and Kihei are great for stand up paddling.

Extended Play. If you've got time to settle in, go to Paia for a few months. Surf Jaws, ride a road bike on the road to Hana or up to

10,023-foot (3,055 m) Haleakala, camp in a backcountry cabin in Haleakala National Park's crater, snorkel Honolua Bay, rent a mountain bike, and go canyoneering. That's a Maui sampler worthy of a month (or 2).

Travel Smart. Water safety is key here. You need open water and surf swimming experience, and you should be an expert wind or kitesurfer. Watch for reefs and rocks along the shore; plenty of windsurfers have shredded their gear and scraped their bodies against the rocks. Learn the currents and local customs. Be ready to share the waves.

33. KAYAKING AND FASTPACKING THE NA PALI COAST (KAUAI, HAWAII)

If you don't quite have the jacked-up temperament for riding on the North Shore (Trip #31) or dropping into Ho'okipa (Trip #32), I've got the place for you. The Na Pali Coast—where *Jurassic Park* was filmed—has stunning, unspoiled lush rainforests, and the 3,000-

foot deep Waimea Canyon. Step back in time and experience the untrammeled island—Kauai.

Na Pali Coast State Wilderness Park is one of the lushest places on earth. It's where the South Pacific island mountains meet the sea. And there are (at least) 2 fabulous reasons to make a pilgrimage here.

First, there's the famed 11-mile (18 km) Kalalau Trail, which is commonly cited as one of the best hikes in the world. It's right up there with the Milford Track in New Zealand (Trip #74), Washington's Wonderland Trail (Trip #4), British Columbia's West Coast Trail (Trip #26), and the John Muir Trail in California's Sierra Nevada (Trip #22). The Kalalau Trail starts at Ke'e Beach, touches Hanakapiai Beach, passes through lush emerald valleys, and meanders atop towering sea cliffs. Built in the 1800s to link early settlements, the out-and-back trail ends in sheer *pali,* or cliffs, at Kalalau Beach.

And for second treat, sea kayak the coast. It's inaccessible by foot, but rests just below the trail. The 17-mile (27 km) coastal kayak route starts from Haena Beach Park and terminates at Polihale State Park. You'll paddle a beautiful, remote stretch of coastline and pitch your tent in campgrounds at Kalalau or Miloli'i.

Don't Miss. Take a day to kayak or paddle the lush Hanalei and Wailua rivers, or snorkel the Blue Lagoon and explore its tide pools and sea caves. You might spot a monk seal or dolphin. Rent a beach-cruiser bike and explore the beautiful town of Hanalei. Like elsewhere in Hawaii, gentle surf breaks, great snorkel spots, and pristine beaches abound. Go stand up paddling!

Logistics. Fly into Honolulu then take a commuter flight to Hanalei. For guided trips, rentals, and car shuttles, check Napali Kayak (www.napalikayak.com), Kayak Kauai (www.kayakkauai .com), or Pedal 'N Paddle (www.pedalnpaddle.com). You can paddle the coast in 1 day, but better to take your time among the surf-carved caves, cascading waterfalls, and trails of the Kalalau and Honopu valleys. For the Kalalau Coast Trail, take a few days, unless you're a runner and want to do 22 miles out and back in 1 stint. You'll need a permit for camping on either trip, so check ahead with the state park (www.hawaiistateparks.org).

Best Time. The coastal campgrounds, Kalalau and Miloli'i, are open between May 15 to September 7. Hike the Kalalau Coast Trail year-round.

Pit Stop. If you're short on time, pick either kayaking or hiking. Or just go fast! Each segment can be done in 1 long day.

Extended Play. Take your time. You can paddle the coastal kayak route in 3 days. Then backpack the 22-mile (round-trip) Kalalau Trail in another 3 days. Stop in to windsurf Maui's Ho'okipa (Trip #32) or surf Oahu's North Shore (Trip #31).

Travel Smart. On the trail, you'll need a tent, mosquito repellent, water-purification goods, rain gear, and a lightweight sleeping bag. On the water, bring a good personal-flotation device (aka life jacket), helmet, and gloves. Hone your water skills. Foul weather, wind, and big waves can plague the open-water passage. And some of the campgrounds may require surf landings.

 34. DIVE AND SNORKEL THE CARIBBEAN: 7,000 ISLANDS

There are enough islands in the Caribbean for a lifetime of exploration. You'll find coral reefs, tiny cays, sandy shores, and open blue water. You'll find a plethora of reefs and cays to choose from in the sundrenched beaches of the Greater and Lesser Antilles and the surrounding islands. The Bahamas, Bermuda, Turks and Caicos, and many Central American countries have beautiful Caribbean Sea coastlines as well.

This mixture of sun, sand, gentle surf, underwater life, and broad, dynamic culture makes the Caribbean a must. It's an especially easy jaunt for East Coasters who can drop down on a quick flight.

The Caribbean is comprised of more than 30 territories, each with its own rich and vibrant culture. You'll fine unique music (calypso, reggae, ska), at least 6 languages (English, Haitian Creole, Papiamento, French, Dutch, and Spanish) and varied religions (Christianity, Rastafari, Santería, and Voodoo).

If you're a diver or snorkeler, this is one of the richest ecosystems in the world. These are some of the best spots for diving and snorkeling:

- Salt Pier, Bonaire, is an underwater wonderland. It's accessible from many hotel beaches, and it has one of the highest concentrations of tropical reef fish. You'll be swimming in a living aquarium.
- RMS Rhone Wreck, Virgin Gorda, in the British Virgin Islands, is a mail steamer that sank in an 1867 hurricane. It's now one of the most famous underwater parks in the world.
- Stingray City in the Grand Cayman Islands is where you can feed stingrays.
- Mona Island in Puerto Rico is like the Caribbean Galápagos, packed with reefs, seawalls, and trenches.
- Saba Island has black sand beaches, black coral, lava flows, shallow dives, and a bazillion fish.
- The West Caicos Wall in Turks and Caicos is a 6,000-foot (1,800 m) vertical reef replete with coral, sponges, tropical fish, barracuda, sea turtles, manta and stingrays, and a collection of hammerhead, reef and nurse sharks. The 22-mile-wide (35 km) Columbus Passage is famous for migrating humpback whales and the 1790 shipwreck HMS *Endymion*.
- Green Outhouse Wall in Roatan, Honduras, has long been a diver's haven for brain coral, sea fans, gorgonians, angelfish,

big scrawled filefish, tangs, durgeons, barracuda, and stingrays.

- Santa Rosa Wall in Cozumel, Mexico, has amazing coral heads, gorgonians, and azure vase and orange elephant ear sponges.
- St. Croix in the U.S. Virgin Islands has wrecks, beaches, and night and wall dives. Check out the arches and ledges of Cow and Calf Rocks in Buck Island, the coal canyons of Cane Bay and Salt River, or the Puerto Rico Trench, at 11,808 feet (3,600 m) down.
- The Yucatán Peninsula in Mexico has the cave-riddled limestone of cenote, a deep sinkhole cave.
- In Cuba, check out Jardines de la Reina (meaning "Gardens of the Queen"), a national park in the forbidden land.

Don't Miss. Go night diving in Roatan, Honduras, or St. Croix, U.S. Virgin Islands, with a guide.

Logistics. Depending on where you go, you will likely fly through either Miami or Dallas/Fort Worth. You can pick an all-inclusive dive resort, or set up your own plan. Rent dive gear from a shop or resort certified through the Professional Association of Diving Instructors (www.padi.com) or the National Association of Underwater Instructors (www.naui.org). At many resorts you can walk right off the beach into the underwater world. For an even more spectacular experience set up boat dives and a guide ahead of time. Want more options? Try Fantasy Island (www.fantasyisland vacations.com) or Anthony's Key Resort (www.anthonyskey.com) in Roatan. The latter has the Roatan Institute for Marine Science. At Bonaire, try Buddy Dive Resort (www.buddydive.com) or Captain Don's Habitat (www.habitatbonaire.com).

Best Time. Many of these spots are open year-round, but in December through April you'll find prime Caribbean weather and escape winter at home.

Pit Stop. If you only have a week, try an all-inclusive dive resort at Bonaire, Roatan, or the U.S. Virgin Islands. You can do only beach dives in those spots. And if you prefer to snorkel, don't worry about missing out: You can view much of the coolest marine life from the surface without dive gear.

Extended Play. Go sailing (Trip #35) and take dive gear, or indulge in flatwater kayaking or kitesurfing.

Travel Smart. If you have a dive emergency or a question about anything related to dive medicine, check out DAN—Divers Alert Network (www.diversalertnetwork.org). It's a nonprofit safety association run by a team of doctors and dive professionals who give medical advice on dive-related issues. Diving has a whole slew of medical risks, which result from pressure differences between the deep ocean and sea level. There are also risk factors if you are flying right after a dive, so consult your local dive doc or textbook.

 ## 35. *SAIL THE VIRGIN ISLANDS*

Go bareboat or full crew. Sail or motor a yacht. Cruise on a monohull or catamaran. In addition to having some of the best diving in the world (Trip #34), the Caribbean offers spectacular sailing. Great winds, fabulous ports, white and black sand beaches, warm aquamarine water, and relatively straightforward navigation make the Virgin Islands an especially desirable spot for sailors.

The Virgin Islands are part of the Leeward Islands in the northern Lesser Antilles. The British Virgin Islands include Tortola, Virgin Gorda, Jost Van Dyke, and Anegada; the U.S. group includes St. Croix, St. John and St. Thomas. The region was first dubbed Santa Ursula y las Once Mil Virgenes, after St. Ursula, the saint of virgins reportedly killed by the Huns in 383. The islands were inhabited by the Arawak and Carib peoples before being ousted by European settlers.

The Virgin Islands are known for having some of the best snorkeling and diving in the world. Many of the bays are protected, but you will find plenty of marinas with beautiful restaurants, like the famous Bitter End Yacht Club (www.beyc.com). It's also 75 to 85 degrees Fahrenheit year-round (24 to 31 degrees C)!

Don't Miss. Check out Cane Garden Bay in northern Tortola. Stop in to kayak, kitesurf, stand-up paddle, or snorkel before cruising through town and grabbing a Bushwacker, a drink made from 4 types of Caribbean rum or a rum-ginger beer concoction called Dark 'n' Stormy. Grab a table and a Mahi Mahi Burger at Myett's Garden and Grille (www.myettent.com) and listen to calypso and reggae. Kayak through the caves of the Bight on Norman Island. Savor Anegada Island conch fritters at the Willie T's floating café (williamthornton.com).

Logistics. Fly through Miami into Christiansted on St. Croix or Charlotte Amalie on St. Thomas. Book a boat through The Moorings (www.moorings.com) or Barefoot Yacht Charters (www.bearefoot yachts.com). For diving, scope out Trip #34; for kitesurfing go to Carib Kiteboarding (www.caribkiteboarding.com) at the famed Bitter End Yacht Club on Virgin Gorda. Most resorts will have dive equipment, kayaks, windsurfing gear, and stand-up paddleboards.

Best Time. Go anytime, year-round. Just be wary during hurricane season, August to October.

Pit Stop. Book a 5-day, fully crewed, and catered boat so you don't have to do anything but show up with a suitcase. Even then, you only need a few summer outfits: flip-flops, boardshorts or bikini, and sun hat are the standard uniform.

Extended Play. Bring dive, snorkel, kayak, or kitesurf gear. Beyond the Virgin Islands, sail the Leeward Island trip—the northern Lesser Antilles—where the winds blow from the east. Anguilla is chocked with white sand beaches, blue water, reefs, and uninhabited cays. Shoal Bay East is one of the best spots for diving and snorkeling and has beautiful Stoney Bay Marine Park. Drop into rustic Saba Island and climb the 1,064 steps to Mount Scenery. Alternatively, sail the Windward Islands—the southern Lesser Antilles—via the easterly trade winds. Martinique (meaning "Island of Flowers") has hikes through lush tropical rainforests like the Gorges de la Falaise.

Travel Smart. Sailing barefoot, or without a skipper, is the real deal. You'll need to know your stuff and probably submit a sailing résumé (Trip #90). Otherwise, book a skippered, catered trip.

 ## 36. DRIVE THE BAJA PENINSULA (MEXICO)

Driving the Baja Peninsula is a pilgrimage that every adrenaline junkie makes at one point in his or her life. The Baja is chock-full of unbelievable beaches and deserts, spectacular marine reefs for snorkeling and kayaking, world-class waves for surfing, steady wind for kiting and windsurfing, and rugged mountains great for bouldering, mountain biking, and even a ski-mountaineering tour.

As one friend told me after his trip, "Baja is good for the soul." The pace is slow, the water is wild, the beer is summer-weight swill, and the fresh dorado, yellow fin and mahi mahi are fabulous.

Driving the full-length of the 775-mile (1,247 km) peninsula is an amazing journey. The road from Tijuana starts in the chaparral and pine-oak woodlands, transitions into the Sonoran desert with its giant cacti and cirio trees, and then extends into desert coastal beaches.

Load up the 4 x 4 or the biggest van you can find. The drive takes about 3 or 4 days to Baja California's southern border, Cabo San Lucas. Better to spend a week if you can. Here's a sampler of amazing pit stops along the way:

- Kayak the Sea of Cortez (more properly Vermilion Sea) out of La Paz. Check out Espiritu Santo Island and the colony of California sea lions. Even better, take a week to paddle from Mulegé to La Paz.
- Windsurf, kitesurf and stand-up paddle in the expat town of Los Barriles or the more primitive, La Ventana. You will find great paddling and dorado fishing here when the wind is down.
- For West Coast waves and steady wind, check out Punta San Carlos, premier kitesurf and windsurf local, especially in the spring. You can book tents and meals through Solo Sports (www.solosports.net)
- Dive and snorkel Cabo Pulmo National Marine Park; the reef hosts 800 marine species including manta rays, yellow jacks, chubs, striped mullets, the olive ridley seat turtle, and seabirds like the yellow-footed gull, great blue heron, and great egrets (www.cabopulmopark.com).

- Surf the famed Todos Santos, one of the best surf breaks in the world for big waves.
- Ski or snowboard Picacho del Diablo, 10,167 feet (3,099 m). In the Sierra de San Pedro Mártir National Park, there's an observatory perched at 9,285 feet (2,830 m) (www.astrossp .unam.mx; www.calforniaalpineguides.com).
- Backpack the popular Sierra de la Laguna Mountains, from San Juan del Aserradero to Picacho de la Laguna, or take the easier trail from Cañon San Bernardo to Boca de la Sierra. Expect some bouldering, wading, swimming, and canyoneering on these 2-day traverses.
- Rock climb around Baja. The Catavina Boulder Field in Desierto Central National Park is one of the best boulder spots. The blooming boojum trees and slew of giant saguaro, giant agave, and prickly pear cacti are a thorny sight.
- Bring a mountain bike, and seek out whatever dirt road, trail, or village you can find. When the wind and waves are down, or your arms are spent from paddling, go surfing or windsurfing.

Don't Miss. Check out the string of Spanish missions built by Jesuits, Franciscans, and Dominicans in the eighteenth century. Santa Rosalia in Mulegé and San Francisco de Borja are highlights, but the latter is only accessible with a 4 x 4. If you time it right, watch California gray whales migrate to the Pacific Northwest and Canada in the spring.

Logistics. You can drive from Tijuana to Cabo San Lucas in several days, but better to take 1 week or 2. Don't drive at night because poor road conditions, livestock, and wildlife make driving treacherous. Groceries, drinking water, and gasoline are easy to come by if you stay on the main road. You'll need a 4 x 4 to reach some of the prime surfing spots on the West Coast. It's not a bad idea to carry 2 spare tires and an extra gas can.

Best Time. You can snorkel, dive, rock climb, or hike year-round. December through February is the best season for surfing at Todos Santos. If you really want to windsurf or kitesurf, the wind and waves on the Pacific Coast are best during the spring.

Pit Stop. Fly down to La Paz or Los Cabos and zip up to Los Barriles for windsurfing and kiting, surfing, or diving and snorkeling. Kayaking is best based out of La Paz. For surfing, windsurfing, and kitesurfing, make a pilgrimage to Punta San Carlos, a ½-day drive from the border. Check out Solo Sports (www.solosports.net) for a fly-in option to Punta San Carlos. They supply all the gear you need for a vast array of activities.

Extended Play. Drive the whole shebang in several months. Some do it annually or leave a vehicle and trailer in Los Barrilles. For real living, gear up with Skype and work remotely. Your boss will never know you're down the Baja.

Travel Smart. If at all possible keep sports gear inside your vehicle, rooftop box, or bags. You don't want to stand out. Much of the water is pure, but play it safe. Take necessary items for purifying or drink bottled water. The street vendors are yummy, but food poisoning is common for foreigners. You'll be in remote places, a long way from help, so be careful.

 37. TRAIL RUN AND MOUNTAIN BIKE COPPER CANYON (MEXICO)

The Barranca del Cobre (Spanish for "Copper Canyon") is even larger and deeper than the Grand Canyon. But there's a good chance you've never heard of this chasm. Tucked in the Sierra Madre Occidental Mountains, the streams and microcanyons coalesce into the Fuerte River, which spills into the Sea of Cortez. The pinyon-oak and madrean conifer forests dot plateaus up to 8,000 feet (2,400 m) and give way to tropical forests as they dive as deep as a mile down to 1,500 feet (457 km) into the volcanic green rhyolite and andesite lava. Military macaws, thick-billed parrots, and coatimundi cruise the campsites.

Herein live the Tarahumara, aka Rarámuri people, meaning "those who run fast." They were made famous by Christopher McDougall's bestseller *Born to Run: A Hidden Tribe, Superathletes, and the Greatest Race the World Has Never Seen.* They are famous long-distance runners who run only in sandals (sans expensive high-tech running clothes or hydration packs).

Come here to see the spectacular canyon. Trail run, trek, or mountain bike the network of trails and visit the scenic splendor of Parque Nacional Barranca del Cobre. Rio Vista Lodge in El Fuerte can serve as a base camp. In El Fuerte, check out the old Spanish fort, a Mexican ballet folklórico, and the Paquimé pottery of the Casas Grandes Indians. For riding mountain bike trails, choose lodge in the town of Creel as a base (www.thelodgeatcreel.com). Visit the Recohuata Hot Springs, the towering rock spires of the Valley of the Monks, and 100-foot-high Cusarare Falls.

Don't Miss. Piedra Volada Falls, or "Flying Stone Falls," is the highest waterfall plunge in Mexico at 1,486 feet (453 m) in Candameña Canyon. Easter is an important and elaborate cultural celebration among the Tarahumara and a wonderful time to visit, or catch the Dia de Candelaria festival in February. Jump into a mountain bike race like Cristo Rey in September or the Copper Canyon race in July.

Logistics. Fly into Los Mochis or catch an express bus from El Paso, Texas. Then head to El Fuerte and grab the historic Ferrocarril Chihuahua al Pacifico train that chugs through 86 tunnels and over 38 bridges. Visit Outpost Wilderness Adventure (www.owa.com) based out of Creel for cross-country mountain bike tours, or Copper Canyon Guides (www.coppercanyonguide.com) for hikes, which include burro and horse support.

Best Time. The best weather, as in not scorching hot, is October to April; July and August can be cool, lush, and wet.

Pit Stop. You can do a fast trip in a week, just day hiking and trail running in the surroundings of El Fuerte or Creel.

Extended Play. Kayak or raft the El Fuerte River among woodpeckers, kiskadees, kingfishers, and cormorants. Rock climb the crags of Chapultepec Park or Cueva de los Leones near Creel. Surf or kayak the coast of Mexico and visit surf town, Sayulita.

Travel Smart. Take insect repellent. Travel low-key. Be cautious running and biking steep trails.

38. SURF TWO OCEANS (COSTA RICA)

Costa Rica is the water sports capital of Central America. Many surfers come here to catch waves on both coasts, the mellow Caribbean Sea and the wild Pacific. And if the surf is flat, buckle up for an amazing array of inland water adventures.

On the Pacific Coast, surf world-class, warm-water waves near the famed ex-pat surf town of Pavones, made infamous by Allan Weisbecker's *In Search of Captain Zero*. Up north catch Potrero Grande, Jaco, Escondida, Boca (some of the longest waves in the country), and Hermosa (some of the most consistent). Rent a 4-wheel-drive to scope out more remote Negra Beach or Witch's Rock near the crocodile-infested Naranjo River mouth in Santa Rosa National Park.

Waves small? No problem. Kayak, mountain bike, stand-up paddle, trail run, windsurf, kitesurf, and tour the national parks. Although the country is small, Costa Rica's tropical forests contain 5 percent of the world's biodiversity in 10 national parks. Other than climbing big mountains, there's not much you can't do here. You just may not have time to do it all!

Don't Miss. Make sure to visit one of the national parks, like the biodiverse Tortuguero, where freshwater rainforest rivers spill into saltwater marshes, lagoons, and wetlands.

Logistics. Fly into San Jose, and if you can, zip out of town right away. Both coasts are a ½-day drive. If you have to bunk in San Jose, pick somewhere close to the airport. You can explore fairly easily with a rental car.

Pit Stop. If you're short on time, go surfing. If you are not an expert surfer, consider stand up paddle surfing. If you can't make it to Costa Rica, check out the fabulous surf town of Sayulita, Mexico.

Extended Play. If you want the multisport experience check out whitewater rafting and kayaking on inland rivers like the Savegre and Pacuare. Lake Arenal is an amazing spot for windsurfing. Puerto Soley, on the Pacific Coast, is also great for windsurfing or kitesurfing. Go diving and snorkeling. Mountain bike the trails of the Dota Valley and the Barva Volcano with Big Mountain Bike Adventures (www.ridebig.com).

If you're a pure surfer, check out more of Central America's wild Pacific Coast, especially El Zonte in El Salvador and Santa Catalina in Panama.

Travel Smart. Get out of San Jose quickly. Travel inconspicuously. Instead of lugging a surfboard, consider renting from a surf camp or a shop. It's much easier to travel light.

39. *KAYAK AND SNORKEL THE BARRIER REEF (BELIZE)*

Belize never quite gets its due. Costa Rica, Mexico, and Panama hog the surf glory, and the Caribbean Islands steal the diving spotlight. But for uncrowded beaches, remote cays, tropical lagoons, and pristine coral, head to Belize. The biotic zone is centered on the longest reef in the western hemisphere, and is augmented with inland jungles, mangrove forests, caves, and Mayan ruins.

A third of the country's wild flora and fauna is protected in parks, preserves, and sanctuaries. The jungles and rainforests are home to jaguars, Baird's tapir, tayra, agouti, and howler monkeys and a smattering of tropical avian sparklers like toucans, trogons, and orependolas.

You'll find a mix of spoken languages (English, Creole, and

Spanish) and a diverse mix of ethnicity (Spanish explorers, Garifuna settlers, Scottish buccaneers, and British colonials).

You can kayak and snorkel the Saddle Caye mangrove wilderness, the remote Queen Cays's white sand beaches, and Glover's Reef. Lighthouse Reef Atoll and Half Moon Caye Wall are rich with staghorn coral, garden eels, eagle rays, sea turtles, and grouper. Belize also has some of the best dive sites in the world, like the Great Blue Hole, a 1,000-foot-wide (305 m), 440-foot-deep (134 m) chasm with hanging stalactites.

Don't Miss. The Belize Zoo and Tropical Education Center has orphaned and injured jaguars as well as crocodiles, king vultures, Jabiru stork, howler monkey, and Baird's tapir (www.belizezoo.org). The Belize Audubon Society manages protected areas including the Cockscomb Jaguar Reserve, Blue Hole National Park and Half Moon Caye Natural Monument (www.belizeaudubon.org).

Logistics. Fly into Belize City, right on the coast. From there, explore via charter flight, boat, or taxi. Island Expeditions (www.islandexpeditions.com) works closely with Belize Zoo and Belize Audubon Society to provide adventure trips coupled with habitat conservation, sustainable development, and ecotourism. Kayak Belize (www.kayakbelize.com) offers kayaking, kayak sailing, diving, and camping.

Best Time. Head to Central America in December through April for the best weather.

Pit Stop. To explore the coast in as few as 5 days, head to Lighthouse Caye and explore Maya Reef. Base your trip out of Bird's Eye View Lodge (www.birdseyeviewbelize.com).

Extended Play. Do it all. Overnight kayak trips, snorkeling, diving, and fishing. Surf Costa Rica (Trip #38). Consider a piggyback trip to Panama, Guatemala, Nicaragua, Honduras, or even Mexico's famed Yucatán where you can drive the Ruta de Maya, dive in

Cozumel, and trek among the big Mayan ruins. Or, *gulp*, zip over to forbidden Cuba.

Travel Smart. Central America is big and caters to the adventure athlete, but many of the cities are bustling, developing metropolises. Be careful of pickpockets and petty theft. Travel inconspicuously. Leave expensive sunglasses and bags at home. Rent dive, surf, and kayak gear so you're not lugging it all over the country. Watch out for sun and mosquitoes. Don't pet the monkeys or any other wild animals. And as hard as it may be, don't try to befriend dogs; rabies still abounds.

Caribbean Sea

COSTA RICA
PANAMA

*The
Galapagos
Islands*

Atlantic
Ocean

VENEZUELA

COLOMBIA

GUYANA
SURINAME

FR.
GUIANA

■ *Quito*
ECUADOR

Equator

PERU

*Macchu
Pichu*

B R A Z I L

■ *Cuzco*

■ *La Paz*
BOLIVIA

■ *La Cumbre*

Pacific
Ocean

PARAGUAY

CHILE

Aconcagua

Portillo

Santiago
■ ■ *Mendoza*

URUGUAY

ARGENTINA

■ *Bariloche*

Atlantic
Ocean

| 0 | 200 | 400 miles |
| 0 | | 400 kilometers |

*Tierra del Fuego
National Park*
■ *Ushuaia*

THIS IS big country.

Venezuela's Angel Falls is the world's highest at 3,212 feet (979 m). The Amazon River is the world's largest by sheer volume, hosting the world's largest, most biodiverse rainforest. The Andes mountain range, stretching 4,300 miles (7,000 km), is the world's most expansive. The Atacama Desert is the world's driest, clocking in 0.04 inches (1 mm) annually. In some spots, no measurable precipitation has ever been recorded. Nestled at 11,975 feet (3,650 m) in the Andes, Bolivia's capital, La Paz, is the world highest. Peru's Lake Titicaca is the world's highest elevated navigable body of water. Puerto Toro, Chile, and Ushuaia, Argentina, are the 2 southernmost permanent communities on earth.

The diversity of South America, in both terrain and culture, will amaze you.

As a multisport playground, it's also less-traveled than many other regions. Ask a world-traveling surfer, and there's a good chance he or she won't have ridden waves in Peru or Chile. Skiers, likewise, often skip the Andes in favor of trips to Europe and Canada.

If you can go on only 1 trip, choose Patagonia. If you can do 2, consider climbing the Bolivian and Ecuadorian volcanoes, skiing the Andes, or surfing Peru. And everyone who's a trekker or hiker should, sooner or later, hike the ancient Inca Trail to the famed and fascinating ruins of the City in the Clouds, Machu Picchu.

Scope out a trip, toss this volume on the table, schedule vacation time, book your ticket, and pack your bags for some of the most spectacular scenery on the globe. Go do, now.

40. HIKE THE INCA TRAIL TO MACHU PICCHU (PERU)

One-time stronghold of the powerful Inca civilization, Machu Picchu was hidden for hundreds of years. When the Spanish conquistadors decimated the natives of Peru, they never found this citadel. When discovered in 1911 by U.S. explorer Hiram Bingham, it was dubbed as the "Lost City of the Incas" or "City in the Clouds," because it's perched at 7,970 feet (2,429 m) in the tropical cloud forest above the lush Urubamba River. Machu Picchu is one of the best preserved of the Inca ruins. Check out unworldly feats of engineering like the cliffside back door to the city, the Inca Bridge, and the polished stone of the Temple of the Sun, which has windows that let light in during the spring and winter solstices.

The Inca Trail is actually a part of a road that connects Machu Picchu with the Inca capital, Cuzco. There are many trails, but the Inca Trail will take you back in time. You will hike through dozens of restored ruins before the trail culminates at Machu Picchu.

Don't Miss. Spend a few days in the delightful, cultural Cuzco. You can check out the markets, the Plaza de Armas public square, and hike past the ruins of Sacsayhuamán. Then plan a couple of days in the Sacred Valley en route to the trailhead. Check out the salt mines of Pichingoto, the Inca agricultural test stations at Moray, the ruins and open market of Pisac, and the quaint town of Ollantaytambo for last-minute pisco (a native alcohol distilled from grapes). Aguas Calientes, the town at the base of Machu Picchu is a fun berg reminiscent of an American ski town.

Logistics. Most trek the Inca Trail in 4 days, 3 nights. That leaves plenty of time to explore Cuzco and the Scared Valley of the Urubamba River. Fly into Lima, and then jump a commuter flight to Cuzco. Most guided treks start in Cuzco. From Aguas Calientes, you must take a train back to Cuzco. A number of outfitters, like Bio Bio (www.bbxrafting.com), Mountain Travel Sobek (www.mtsobek .com), and Wilderness Travel (www.wildernesstravel.com), run this classic trip.

Pit Stop. If you're short on time, you can hike the trail in 1 or 2 nights. It's only 25 miles (40 km) through the tropical cloud forest, but you'll want to take some time to admire the many ruins along the trail. You can also speed through the Sacred Valley, just touching down at Pisac and Ollantaytambo.

Extended Play. Not enough hiking? Once at Machu Picchu, you can hike either Huayna Picchu or Machu Picchu, the 2 mountains that flank the ruins.

If you have a couple weeks, there are some fabulous add-ons in Peru. You can zip up to Lake Titicaca and explore Amantani Island, populated by Quechua-speaking native Peruvians. Explore the cultural city of Arequipa. My favorite is a 3-day excursion to the far southeastern area of Peru, the Amazon Basin. Fly to Puerto Maldonado, catch a dory up the Madre de Dios River, and spend a few nights at one of many ecolodges such as Inkaterra Reserva Amazonica (www.inkaterra.com). Or surf the longest left-hand wave in the world at Chicama, on the north coast.

Travel Smart. Don't forget bug spray. There are all kinds of micro-insects on the Inca Trail. Although it's tropical, there's almost never snow, but expect rain. There'll be lots of it in the cloud forest. Expect sun, too. Bring a sun hat, long-sleeve nylon shirts, and long pants. The highest point on the trail is Abra de Warmiwanuska (meaning "Dead Woman's Pass"), at 13,779 feet (4,198 m) so mountain sickness can occur.

41. EXPLORE DARWIN'S ISLES: THE GALÁPAGOS (ECUADOR)

It's one of those places you have to experience to understand the awe of nature.

Originally called Insulae de los Galopegos ("Islands of the Turtles"), Ecuador's offshore Galápagos Islands are a nature-lover's and an adventure-seeker's delight. The giant tortoise is the signature species. You'll also find iguana, sea cucumbers, flightless cormorants, magnificent frigate birds, eagles, golden rays, flamingos, wave albatross, blue-footed booby, sea lions, and penguins. Scope out a few of the 13 species of finch, including 4 mockingbird varietals, the famed birds that inspired Charles Darwin's 1859 treatise, *On the Origin of Species*.

The best way to see the Galápagos in a short period of time is on an organized boat trip. In a week you can cruise to several islands in the archipelago. In Isabela, occupy a whole week surfing the breaks, trail running the volcano, and snorkeling. On Floreana and Champion you'll find premier snorkeling at Post Office Bay.

Find a guide geared toward adventure who's also willing to take you on inland hikes or tour in a *panga*, aka dinghy.

Don't Miss. On Isabela Island, surf the waves, kayak Puerto Villamil, and hike the Sierra Negra, the second largest volcanic caldera in the world. Snorkel the lava tunnels, a labyrinth of volcanic tubes alongside the sea turtle highway. And don't forget to check out the Charles Darwin Research Station on Santa Cruz Island.

Logistics. Fly into Quito, Ecuador, a colorful town nestled in a basin in the Andes. Catch a commuter flight from Baltra Island in the Galápagos. Most of the adventure companies run small-boat trips including Bio Bio (www.bbxrafting.com), Mountain Travel Sobek (www.mtsobek.com), and Wilderness Travel (www.wilder nesstravel.com). One outfitter, ROW Adventures (www.rowadven tures.com), makes use of local hotels and camps on pristine, secluded beaches. Looking for a dive tour? Try Buddy Dive (www .buddydive.com), which runs the Motor Catamaran Seaman II.

Pit Stop. It's difficult to do this trip in a short amount of time; there's just so much to see. But if you can only accommodate a 1-stop jaunt, hit Puerto Villamil on Isabela Island where you can surf, hike the Sierra Negra volcano, and snorkel and kayak Las Tintoreras Lagoon.

Extended Play. Book a 3-week trip. This will give you time to see and do it all, even spend some time in Quito. You can also couple the trip with a volcano climb of Ecuador's volcanoes (Trip #44) or surfing the waves of Peru.

Travel Smart. Bring water shoes, kayaking jacket and gloves, and snorkel gear. This is the tropics, so a sun hat, shielding clothing, and sunscreen are essential. Oh, and don't forget hiking shoes for the ubiquitous lava! You're a long way from help so be cautious. Rent surfboards and kayaks. It's a hassle to haul them to the islands.

42. *EXPLORE THE LAND OF GIANTS (PATAGONIA, CHILE, AND ARGENTINA)*

Magellan called this place the "Land of Giants" back in 1520 because the Tehuelche natives towered over the rather short Spanish explorers. Today, Patagonia is still the land of giants: giant mountains, giant fjords, and giant rivers. The scenery reigns on an epic scale.

You may not need to keep reading. No doubt you've heard about the magic, splendor, and wild ruggedness of this legendary place. Towering granite spires, glaciate peaks, deep fjords, Alpine lakes, emerald valleys, and windy steppes abound. The Patagonia region of southern Chile and Argentina rivals the southern New Zealand fjord lands and remote British Columbia coastal range for its spectacular natural landscape.

The gateway to this wondrous land is the ski town of San Carlos de Bariloche, often dubbed the "Switzerland" of South America. The treks through Chile's Torres del Paine and Argentina's Los Glaciares National Park are classic trips of the region.

The massive granite spires of Cerro Torre and Fitzroy from Los Glaciares is the view of a lifetime. In Torres del Paine, trek among rocky spires, jagged peaks, cyan lakes, and wildflower-spackled meadows.

Don't Miss. Spend a night in Buenos Aires, the quintessential cosmopolitan South American city. In the spring, take a few days and ski at Bariloche.

Logistics. Fly to Buenos Aires; then connect to San Carlos de Bariloche. Pick a base camp like the Paine Grand Lodge (www .verticepatagonia.com) near Lake Pehoé. Rent a car or hire a guide to maximize time. Try one of the big companies like Wilderness Travel (www.wildernesstravel.com) or Mountain Travel Sobek (www.mtsobek.com), or one of the smaller outfitters like Bio Bio Expeditions (www.bbxrafting.com).

Pit Stop. If you're short on time, pick 1 of the 2 national parks, and 1 of the 3 impressive hikes in Torres del Paine: Gray Glacier, the Mighty Torres, and the French Valley.

Extended Play. Where to start! Raft the Rio Futaleufú (Trip #45), or float the trifecta: Rio Futaleufú, Rio Azul, and Rio Espolon. There's no end. Go horseback riding or mountain biking. Cast a rod for some of the world's best brown and rainbow trout. Trail run some of the spectacular stream and lake-side trails. Scale the summit of Fitzroy. Fly down to Ushuaia and check out Tierra del Fuego National Park.

Travel Smart. When traveling above 8,000 feet in the national parks, pay attention to signs of altitude illness. Use plenty of sunscreen and carry warm clothing. The sun can blister during the day in the Andes, and the temperatures are downright frigid at night.

Use a personal-flotation device and helmet when rafting or kayaking. Most outfitters provide them.

43. RIDE FROZEN WAVES: SKI AND SNOWBOARD (CHILE)

The name Portillo brings a shiver of envy for every skier and snowboarder with a tick list. The famous banana yellow lodge nestled on the Chilean-Argentine border is far removed from the glitzy glamor of the ski villages to the north. Ascend the twisty-turny road to Paso de los Libertadores on 32 hair-raising switchbacks to enter the deep Andes. Once at 10,000 feet (3,050 m), Old-World charm meets beautiful mountains with a splash of modern amenity. The expansive peaks are uncrowded and pristine. On the days you aren't carving tracks in deep powder, you'll find clear skies, warm sun on the slopes. You'll rarely find slush or crud on these slopes. The reason: The Andes are so high and dry that snow doesn't melt. It dissipates. Perfect.

The slopes at Portillo are perfect for the whole family or the expert glisse alpinist looking for big mountain backcountry. You'll find intermediate groomers on the Juncalillo, backcountry above Roca Jack, heli-skiing above the expansive ice-covered Inca Lake, and out-of-bounds hiking up the world-renowned Super C Couloir or "Train Run," which drops 2,000 feet (610 m) from Argentina into Chile.

And the fabulous hospitality at Portillo, with its 1:1 staff-client ratio, augmented by delectable Chilean tilapia and sea bass, spicy Malbec, citrusy Pisco Sours, and fresh produce from the Santiago Valley.

Don't Miss. Go heli-skiing or backcountry touring. In cosmo-politan Santiago, take the subway to Mercado Central fish market. Donde Augusto's is the best spot for conger eel and chips. Visit the artisan market at Los Dominicos to sample fresh-baked empana-das, Chilean alpaca sweaters, and hand-painted pottery. Mountain bike the single track up Cerro San Cristóbal or hike steps to the old fortress at Cerro Santa Lucia, both hilltop parks with spectacular panoramic views. Run the Rio Mapocho riverside trail through the banking district. Book an afternoon wine tasting or make an over-night junket to Valparaiso on the Pacific Coast (www.santiago adventures.com).

Logistics. Check in for an all-inclusive week at the famed, Euro-style lodge known simply as Ski Portillo (www.skiportillo.com). With direct flights to Santiago, it's hard to find an easier trip if you've only got a week to spare and you're toting ski gear. Like a cruise ship for die-hard skiers, the ski week includes lift tickets, 4 *delicioso* daily meals, outdoor pool and Internet access (no pesky "resort charge"), gym, game room, and a theater with nightly pro-grams ranging from ski flicks to feature films. Hire a local guide for lift access, backcountry hikes, or heli-skiing right from the hotel. Sign up for a guided camp like Chris Davenport's "Ski with the Superstars" (www.steepskiing.com) or Kim Reichhelm's family ski tours (www.skiwithkim.com).

Pit Stop. If you're just passing through, spend a few days in the dorm-like hostel at Ski Portillo and rent ski gear. Or scope out the

Santiago ski resort of Valle Nevado (www.vallenevado.com), an easy ½-hour jaunt right from the city where you can sleep cheap at La Chimba Hostel (www.lachimba.com) in the artsy Barrio Bellavista neighborhood.

Extended Play. Take an extra week and hike among the green canyons, expansive salt flats, flocks of flamingos, giant cacti, and sulfurous geysers of the Altiplano and Atacama Deserts. Fly to the colorful village of San Pedro and book a night at the Tierra Atacama Hotel and Spa (www.tierraatacama.com). Alternatively, check out Las Leñas (www.laslenas.com), a ski resort in Argentina a few hours from the famed wine country of Mendoza. Have a month? Couple your Portillo trip with a trek to Machu Picchu, Peru (Trip #40) or a boat tour of the Ecuador's Galápagos Islands (Trip #41).

Travel Smart. Portillo has fabulous skiing for all skill levels, but don't go if you're out of shape. You'll want to maximize your ski week. Watch for signs of acute mountain sickness. Get plenty of rest, drink lots of fluid, and ask your doctor about acetazolamide (Diamox), a safe, effective medicine to prevent that nasty high-altitude headache. Guard against cold—hypothermia and frost-bite—by wearing polyester or Merino wool underwear, warm socks, and a down sweater (a light, cozy, indispensible layer). Temperatures in the high peaks can reach near 60 degrees Fahrenheit (15 degrees C) midday and the reflective power of the snow can amplify the sun's rays so take sunscreen lip balm, sunglasses, and dark ski goggles.

44. CLIMB AND SKI THE RING OF FIRE (ECUADOR, BOLIVIA, AND MEXICO)

The Ring of Fire—famous for its basalt and andesite lava and snowcapped peaks—stands out among the seas of green forest volcanoes in the region.

What is the Ring of Fire? It's the string of active and dormant volcanoes that encircle the Pacific Ocean by way of Japan's Mount Fuji, North America's West Coast, and peaks in South and Central America.

Volcano climbing is different from other forms of climbing. The peaks stick out among the lowlands with open snowfields and surprise weather.

None are more sought out than the Ecuadorian greats. Illiniza Norte (16,818 ft/5,126 m), Cotopaxi (19,348 ft/5,896 m), Cayambe (18,997 ft/5,790 m), and Chimborazo (20,701ft/6,268 m) are all nestled high in the mountains between the Pacific surf and Amazon rainforest. The 2 most accessible: Cayambe and Cotopaxi, have climbers' huts at 15,000 feet (4,500 m) that make ascending without a snowbound tent doable. Acclimatize on Rucu Pichincha (13,451 ft/ 4,100 m), a peak outside of Quito with a teleferico that carries you halfway up or on Tungurahua, a well-known trekking peak (16,452 ft/5,015 m).

Don't Miss. Zip 15 miles (24 km) north of Quito and set foot on both sides of the equator.

Logistics. Fly into the high-altitude basin of Quito, a colorful town just 15 miles (24 km) south of the equator. Book through Rainier Mountaineering (www.rmiguides.com), Mountain Guides International (mountainguidesinternational.com), International

Mountain Guides (www.mountainguides.com), or Mountain Madness (www.mountainmadness.com).

Best Time. Go December through February for climbing. For skiing you'll want to go during South America's spring, July through November.

Pit Stop. Book an express climb with Rainier Mountaineering and summit Cotopaxi in a little over a week.

Extended Play. There are a slew of volcanoes on the Central and South American junkie tick list. Check out Mexico's Ixtaccihuatl (17,338 ft/ 5,285 m) and Orizaba (18,880 ft/5,755 m), or pop down to Bolivia for remote, spectacular peaks in the Cordillera Real, like Pequeño Alpamayo (17,482 ft/5,329 m), Huayna Potosi (19,974 ft/6,088 m), and Illimani (21,200 ft/6,462 m). Combine a climb with a mountain-biking junket in one of the newest hot spots for freeriders—Sorata, Bolivia (Trip #46).

Travel Smart. When climbing volcanoes you may encounter heavy snow, glaciers, and tempestuous weather. There's also a chance of volcanic activities, such as eruptions or earthquakes. Volcanoes often stick out among the lowlands like weather magnets. Learn crevasse rescue and avalanche safety.

☑ 45. *PADDLE THE FUTALEUFÚ (CHILE)*

Chile's Futaleufú was formed from the glacier meltwater off the Patagonia Andes and it offers some of best churning whitewater in the world. In fact, Patagonia is widely recognized as one of the 4 best spots in the world for whitewater alongside Northern California, Norway, and New Zealand.

The headwaters of the Futaleufú River trickle out of Argentina, then weave through a remote and utterly spectacular valley in Southern Chile. This region was made famous by *Butch Cassidy and the Sundance Kid*. Float through emerald forests, aquamarine lakes, and wide-open steppes. When the rapids hit, you'll run giant waves and holes. The 6-mile (10 km) stretch downriver from the Puente Futaleufú has hundreds of rapids including El Cojin (meaning "the cushion"), Mundaca, and the c\Class V Casa de Piedra ("House of Rock"). The run finishes at Inferno Canyon with Class V Zeta and Throne Room. The runs are so gnarly that some guides choose to portage this churning froth.

Don't Miss. Spend a night in Bariloche, Argentina, a southern ski and outdoor town. Fly or spin cast for world-famous rainbow trout. Feast on Chilean asado—lamb and potatoes roasted over coals right on the river.

Logistics. Fly into Buenos Aires. Then take a commuter flight to the mountain ski town of San Carlos de Bariloche. Lake Nahuel Huapi's base camp is the "Switzerland" of South America is lined with craggy peaks reminiscent of the Alps. Check out Bio Bio (www.bbxrafting.com), one of the most reputable guide operations.

Best Time. Rafting and kayaking are best in December to March, the South American summer season.

Pit Stop. Drop in for a week to run the Futaleufú.

Extended Play. Combine the raft trip with a Patagonian multi-sport extravaganza: hiking, horseback riding, trail running, and mountain biking in the spectacular national parks (Trip #42). Paddle the Rio Azul as well as the Futaleufú. Hit Chile's Torres del Paine and Argentina's famous Fitzroy spires.

Travel Smart. Whitewater rafting and kayaking require a guide unless you're pro. Wear a helmet, a personal-flotation device, and river garb including boat sandals and sun-protective clothing. Pack your gear in dry bags. Make sure you scout all the rapids and know what to do if you get stuck in an eddy or wrapped around a boulder.

☑ 46. MOUNTAIN BIKE THE WORLD'S MOST DANGEROUS ROAD (BOLIVIA)

Whether you're a freeride downhiller or cross-country climber, you don't want to miss Bolivia's Death Road (aka El Camino de la Muerte). The 40-mile (64 km), 11,800-foot (3,600 m) descent starts in the high plains, surrounded by the snowcapped Andes, and winds into the sweltering Amazonia. This long ride is known as the "World's Most Dangerous Road."

You'll begin in the desolate La Cumbre, Bolivia, perched at 15,400 feet (4,700 m) beneath towering Huayna Potosi peak 19,973 feet (6,088 m). Then the road winds through open fields, llama and alpaca ranches, tiny villages, cliffs, and raging waterfalls. You'll ultimately cruise into the dank jungle of the Amazon Basin.

Don't Miss. In Yolosa, toward the end of the ride, catch a night at the La Senda Verde cabins. Take a dip in the river and tour the La Senda Verde Animal Refuge.

Logistics. Fly into La Paz and book a tour through Gravity Bolivia (www.gravitybolivia.com). They can arrange a shuttle to and from La Cumbre as well as a vehicle shuttle to the top of the ride.

Best Time. To miss rain and heat, go in April to May or September to November.

Pit Stop. You can do the ride in a 1-day, round-trip trek from La Paz. Shuttle to La Cumbre, drop the road in 4 to 5 hours, and shuttle back to La Paz. Alternatively, pick Ghost Ride, right outside of La Paz. It starts at 15,900 feet (4,850 m) and descends double and single track to the El Castillo del Loro castle.

Extended Play. Try Sorata, some of the best, undiscovered single track in the world. Pick from 10,000-foot (3,050 m) descents, shuttle rides, and cross-country single tracks alike. Take a tour to Rurrenabanque, in the Bolivian Amazon. Even better, try one of the many off-road mountain bike routes in Central and South America:

- Pedal part of the 400 miles (640 km) of Copper Canyon, Mexico (Trip #37)
- Drop the 7,000-foot (2,100 m), 12-mile (19 km) downhill in Mérida, Venezuela, and zip through coffee plantations
- Ride the 15.5-mile (25 km) Isla Ometepe trail between volcanoes in once-forbidden Nicaragua
- Jump on the network of trails in Iguazú National Park in Argentina and Brazil
- Scope out the adventure sports hub of Salta, Argentina
- Ride Costa Rica's Arenal Volcano (Trip #38)
- Drop into Peru's Sacred Valley for downhill and cross-country trails, coupled with an Inca Trail hike to Machu Picchu (Trip #40)

You can book worldwide mountain bike adventures in Costa Rica, Peru, Morocco, New Zealand, and Iceland though Big Mountain Bike Adventures (www.ridebig.com).

Travel Smart. The World Most Dangerous Road is downhill mountain biking so you may want to consider armor: at least knee and elbow pads. Bring a hydration pack with 3 liters of water, food, and a repair kit for your bike and body. Make sure your bike is in excellent condition. You may want to consider renting, since dragging a bike on an airplane is costly. Ride cautiously; this isn't the spot to make the biggest drops or the fastest descent of your life. Don't count on search and rescue or a helicopter in Bolivia.

47. *CLIMB ACONCAGUA: THE SEVEN SUMMITS, SOUTH AMERICA (ARGENTINA)*

Cerro Aconcagua is South America's crown jewel. Situated on the Chilean-Argentinean border, a mere 90 miles (145 km) from the Pacific Ocean, it's a long climb to the 22,841-foot (6,962 m) peak, the second highest of the Seven Summits. Matthias Zurbriggen embarked on the first climb in 1897 via the Ruta Normal (meaning "Normal Route"), which is still the most commonly used route. You will find no technical rock or ice on this trek. In fact, many call it a "long walk." It does, however, require proficiency in crampons and fixed ropes, high-altitude climbing, and living 2 weeks in a tent. And because of the sheer size of these mountains, it's still a major undertaking. Don't be fooled.

From Los Penitentes, the neighboring ski-town hub, you'll check in at the Horcones Ranger Station. Then begin your trek up the spectacular winding Rio Horcones. Spend a few days acclimatizing at Plaza de Mulas, the international tent city of climbers, porters, rescue police, cooks, and rangers at 14,108 feet (4,300 m). Work your way higher up Horcones Valley to one of a series of base camps: Plaza Canada, Cólera, or Nido de Cóndores. There are shelters in Refugio Berlin at 19,455 feet (5,930 m). In 1 day, you can make it from the Berlin shelter along the Gran Acarreo Glacier to the summit.

Don't Miss. Tour the famed wine country of Mendoza. Raft the Mendoza River and walk on the Inca roads.

Logistics. Fly into Buenos Aires and take a commuter flight to Mendoza. You'll land right in the famed Malbec wine country of Mendoza. Drive International Route 7, which connects Mendoza, Santiago, and Los Penitentes. This mountain town is a ski hub, nestled at 9,000 feet (2,743 m). Depending on the route you choose, it's approximately a 2-week journey to the summit. You'll hike through rugged forests and streams to the stark landscape of glacial moraines, scree fields, and icy couloirs. Check out Aconcagua Expeditions (www.aconcaguaexpeditions.com) or Rainier Mountaineering (www.rmiguides.com) for expeditions.

Best Time. December, midsummer in Argentina, is the best month for climbing.

Pit Stop. Like most of the Seven Summits, there's no quick way route. If you're not a Seven Summits climber, ski Las Leñas in

Argentina, or Portillo in Chile (Trip #43). Consider climbing and skiing one of the volcanoes of Ecuador, Bolivia, or Mexico (Trip #44.)

Extended Play. If you have time, drive to Santiago and the Valparaiso coast. Spend time rafting, horseback riding, canyoneering, kayaking, or rock climbing in Mendoza. You can bunk at the Pueblo del Rio Resort. Argentina Rafting (www.argentinarafting .com) leads 2-day runs on the Potrerillos River. Mountain bike the Potrerillos Valley, including the famous Rucahue downhill. Consider a visit to Salta, a wine-making town where you can hike the colorful hills of Nevado de Cachi valley, sample artisan cheese, view Spanish colonial buildings, and listen to *musica folklorica*.

Travel Smart. Guard against altitude illness, hypothermia, and frostbite. A 3-week expedition can cause fatigue, malnutrition, and dehydration. Eating well, sleeping plenty, and drinking lots of fluids are your first steps to a successful climb.

WHEN YOU think of Europe, civilized cities, history, ancient architecture, and a deep, rich *sportif* culture come to mind. Aside from the majestic landscape and populous cities, Europe has some of the best alpine climbing, mountain biking, and whitewater in the world. Add in its rich history and culture and you've got a vibrant and enchanting athletic playland.

One of the great things about Europe is its relative ease of travel; mass transit is sophisticated and relatively safe. If you're not ready to jump into the wilds of Africa, the remoteness of the Andes, or the complexity of Indochina, go to Europe.

But just because many European countries are refined and cultured, doesn't mean you won't find some of the gnarliest mountains, hair-raising trails, white-knuckle rivers, and scary canyons on earth. You'll get an adrenaline rush that will push your pulse near max.

If you want to head to the Alps, start with the extreme-sports capital of the world, Chamonix, France. If you're a more casual traveler, try the quaint, quiet, breathtaking berg of Interlaken, Switzerland. You can find even more remote adventure with less fanfare in Scandinavia, Spain, or Eastern Europe.

My advice: Don't try to do all of Europe in 1 trip—unless you can take a month or 2. Pick 1 region and 1 sport. Then go back as much as your budget allows. People do successfully crisscross Europe, and hit a half dozen countries in as few as 2 weeks. I tend to favor a more in-depth adventure, experiencing 1 place, 1 sport, and 1 fabulous trip.

If you can only go on 1 trip, try one of my most cherished tours: ski mountaineering the legendary Haute Route from Chamonix, France, via Italy, to Zermatt, Switzerland. It is one of the most scenic, demanding, thrilling, and cultural trips you can imagine.

If you're a mountain biker, go *dolobiking* in the jaw-dropping peaks of the Italian Dolomites. For something to kick the heart rate into double digits, try circumnavigating Mont Blanc on foot.

Not only is Europe easy to get to, you can usually find good ticket deals, easy gear rentals, reasonably priced lodging or camping, and delectable food from street vendors, markets, and family-run cafés.

Get on it.

48. SKI MOUNTAINEER THE ALPS: THE HAUTE ROUTE (FRANCE, ITALY, AND SWITZERLAND)

If you're a backcountry skier, mention of the Haute Route probably sends a shiver down your spine.

This is, by far, my favorite trip of all—have I mentioned that?

The Haute Route, or High Route, is the most sought-after ski traverse in backcountry skiing (and snowboarding, but more on that later). It's ski mountaineering mixed with old-world ski culture. Ski with a daypack, and a cadre full of sharp pointy objects: ski crampons, boot crampons, and Piolet (ice ax). Duck into refurbished Swiss Alpine Club huts perched at 12,000 feet (3,658 m) in the middle of an expansive crevassed glacier. The huts are fully staffed and stocked via helicopter. Grab a soup and sweet, floral tea for lunch; *rosti* (potato and meat dish) for dinner; and muesli—a dried fruit and oat cereal—for breakfast. You'll be assigned a bunk with a pillow, mattress, and comforter. Just roll out your travel sheet.

Sure, you can embark on hut-to-hut trips elsewhere—other parts of Europe, Colorado, and British Columbia—but none encompass 3 countries, 7 days, majestic Alpine glaciers, and fully catered huts populated with adventurers from all over the world.

The Haute Route, pronounced "oat root," was first climbed in the mid-1800s, but wasn't skied until 1911. It begins in Chamonix, France, at the foot of famed Mont Blanc, the origin of mountaineering and the epicenter of extreme skiing. From there you'll traverse the majestic glaciers and snowfields of the Alps.

Unless you're interested in technical ice and glacier climbing, choose the modern Verbier "skiers" route that offers more downhill turns.

Don't Miss. Spend a few days at both ends in Chamonix and Zermatt, these 2 towns will show you the extremes of the Alpine ski culture. In Chamonix, you'll see people jump on city buses dressed in full ski regalia—boots, climbing harness with ice screws, big packs with climbing ropes, and helmets strapped atop. You'll land in Zermatt, a glitzy, car-free town at the base of iconoclastic Matterhorn, first climbed in 1865 by Edward Whymper (14,690 ft/4,478 m). You glide alongside skiers wearing fur coats!

Logistics. Fly into Zurich or Geneva; both have trains and shuttles to Chamonix or Zermatt. The trains run frequently and operate like Swiss clockwork: precisely on time. You can do the route either way, but for the best experience you should ski from Chamonix to Zermatt. You can try it yourself... if you're an expert at glacier travel, avalanche avoidance, whiteout navigation, and booking lodging in French and German. My advice is to pick a reputable outfitter like Northwest Mountain School (www.mountainschool.com) or Timberline Mountain Guides (www.timberlinemtguides.com).

Best Time. The Haute Route ski season is late March to May. Some prefer early trips for better snow, and others later in the season for clearer weather.

Pit Stop. Try the shorter, safer, low-angle Silvretta Route, that begins and ends near the St. Anton ski resort in Galtür, Austria, on the Swiss-Austrian border. Or spend a week in Chamonix and take guided day trips through the Alps.

Extended Play. If you want to live the dream, embark on the European ski mountaineering trifecta: the infamous peaks of the

Eiger, Mönch, and Jungfrau along the Berner Oberland route (Trip #49). Then take a few days of R & R in the famed Interlaken. Or try the Ortler Circuit in Stelvio National Park in Northern Italy; the loop begins and ends in the rustic ski village of Bormio, Italy (or start with this tour if you want nicer huts and better coffee).

Travel Smart. For the Haute Route you'll need good quality winter clothing and alpine touring (aka randonee) or telemark skis with skins, ski crampons, boot crampons, climbing harness, and an ice ax. You can try it with a split snowboard, but snowboards don't lend themselves to touring long traverses of varied terrain with frequent tool changes; you'll need to change often among boot crampons, ski crampons, and ski skins. I don't recommend a solid snowboard with snowshoes or approach skis because they're slow and require extra gear. You'll need expert glacier travel, white-out navigation, avalanche avoidance, and crevasse rescue skills.

49. SKI THE GLACIERS: THE BERNER OBERLAND (SWITZERLAND)

The Berner, or Bernese, Oberland is one of the most beautiful collection of peaks on earth. It's home to the famed triple-threat peaks of the Eiger, Mönch, and Jungfrau. After the Haute Route (Trip #48), this is one of the most popular ski tours in the world.

Crash in Swiss Alpine Club huts and enjoy the meticulously clean accommodations, hearty meals, and well-furbished bunks. You'll need a travel sheet, a daypack, and a wad of Swiss francs to buy $10 cans of Swiss beer and $10 bottles of water. But it's worth it. You'll pop into a hotel at 12,000 feet (3,700 m) perched on a rocky outcrop in the middle of a giant glacier.

More technical and physically demanding than the Haute Route, the Berner usually begins with a sporty ride up the Jungfraujoch train with tracks that pierce the Eiger. Then you'll ascend glaciers, climb via ferrata (iron rungs and ladders fixed to the rock), and bag Trugberg (12,687 ft/3,867 m), Gross Wannenhorn (12,812 ft/3,905 m), and the highest peak in the Berner Alps, the Finsteraarhorn (14,033 ft/4,274m).

Don't Miss. Ski a day at Kleine Scheidegg and take the Jungfraubahn, Europe's highest railway which has been in operation since 1896. At the top, check out the Sphinx Observatory and the Great Aletsch Glacier.

Logistics. Start in Interlaken and take a guided tour with Northwest Mountain School (www.mountainschool.com). Stay at Balmers, Europe's oldest and most famous hostel (www.balmers .com); it's a gathering place for travelers from all over the world. Or book a night at the upscale Hotel Bellevue des Alpes (www .scheidegg-hotels.ch) scene of the 1974 film *The Eiger Sanction.*

Best Time. Late March through early May is ski season in the high Alpine glaciers. Snow is better earlier in the season, but the weather is better later.

Pit Stop. Pick 1 hut, ski for a few days. Hang out in Interlaken and ski at Kleine Scheidegg. Or hunker in the undiscovered high Alpine hamlet of Mürren.

Extended Play. Interlaken could easily have had its own chapter. The Lauterbrunnen Valley has spectacular canyoneering. You can mountain bike, hike, trail run, ski, snowboard, bungee jump, BASE jump, raft, kayak, ice climb, paraglide, or skydive. Like Chamonix, Whistler, and Queensland, this is reaped in pure mountain lifestyle.

Want a rugged trip in summer? Hike the Alpine Pass Route from Sargan to Geneva, Switzerland, totaling 220 miles (350 km). Block off 2 to 3 weeks to get over the 16 high-mountain passes. Or ski all 3 Grand Tours of the Alps: the Haute Route (Trip #48) and Ortler Circuit based out of Bormio, Italy.

Travel Smart. Skiing on glaciers is replete with crevasse and avalanche danger. And then add in altitude, hypothermia, frostbite, and sun exposure. Blisters and sunburn can be the most debilitating. Because you're above tree line, the skies can spew spectacular bluebird sun or a torrent of wind, snow, and rain. Because you're in the Alps, rescue requires payment; get Swiss rescue insurance.

50. CLIMB VIA FERRATTA AND MOUNTAIN BIKE THE DOLOMITES (ITALY)

Can't quite swing the technical ascent of a massive Italian rock face? No problem. Just use a ladder. Forget the fact that you'll be climbing hundreds of feet up a vertical stone cliff.

Via Ferrata is Italian for "Road of Iron" (called *Klettersteig* in German for "climbing path"). Via Ferratta is comprised of some 400 technical hiking routes laced with cables, ladders, rungs, steps, stairs, bridges, and other fixed devices. That means all you need are hiking boots and basic safety gear.

The first Via Ferrata route was hammered into rock as far back as 1492 when guide Antoine de Ville used a ladder to ascend Mont Aiguille. In 1880, Alpine guides of Madonna di Campiglio in the Dolomites tacked in more routes and many more Via Ferratta were constructed during World War I.

Search out the iron trails near the ski and outdoor berg of Cortina d'Ampezzo. One of the most famous, Meneghel's Ladder, was constructed in 1907 when Luigi Gillarduzzi placed 200 iron pins in the high-alpine refuge Cantore Hut. One of the longest trails is Gianni Costantini, and the historic Lagazuoi Tunnels pierces Monte Lagazuoi via rock tubes that date back to World War I. Ivano Dibona traverses Monte Cristallo ridge and passes many World War I fortification areas. Bolver-Lugli reaches 9,859 feet (3,005 m) up Cimon della Pala, a peak referred to as the Matterhorn of the Dolomites because of its craggy summit pyramid. (*Hint:* You can bivouac in the Fiamme Gialle shelter before heading to the summit.)

If Via Ferrata isn't enough, you'll also find some of the best mountain biking in the world. The scenery is so unique and the trails so technical, riders call it *dolobiking*.

Don't Miss. If you can, book a night or 2 in a hut, high in the Dolomites. Alternatively, hang out in Cortina d'Ampezzo, host of the 1956 Winter Olympics and the mountains where *Cliffhanger* and the Bond flick *For Your Eyes Only* were filmed. Check out Santa Croce Sanctuary, built in 1484, and the ultra-scenic Fanes-Senes-Braies Nature Park.

Logistics. Fly into any of Italy's major cities and make your way to Cortina d'Ampezzo. For Via Ferrata hiking, go with a guide service like Guide Dolomiti (www.guidedolomiti.com) or HighPoint Mountain guides (www.mountainguides.co.uk). For mountain biking, check out Dolomite Sport (dolomitesport.com) or Mountain Pass Alta Badia for lift access (www.mountainpass.it).

Best Time. June through August is best for good weather, but you may want to go in September or October to avoid crowds.

Pit Stop. Book a long weekend in Italy's picturesque high mountain Lake Garda, where you can climb, mountain bike, windsurf, and kitesurf.

Extended Play. Rock climb this spectacular granite; you'll find free climbs, aid routes, and bolted ascents. Ski or snowboard at Cortina if you're there in early spring. To indulge your urban, cultural side, tack on this ancient Tuscan town of Florence. You can spy works from Michelangelo and Da Vinci and tour the catacombs where they learned their craft. For R & R, stop in the fabulous Cinque Terre, aka the Italian Riviera, where you can relax and ride great single-track mountain biking trails.

Travel Smart. For Via Ferratta routes, you'll need basic mountain-hiking gear: boots, clothing, pack. You'll also need a helmet in case of rockfall, a climbing harness, and a ferrata set (webbing sewn into a pair of 3-foot lengths with carabiners on the end of each piece, which allows you to clip into a cable for safety).

☑ 51. CIRCUMNAVIGATE THE WHITE MOUNTAIN: THE MONT BLANC CIRCUIT (CHAMONIX, FRANCE)

Chamonix. There's a certain fear that should run down your spine with the mention of this town. Indeed, this is extreme sports central. The birthplace of mountaineering. Center point of big-mountain skiing. The pinnacle for age-old sports like ski mountaineering and rock climbing, as well as daredevil ones like speed skiing (aka ski foiling), BASE jumping, and paragliding.

There are few places in the world where you'll stroll downtown for dinner, and sit next to someone ordering food in full ski-mountaineering regalia: harness still buckled around waist with a few ice screws dangling against the chair.

This is Chamonix. Bold, rugged, extreme.

For something simple, as far as this town goes, run or trek the famed Mont Blanc Circuit, which circumnavigates the massive 15,782-foot (4,810 m) mountain via Italy and Switzerland. You can travel around the "White Mountain" among glaciers, wildflower-chocked meadows, spectacular views, jagged peaks, and world-class ski towns like Courmayeur. The 100-mile (151 km) circuit around Mont Blanc will feel like walking inside a postcard, every single day.

Don't Miss. If you come in spring, don't miss the gravity-defying tour of the Mer de Glasse up the Aguille du Midi tram and down the Vallee Blanche Glacier. It's a ½-day ski mountaineering descent that will take you on a 6,000-foot run.

Logistics. Fly into Geneva, and then it's an easy shuttle or train ride to Chamonix Valley. Check out quiet Hôtel de l'Arve (www .hotelarve-chamonix.com/en/) right on the main walking street. For more raucous nightlife try the Hotel Gustavia close to the *bahnhof* (train station) (www.hotelgustavia.eu). Book a trip with the oldest guide service in the world, Compagnie des Guides de Chamonix (www.chamonix-guides.com).

Best Time. To hike, mountain run, or mountain bike the Mont Blanc Circuit schedule a September trip when the weather is grand and the crowds have dispersed. If you want to ski or snowboard, go during the winter or early spring. If you want to climb Mont Blanc, summer is the main season.

Pit Stop. Book a week in the snow: resort skiing, ski mountaineering day tours, and skate skiing for light days; there's a track for the latter right through town.

Extended Play. Ski the famed extreme skiing valley of La Grave (go with a guide!). Traverse the Haute Route (Trip #48). Cycle a leg of the Tour de France (Trip #53). If that isn't enough, ski one of the 4 resorts such as Les Grands Montets, or skate ski, road bike, mountain bike, paddle, rock climb . . . the list does not end. This is a great spot to try a new sport like speed skiing (aka ski foiling) or paragliding (go tandem with a guide). Or embark on one of the most difficult, famed ascents in Europe: climb Mont Blanc via the Voie Royale route and the Vallot cabin (again, go guided).

Travel Smart. Chamonix is the center, and perhaps birthplace, of extreme mountain sports. Don't try to do it all. These mountains are more than big: They are gigantic, steep, rocky, and glaciated (as in crevassed). The trams are built in unworldly places. The entrances to some of the ski lines require rappels. The ski hills are all perched thousands of feet off the valley floor and many of the descent lines end in cliffs (you have to know the routes to ski all the way to town). So go guided. And, don't try to keep up with the locals!

52. RUN 26 MILES AND 386 YARDS: MARATHON DU MEDOC (FRANCE)

According to the ancient historian Herodotus, Pheidippides ran from Sparta to Athens during the Battle of Marathon, back in 490 BC. Round-trip it was more like an ultramarathon: 150 miles (240 km). Eons later, in 1896, the 26-mile, 385-yard marathon, became one of the original Olympic events. The length started with roughly the distance from Marathon to Athens (25 miles/40km). At the 1908 Olympics in London, the route was set as the distance from Windsor Castle to the

White City Stadium plus 1 lap on the track. Now, there are hundreds of marathons all over the world.

If you haven't run a marathon, you probably will. It's a rite of passage for the adrenaline junkie. Eventually you may even try an ultramarathon (Trip #2). There are spectacularly scenic marathons—rural and urban alike—like the ones in Bar Harbor, Maine; Steamboat Springs, Colorado; and San Francisco. There are intercontinental ones like the Intercontinental Istanbul Eurasia Marathon. You can run the distance along the Great Wall of China, in South Africa, or across parts of Iceland or Greenland.

If you want to go for the top, the official world record is held by Kenyan Patrick Makau, who ran the 2011 Berlin Marathon in 2 hours, 3 minutes, and 38 seconds. That's about 4.7 minute miles—most of us can't run 1 mile that fast!

Not an ultra-competitive runner, or never done a marathon? Check out Medoc. The zany Medoc run started in 1984, nestled in beautiful French Bordeaux wine country. You can run it full on or dress up (some say this is a requirement) depending on the year's theme. In past years themes have covered the animal kingdom, the circus, and historical figures. Because the route meanders through some 50 châteaux, you may be tempted to sip wine at the aid stations, but wait until you're finished with the event. The toughest decision is whether to do it for fun, or competition. Do you prefer wine and costumes, or sweaty spandex, sports drinks, and way more pain?

Don't Miss. Check out the wineries of Bordeaux and the surf town of Biarritz. And spend a few days in the City of Lights, Paris.

Logistics. Fly into Paris, and then take a KLM Cityhopper to Bordeaux. You have to sign up in February (www.marathondume doc.com).

Best Time. The Medoc marathon usually takes place on the Saturday of the first full weekend in September.

Pit Stop. Book a 10-day trip. That's enough time to get there, run the marathon, tour Bordeaux, surf a few waves on the coast, and get home.

Extended Play. Qualify for and then run the Boston Marathon (www.baa.org); it seems daunting, but you can do it!

Travel Smart. Most marathons take 3 to 5 hours, and have aid stations every couple of miles. You'll want to follow a training program for 6 months in advance. During the race you'll want to stay hydrated, and avoid depletion of electrolytes, which can result in nausea, vomiting, dizziness, and cramps. Basically, try to slug a sports drink every aid station and eat some sort of quick-energy food, like a banana, or the more high-tech gels and goos (which some people love, and others hate). Don't be afraid to run-walk. And pace yourself—starting out at your half-marathon pace can be a disaster.

53. CYCLE THE TOUR DE FRANCE: ALPE D'HUEZ (FRANCE)

The Tour de France is touted as one of the most difficult cycling races, even sporting events, in the world. And for good reason. The 3-week, 2,200-mile (3,600 km) cycling stage race forges up mountain passes, across long stretches of rural roads, over cobblestones, and in and out of multiple countries. The Tour started in 1903 and is one of the 3, 3-weeklong Grand Tours of cycling, which include the Giro d'Italia (Italy) and the Vuelta a España (Spain).

If you're a roadie, any kind of biker really, then you must ride at least 1 stage of the Tour. And if you're only going to ride one, ride the most difficult, most famous, and most thrilling: Alp d'Huez. If the 9.4-mile long (15.2 km), 3,770-foot climb (1,150 m), 7.9 percent average grade ascent in the Dauphiné Alps isn't enough, you'll go through 21 vertiginous switch-backs to the top. Go for it, at whatever pace you want.

Don't Miss. Spend a few nights in Chamonix, the birthplace of mountaineering and the world epicenter for extreme sports (Trip #51). The quaint village is all things *sportif*: trail run, mountain bike, ski, climb, and paddle. If you have time, cycle the backroads of the bucolic Provence region.

Logistics. Fly into Geneva or Lyon, and catch a train to either Chamonix or, if you're more of an urban type, Grenoble. The Alp d'Huez ride starts in the town of Le Bourg-d'Oisans. You can extend it up to Col de Poutran and Lac Besson—11.6 miles longer (18.7 km) and 3,970 feet higher (1,210 m)—if you're not tired. To make it simple, rent a bike from More Than 21 Bends in Le Bourg-d'Oisans (www.morethan21bends.com). The bike shop can also help with a guide, lodging, and transfer from Grenoble.

Best Time. Go anytime spring to fall, as long as the snow has melted off the peak. For great weather, fewer tourists, and better airfare, go in September or October.

Pit Stop. Because the Tour de France has been operating for over a century and the routes vary from year to year, you can ride a portion of the tour from almost anywhere in France: the Atlantic Coast, the Mediterranean Rivera, Massif Central, the Pyrenees, or the wine country of Bordeaux or Lorraine. Find a bike shop, rent a steed, and ride a route.

Extended Play. If you're a roadie nut, you'll probably want to cycle for a week, every day, all day. Alternatively, hang out in France for as long as you can and rock climb southern France, ski the Haute Route in the spring (Trip #48), or run the Medoc marathon in the fall (Trip #52). Any of these can be combined with cycling for a fabulous 2-week trip.

Or, *gulp,* ride a route on each of the Grand Tours: France, Spain, and Italy (probably in 3 separate trips). In Italy, check out the spectacular scenery in Tuscany, the lake region of the north, or the Dolomites. In Spain, explore the cycling community of Girona.

Travel Smart. Take your own shoes, pedals, helmet and kit (aka bike clothing). If you want to bring your bike, pack it carefully in a bike carrier and check on airline fees. Use caution on roads, especially on the downhill portions. This isn't the place to push the limit.

☑ 54. *ROAD BIKE THROUGH EUROPE*

Cycling through Europe will give you a very different perspective from a motorized trek.

You'll meet loads of friendly people, you'll get incredibly fit, and you'll be able to stick to a lower budget. The real boon is the fantastic perspective from a bike saddle. You'll move slowly through cultures, countries, and landscape drenched in centuries-old history.

There is nearly unlimited cycling, so you'll want to focus on a particular region. Scope out one of these areas:

- The Lake District outside Salzburg, Austria
- The national parks of Dalmatia, Croatia
- Circumnavigate the Baltic Sea
- Tuscany, Italy
- France's Loire Valley
- Switzerland's Alps
- The Romantic Road, Bavaria, and Danube River, Germany

Don't Miss. Stop in to see the Spring Classics in Belgium, center of the road-biking universe. Catch a cobblestone race like the famous Tour of Flanders (in Dutch *Ronde van Vlaanderen*).

Logistics. Get either a cyclo-cross or a touring bike. It's a bit heavier, but more durable and less expensive than a carbon roadie. Pack gear in panniers; try not to go too heavy and not to put too much gear on the front wheel. If you plan to camp, you'll need a sleeping bag, micro tent, small stove, and just bare-essential clothing. Hostels or guest houses are also viable options. For tours, check out Bike Tours Direct (www.biketoursdirect.com). Adventure Cycling Association (www.adventurecycling.org) has tons of information as does the famed late bike wrench (aka mechanic) Sheldon Brown's posthumously managed Web site (sheldonbrown.com). If you're riding a short trip, consider renting because packing a bike on a plane is expensive and a chore!

Best Time. In the summer you'll have the best chance of clear weather, but fall will have fewer tourists. Southern Europe or Belgium, Denmark, and Holland are the best spots for spring cycling.

Pit Stop. Pick 1 region, ride for 1 week, and don't stress about trying to see it all. Avoid big cities; they will be there when you hang up the bike—if that ever happens.

Extended Play. Traverse the whole continent in 1 month (or more). Go north to south, from London to Istanbul, or west to east from Paris to Istanbul. Either way, touch down in Istanbul, one of my favorite cities in the world. You can take the Orient Express back to Paris.

Travel Smart. Pack light, and make sure you have a credit card handy for emergencies. Road safety is paramount. Carry a bike-repair kit. Also, make sure you ride safely, especially with a fully loaded bike. And watch out for cars!

 ## 55. *MOUNTAIN BIKE THROUGH EUROPE*

Europe has a long-standing history of road biking, cyclo-cross, and long-distance bike touring. It also happens to have some of the best mountain bike trails on the globe.

Downhillers and freeriders should check out the Portes du Soleil tour that spans 12 ski and bike resorts between Geneva, Switzerland, and Chamonix, France (en.portesdusoleil.com). Ride

Sauze d'Oulx, near Turin, Italy (www.sauzeonline.com), or cycle through the famed Cinque Terre Riviera.

Cross-country riders can ride from Chamonix to Zermatt via Verbier (like the skiers Haute Route, Trip #48). Blast the trails near Lake Garda, Italy. Ride Bubión, Spain, in the Sierra Nevada range (www.switch-backs.com) or the Almanzora Valley in the Sierra de los Filabres Mountains (www.mountainbikingspain.com).

Don't Miss. If you're a freerider, check out one of the best bike parks in Europe, the Hafjell Bike Park in Lillehammer, Norway (www.hafjell.no).

Logistics. Ride the Alps (www.ridethealps.com) and Mountain Bike Europe (www.mountainbikeeurope.com) can set you up with tours and rentals. If you can rent, bring your own clothing kit, helmet, shoes, pedals, and hydration pack. You may also want to have your measurements handy so you can quickly size a rental bike.

Best Time. Summer is the best time for clear weather. Spring can have fabulous weather and great trail conditions, but rain and snow in the mountains can stymie a spin.

Pit Stop. Couple a 1- or 2-day ride with another trip. Bike stores are plentiful in Europe for rentals.

Extended Play. Go on a weeklong tour of the Alps with Ride the Alps (www.ridethealps.com) or try the Alpenrock or Cloud-raked tours from Big Mountain Adventures (www.ridebig.com).

Travel Smart. Bring a hydration pack, helmet, and small repair kit. Don't rely on bike shops for safety gear. Arm yourself with basic trail-repair skills, like changing a flat, fixing a chain, and adjusting derailers. Since you'll be riding new trails, this isn't the best time to huck big cliffs. Trails in Europe can be advanced. Rescue in Europe's mountains costs money so sign up for travel and rescue insurance, and go with a partner.

Better ruins than Rome. Open aquamarine seas. Rugged rocky coastlines.

This is the spectacular Turquoise Coast, aka the Turkish Riviera, on the Aegean Sea. In addition to the spectacular sea views, you'll find well-preserved archaeological ruins, like the Mausoleum of Maussollos in Halicarnassus and the Temple of Artemis in Ephesus, the remains of which are part of the Seven Wonders of the Ancient World. In Cappadocia, you can cruise among lava-encrusted buildings from centuries past. You should also scope out the Byzantine castle of Simena and ruins at Ship Island.

And after a bit of exploring, refresh on a gullet, a dual-mast wood sailboat traditionally found on the southwest coast of Turkey. It's a Turkish word, modified from the French *gouelette*, which means "schooner." Most are built in the Turkish marine community of Bodrum. Modern incarnations do include motors!

This coastline is a mix of ruins and magic, culture and adventure. Make sure you get out to snorkel, kayak, stand-up paddle, or cast a line.

Don't Miss. Istanbul is one of the coolest cities on the planet. It's where Europe meets Asia. Tour the Blue Mosque, Hagia Sophia, and Grand Bazaar, the largest covered market in the world. Check out the separate spice and silk markets, too. Even take a Turkish bath— if you dare!

Logistics. Make your way to one of the most bustling cities in Europe and gateway to Asia. Book a boat through Blue Cruise (www.bluecruise.org). They offer private charters with small 3-cabin boats or larger ones that accommodate nearly 10 people. Or just grab a cabin on a scheduled cruise. Cruises begin in Bodrum, Marmaris, Fethiye, or Antalya. A weeklong sail is ideal.

Best Time. Pick September and October for beautiful weather and calm seas.

Pit Stop. If you can't make the full week, book a 3-night cruise from Marmaris to Fethiye along the Lycian Coast.

Extended Play. Looking for another sail? Check out the famed Dalmatian Coast from Split to Dubrovnik in Croatia. Make your way to Athens and zip over to one of the islands in the Cyclades: Mykonos, Tinos, Delos, Naxos, Amorgos, and the famed Santorini, with its rugged trails, whitewashed blue-roofed villages, and spectacular coastal kayaking. Or stay in Athens, another fascinating, bustling city with a rich history.

Travel Smart. You're sailing, so make sure you head out in fair weather and bring survival gear, or rent a skippered boat. And don't forget the sunscreen.

57. SEA KAYAK THE ARCTIC TRIFECTA (NORWAY, GREENLAND, AND ICELAND)

The Arctic: the trip of a lifetime.

You may not be able to climb the big walls of Baffin Island, dogsled the North Pole, or ski across Greenland. But you can get within 10 degrees of our planet's most northern point via icebreaker or ice-strengthened small cruise ship. One of the world's undiscovered wonders is kayaking a trifecta of Arctic countries: Norway's Spitsbergen Island, Greenland, and Iceland.

Paddle alongside bearded, ringed, and harp seals; walrus, beluga, and bowhead whales; and the elusive king of the arctic, *Ursus maritimus*, polar bears. On Spitsbergen, scope out Arctic terns, skuas, long-tailed ducks, kittiwakes, and Glaucous Gulls along with Spitsbergen reindeer.

Don't Miss. On Spitsbergen, visit the European Centre for Arctic Environmental Research in Ny-Ålesund and hike the remote glaciers, steep fjords, and grassy tundra in search of wildlife.

Logistics. Bag all 3 with Quark Expeditions (www.quarkexpe ditions.com). Fly into Reykjavik, catch the boat northbound or take a commuter flight to Longyearbyen on Spitsbergen Island and catch a southbound tour. Quark arranges the kayak and zodiacs for shore exploration.

Best Time. Quark runs tours in August, great for calm seas and long days.

Pit Stop. If you don't have time for all 3, pop into Iceland for ski touring, hiking, mountain biking, or trail running.

Extended Play. After the ship tour, spend a week in Iceland, the "Land of Fire and Ice," among the geysers, percolating mud pools, rhyolite crags, lava fields, hot springs, and glaciers. Drive from glaciers to active volcanoes on a road that circumnavigates the whole country. Run the Reykjavik Marathon (www.marathon.is). Ski the backcountry with Icelandic Mountain Guides (www.mountain guides.is). Mountain bike the pristine single track alongside the Eyjafjorour Fjord, Jokulsargljufur National Park, Eyjafjallajokull Volcano, and the Langjökull Glacier with Big Mountain Bike Adventures (www.ridebig.com). You can spend at least 2 weeks adventuring in Iceland.

Travel Smart. This is the Arctic. Even if you're not kayaking, the weather is cold and blustery year-round. If in a kayak, make sure you wear a personal-floatation device, go in a group, and learn cold-water survival skills. If you dump the boat in cold water, you'll have about 2 minutes to get your breathing under control, about 20 minutes to get back in the kayak, and about 2 hours before you become exhausted and hypothermic.

58. WHITEWATER RAFT OR KAYAK THE SJOA RIVER (NORWAY)

Along with Chile, New Zealand, and California, Norway has some of the best whitewater in the world. If you run just 1 river, head to the Sjoa. It begins in the headwaters in the Jotunheimen Mountains, dumps massive whitewater through Jotunheimen National Park, meanders through the Ridderspranget ravine, and eventually spills into the Gudbrandsdalslágen River. The Sjoa dishes up Class II through IV rapids.

Kayaking not for you? Go rafting, catarafting (pontoon catamaran), or riverboarding. But be advised, some parts of this river are for experts only, and others are simply not navigable.

Don't Miss. If you can, book a trip around the Sjoa River Festival in mid-July (www.sjoariverfestival.no).

Logistics. Fly to Oslo or Copenhagen and make your way to Heidal via rental car or train. Hang out at Sjoa Kayak Camp (www.sjoariverfestival.no) where you can pitch a tent or book a dorm bed, rent gear, take a sauna, grab a guide, and get a shuttle to and from the creek. Sjoa Rafting (en.sjoarafting.no), Heidal Rafting (www.heidalrafting.no), and Sjoa Rafting Center (www.sjoaraftingsenter.no) all have guided trips, rentals, and gear.

Best Time. May to September is best for river flow and good weather.

Pit Stop. If you're touring Scandinavia, it's easy to make a 1- or 2-day run down the Sjoa River.

Extended Play. Rent a road bike and spin the beautiful Scandinavian countryside. Hit 1, or all of the clean, cosmopolitan, seaside cities: Copenhagen, Oslo, Helsinki, Amsterdam, and Stockholm. They all have cultural history, great road biking, and fabulous whitewater and flatwater kayaking. Check out the Spring Classics, the famous road bike races in Belgium. Climb Norway's glaciers, or mountain bike one of the best parks in the world, Hafjell Bike Park near Lillehammer (Trip #55).

Travel Smart. Go guided down this river. Wear a helmet and personal-floatation device. And if you get dunked, make sure to get your feet out in front of you to fend off rocks and swim to shore.

59. CLIMB MOUNT ELBRUS: THE SEVEN SUMMITS, EUROPE (UKRAINE)

Although Mont Blanc gets the glory for being the birthplace of mountaineering, Mount Elbrus is the crown of Europe, the highest peak on the continent.

Nestled in Ukraine's Caucasus Range, between the Black and Caspian seas, the volcanic peak tops out at 18,510 feet (5,642 m). Dubbed Mingi Taw, or "resembling a thousand mountains" in the Balkar language, Elbrus is massive. F. Crauford Grove and Peter Knubel first ascended the mountain in 1874.

You'll not only have bragging rights for topping the highest peak in Europe, you can climb Elbrus in just a week. You can also take a lift up the mountain and sleep in the quaint Barrels or Diesel huts. You'll just need a daypack. It's not super technical or time consuming like most of the Seven Summits.

Don't Miss. You can attack Elbrus from Moscow. Red Square, Lenin's Tomb, St. Basil onion domes, and the GUM department store are all must-sees in Russia's capital. You can also take a short flight to St. Petersburg, often called the Venice of the North. The architecture in St. Petersburg is spectacular and the Hermitage is one of the biggest museums in the world (www.hermitagemuseum .org) with some 3 million pieces.

Logistics. Fly into Moscow then take a commuter flight to Mineralnye Vody, a small mountain town. Then take a bus or shuttle to the ski town of Azau in the Baksan Valley at 7,500 feet (2,286 m). You'll hike or ride the lift up the south side of Elbrus to 12,000 feet (3,658 m) then hike to the Barrels or Diesel huts. Climb to the summit via Pastukhova Rocks. For guides, check out International Mountain Guides (www.mountainguides.com) and Alpine Ascents International (www.alpineascents.com).

Best Time. Summer is prime climbing season. Winter is best for skiing in the area.

Pit Stop. The resort tram operates in winter and summer so you can access the upper mountain in both seasons. From there, book a snowcat to Pastukhova Rocks at 15,000 feet (4,572 m). It makes for a speedy ascent.

Extended Play. Climb the second crown jewel of Europe: Mont Blanc (Trip #51).

Travel Smart. It's a mountain, so bring warm clothes, plenty of food and water, and go with a guide.

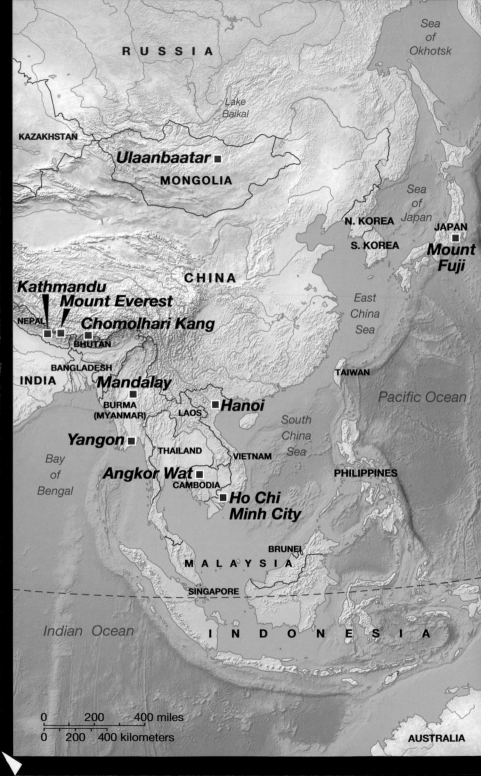

AS THE largest and most populated continent, Asia is home to nearly half of the world's 7 billion people. It also has some of the most varied geography with its thick forests and volcanoes in the north, ancient cloud kingdoms in the center of the continent, and pristine beaches in the south. And then there's India, a subcontinent of its own.

Since Asia comprises 30 percent of the world's landmass, you could plan 100 trips to this continent alone. Unlike many of the other regions in this book, much of it is undiscovered and less trav eled. There are rivers that have yet to be run, mountains to be climbed, and trails waiting to be explored. At the same time, the continent also has some of the world's most fascinating cities: Istanbul, which straddles the European/Asian border; Singapore, with its futuristic architecture; and Mumbai, where all things India coalesce into chaotic and colorful energy.

Indeed, it's a long way from North America. It's slightly challenging to get around and difficult to readily rent big gear like kayaks, rafts, skis, or bikes. So consider a trek for your first trip here or think about going fully guided, so gear will be provided.

Where to begin? For something simple, start with a backcountry ski tour of Hokkaido, Japan, a surf trip in Indonesia, or a bicycle tour of Indochina. For those with more time, flexibility, and a keen sense of adventure, head to India, China, and Nepal. For some of the more remote countries, like Mongolia, New Guinea, or Bhutan, consider a guided trek because it's fairly complicated travel on your own efficiently.

Few people can drop thousands of dollars, shirk a few months of work, commit to a year of training and climb to the summit of the highest peak in the world. The trek to Everest Base Camp is simpler, less expensive, less risky, and allows you to explore the wonders of Nepal as well as get a taste of what a big climbing expedition is like. You can immerse yourself in the cultural duality of the working mountaineers, the Sherpas, and their paying clients.

The trek weaves in and out of Sherpa villages, through spectacular rhododendron forests and the high altitude mountains of the famed Himalayan peaks. Namche Bazaar, the gateway to the big mountains, is a central meeting place for Sherpas and Tibetans either buying or selling supplies in the markets. Check out the bakeries, tea shops, museums, monasteries, and Sagarmatha National Park Visitor's Center. Higher up on the trek, in Tengboche, you'll find the largest Sherpa monastery in Nepal. Further on the trail, you'll pass through Dingboche, Lobuje, and Gorak Shep, with optional hiking to Ama Dablam Base Camp.

Don't Miss. If completing the trek to Everest Base Camp is your goal, get in shape, pay attention to your health, and go guided. You may not have another opportunity.

Logistics. Fly into Kathmandu, Nepal, most likely via Bangkok. Nepal is a bustling outdoor and cultural city. Most guides book at the Hotel Yak & Yeti (www.yakandyeti.com). Fly to Lukla, via the hairball landing at "Airstrip in the Sky," aka Short Take Off and Landing. From Lukla, you'll trek up the Dudh Kosi River, passing through Namche Bazaar, Tengboche, and Pheriche to Everest Base Camp at 17,575 feet (5,357 m). Then spin around and head back down in half the time. You can go lodge to lodge, or camp. Find a guide through Mountain Travel Sobek (www.mtsobek.com), Wilderness Travel (www.wildernesstravel.com), Bio Bio Expeditions (www.bbxrafting.com), or one of many other outfitters.

Best Time. March and April, before the summer monsoons, are the best climbing months. October and November are also viable.

Pit Stop. If you want to do a shorter trek, hike into Namche Bazaar and Tengboche. That'll take about 2 weeks.

Extended Play. Add on the Annapurna Circuit, which includes rafting and wildlife viewing. You'll have to fly from Kathmandu to Pokhara. Then hike the rhododendron forests, raft the Seti River, and visit the Royal Chitwan National Park—home of Bengal tigers and one-horned rhinos. Or, *gulp,* climb Mount Everest (Trip #66).

Travel Smart. Acute mountain sickness is a big risk on this trek. Basic treatment is fairly straightforward: Go down. Unfortunately it can cause a wrinkle in a trip. Taking prophylactic meds, like acetazolamide, helps prevent onset. You can also mitigate risk by ascending slowly, staying hydrated, and making sure you're in great shape. Travelers' diarrhea is also big issue that can also make you dehydrated. Hypothermia and frostbite are also possible. Fortunately, you can get help. There's a travel clinic in Kathmandu, CIWEC (ciwec-clinic.com), and the Himalayan Rescue Association operates clinics at Pheriche and Everest Base Camp (www.himalayanrescue.org).

61. TRAVEL INTO MONGOLIA: READ ABOUT, THEN EXPLORE THE EXOTIC

Adrenaline junkies read a ton. We pore over guidebooks, devour modern adventure narratives, and revere historical expedition stories. Adventure travel books are our escape, connection, and inspiration. There's nothing better than being absorbed in a book, and then heading into the wild lands. There are two quintessential books for exploring the wonders of Mongolia: *Dateline Mongolia: An American Journalist in Nomad's Land,* by Michael Kohn, about his years working as a local reporter, and *Wild East: Travels in New Mongolia,* by Jill Lawless, about the emergence of the country after centuries of isolation.

From Genghis Khan to nomadic tribes, from the steppes of the big continent to the dunes of the Gobi desert, from the vast wetlands to the Flaming Cliffs, Mongolia is one of the most remote, rugged, and rarely traveled lands. You can camp in yurts, or gers, in which many of the nomads still live. You'll see wild horses, snow leopards, Argali mountain sheep, Saker falcons, and Bactrian camels.

There are several circuits you can trek in Mongolia. Outside the capital of Ulaanbaatar, visit the Hustain Nuruu National Park to spy wild horses; the ruins of Kharakhorum, Genghis Khan's capital; and Khorgo-Terkhiin Tsagaan Nuur National Park set on Great White Lake. Try the Gobi Desert Circuit and see the dinosaur fossil beds at the Flaming Cliffs near Gobi Gurvansaikhan National Park, and the "singing sands" of the 60-mile-long (97 km), 2,500-foot- (760 m) high Khongoryn Els sand dunes.

Don't Miss. Check out the Gandan Monastery and the temples of Megjid Janraisig and Kalachakra in Ulaanbaatar. There's a National History Museum with relics and dinosaur bones and eggs.

Logistics. Fly into Ulaanbaatar via Seoul, Korea. Check out the Three Camel Lodge, nestled near the Khongoryn Els sand dunes (www.threecamellodge.com). The yurts are made of felt stretched over wood frames. Inside you'll find beds and small stoves for heating. The lodge serves as a base for wildlife and scientific study. There are replanted native trees that assist migratory bird populations that come through Mount Bulagtai. The lodge is powered by solar and wind energy.

Best Time. Head to this wild land from June through September for the best weather.

Pit Stop. It's hard to make a quick trip, but if you only have a few days, visit the Three Camel Lodge and explore the beautiful Gobi surroundings.

Extended Play. You can climb Mongolia's highest peak Mount Khuiten (14,350 ft/4,374 m). Visit the Tsagaan Salaa petroglyphs at Tsagaan Salaa and trek in the high Altai Mountains among the Potanin Glacier. Or head back to the library or your favorite bookstore, pick up a historic narrative, and explore other Asian landscapes:

- Heinrich Harrer's *Seven Years in Tibet* recounts his years in Lhasa.
- Eric Hansen's *Stranger in the Forest: On Foot Across Borneo*

describes exploration of the rainforest jungles, Mount Kinabalu, and the thick Danum Valley mangrove jungles.

- Consume another of Eric Hansen's tales, *Motoring with Mohammed: Journeys to Yemen and the Red Sea,* and then check out Yemen and then stop in Dubai, the world's most modern city.
- Peter Matthiessen wrote *The Snow Leopard,* a classic about his travels in Mustang, Nepal.

Travel Smart. Keep in mind, when traveling to remote lands, medical care is not readily available and evacuation is difficult. Don't take big risks by hucking cliffs or pushing yourself to the limit. Take a medical kit, and know how to use it. Ward off the basics: dehydration, hypothermia, heat exhaustion, sun exposure, and the bane of trekkers--blisters. Watch for insect bites and avoid bites from any and all dogs. Many can carry rabies.

62. TREK SHANGRI-LA IN THE CLOUD KINGDOM (BHUTAN)

In James Hilton's 1933 book, *Lost Horizon,* the mysterious, harmonious, isolated Shangri-La was depicted as a pure mountain paradise where people lived long and happy lives. Today, the cloud kingdom of Bhutan has been called the world's last Shangri-La.

Once closed to Western travel and shrouded in mystery, the mountains, temples, rice paddies, and villages of Bhutan are now a must-see in this mountain kingdom. In addition to epic peaks and spectacular scenic trials, you'll find ancient monasteries, artisan crafts, vibrant festivals, and beautiful temples in this once-forbidden land.

The pinnacle of adventure in Bhutan is the trek to Mount Chomolhari (23,997 ft/7,314 m), where you'll (hopefully) spy the elusive blue sheep and snow leopards. Walk through the Soi Yaksa Valley and hike, trail run, or bike in the mountains of Phobjika, where the black-necked crane winter, and rhododendrons, dwarf bamboo, and gray langur monkeys reside. You'll also want to check out the mountain villages of Paro, Punakha, and Thimphu as well as the *dzongs*, aka fortresses, and citadels in the cliffs. And definitely raft the Drangme Chhu River.

Don't Miss. Outside Paro, visit the cliffside monastery at Taktsang: the "Tiger's Nest."

Logistics. From Bangkok, fly to the Paro Valley in Bhutan. Book a trek through one of the big outfitters like Mountain Travel Sobek (www.mtsobek.com) or Wilderness Travel (www.wildernesstravel.com). The smaller Bio Bio Expeditions (www.bbxrafting.com) has rafting trips down the Drangme Chhu River.

Best Time. October and November have the best weather.

Pit Stop. You can make a 5-day trip to Paro and its surroundings, but you'll miss the Cholo trek unless you have more time.

Extended Play. Combine Bhutan with a trip to Nepal, and trekking the Himalaya. Hit up Bangkok and then head to the beautiful Thai beaches. Alternatively, touch down in another hidden and once-forbidden land, Burma, now known as Myanmar (Trip #65). Or visit India and raft the Grand Canyon of the Himalayas, the Zanskar River with Bio Bio Expeditions (www.bbxrafting.com).

Travel Smart. Like many remote regions, medical care is not readily available. Go prepared with a medical kit, knowledge of wilderness and travel first aid, and a healthy dose of caution.

Emerald jungles, pristine beaches, expansive rice fields. Cycling through Indochina—a name that started with French colonization of what is now Vietnam, Cambodia, and Laos in the late 1800s—is a biker's dream trip. Riding the lowland route along the Vietnam coast, you'll see more of this country than you ever could from a bus or car.

You can choose from two primary itineraries. The first is a spin from Ho Chi Minh City, formerly Saigon, to Hanoi along the coast. You'll travel through the towns of Hoi An and Hue. Alternatively, pedal from Ho Chi Minh City to Angkor, Cambodia, to the famed temples of Angkor Wat, via the backroads, banana plantations, and sugar cane fields of the Mekong Delta.

Don't Miss. Angkor Wat is one of the largest and most well-preserved ancient cities, much like Peru's Machu Picchu (Trip #40). If you want to stay in Vietnam, rent a kayak in Hanoi and paddle through Halong Bay.

Logistics. From Bangkok, take a commuter flight to Ho Chi Minh City or Hanoi. Book a cycle tour through Recreational Equipment Inc. (www.rei.com) for a 10-day tour.

Best Time. Avoid heat and bugs by picking a window between November and January.

Pit Stop. Enjoy day rides around Ho Chi Minh City, kayak Halong Bay for an afternoon, and zip over to Angkor Wat, all in less than a week.

Extended Play. If you want to see the whole country, ride along the coast through Nha Trang, Hoi An, and Hue all the way to Hanoi. Once in Hanoi, rent a kayak and paddle Halong Bay and hike the Pu Luong Nature Reserve. Then either ride or drive to Angkor Wat, making a pit stop in Laos. Drop into Malaysia and then visit nearby Singapore, one of the world's most modern countries. Hit up the waves of Bali, Indonesia, for some excellent surfing.

Travel Smart. Guard against bugs and heat with lightweight cycle clothing. Try to avoid riding in the midday heat and humidity. Cycling can be dangerous if you're overloaded with panniers. Your bike won't steer well or stop quickly, and hoofing it up hills will take loads of energy. Staying in hotels and inns will allow you to forego camping gear. Watch out for cars!

✓ 64. BACKCOUNTRY SKI HOKKAIDO: LAND OF THE RISING SUN (JAPAN)

Sheets of snow, deep powder, lava-rock moonscapes, and bubbling hot springs. This is backcountry skiing on Hokkaido, the second largest island in Japan. In this still undiscovered marvel of an adventure playland, you'll largely have the slopes to yourself.

There are, however, amenities available so you won't have to rough it in a tent. There are 3 volcanoes to shred: Daisetsuzan, Yotei, and Asahidake. Niseko and Furano are the 2 main areas for skiing and snowboarding on Hokkaido. Both have excellent backcountry and sidecountry (just out of bounds) areas for the more adventurous types.

Don't Miss. Take the time to climb Mount Fuji, the 12,389-foot (3,776 m) stratovolcano, 1 of the 3 Holy Mountains of Japan. Meaning "wealth," Fuji is arguably one of the most heavily trafficked peaks in the world, with some 300,000 ascents annually. You won't necessarily find solace in the crowds, but climbing one of the world's most sacred peaks is worthy of the tick list.

Logistics. Fly into Tokyo and take the underwater railway through the Seikan Tunnel to Sapporo, or just hop a commuter flight. Hire a guide with Hokkaido Powder Guides (www.hokkaido powderguides.com). They have 2 bases of operation, one at Niseko Ski Resort in the Niseko Mountains and one in Furano in the Daisetsuzan Range. Use Hakusou Hot Spring Lodges in Kamiho as a base near Mount Tokachi in Daisetsuzan National Park. In the Niseko area, check out Goshi Hot Springs Lodge, among boiling, sulfer-laden volcano pits.

Best Time. December through March is prime ski season.

Pit Stop. Zip over to Japan and spend a week, or even just 4 days, at Niseko Ski Resort for lift skiing or sidecountry touring.

Extended Play. Kayak the coast. Explore the beautiful national parks. Book a night in culturally rich Kyoto and wander the urban jungle of Tokyo. And climb Mount Fuji! You can also zip over to Russia's far-east Kuril Islands and Kamchatka—a remote and beautiful wildlife-laden land.

Travel Smart. Backcountry skiing and snowboarding bring the usual mountain hazards. Hypothermia, frostbite, and altitude illness are largely preventable with quality clothing and cautious ascent. Avalanches are prevalent in the mountains so go with a guide. You'll be safer and have a better time with someone who knows where to find the best powder.

Mysterious, untrammeled, and breathtakingly beautiful. From its beaches on the Bay of Bengal, to the thick tropical jungles, and snow-covered Himalayan foothills, Myanmar is a sight to behold. Long closed to foreign travel, the Republic of the Union of Myanmar (formerly Burma) has just recently opened to tourism. Touch down in Yangon and see the Shwedagon Pagoda; visit Mandalay and trawl the temples of Bagan. This country is as culturally diverse as it is scenic. You'll see men dressed in *longyi,* a kind of long shirt, and women wearing *thanka,* traditional Burmese makeup, and chewing betel leaves.

If you can find a canoe, kayak, or longboat, paddle among the monasteries, markets, and temples on Inle Lake, or bike to the hot springs in Kaundaing. Then go sea kayaking in the Mergui Islands.

Don't Miss. Try the wonderful food, a fusion of Indian, Chinese, and Shan. *Mohinga,* made of vermicelli noodles, fish sauce, coriander, and chile is a breakfast staple. Stop at Black Canyon Coffee in Mandalay.

Logistics. The best way to explore is with a guided group. Check the U.S. State Department advisory (www.travel.state.gov) and get a visa in advance. Fly through Singapore or Bangkok. Be prepared with plenty of cash. You can't rely on credit or debit cards in Myanmar. Both Wilderness Travel (www.wildernesstravel.com) and Mountain Travel Sobek (www.mtsobek.com) run guided trips. Several outfitters run sailing and kayaking trips including Paddle Asia (paddleasia.com).

Best Time. To avoid heat and monsoons, go between October and February.

Pit Stop. Visit Mandalay, a rich cultural mecca.

Extended Play. Surf Indonesia, cycle Vietnam, and trek Bhutan. All are close-by. Or spend a month on the Burma Road from Kunming, China, to Yangon, Burma, via Wilderness Travel (www .wildernesstravel.com).

Travel Smart. Hampered for decades with political unrest and extreme poverty, tourism is just beginning to develop as an industry. Bring cash, and know where the U.S. embassies are. Consider registering with the U.S. State Department's Smart Traveler Enrollment Program, which allows you to enter information into a database for better emergency assistance.

66. CLIMB MOUNT EVEREST: THE SEVEN SUMMITS, ASIA (NEPAL)

Climbing to the summit of Mount Everest is one of the most grueling achievements humanly possible. Next to the Tour de France (Trip #53), the Race Across America (Trip #23), and the Pacific Crest Trail (Trip #22), this is about as punishing as it gets. The peak punches more than 5 miles into the sky, grazing the jet stream. You probably need to go fully guided. And, be very careful. This is one of the most dangerous trips in the book.

Chomolungma, a Tibetan name meaning "Holy Mother," juts 29,029 feet (8,848 m high). The Royal Geographic Society named the mountain Everest in 1865 after geographer George Everest who was chiefly responsible for the Great Trigonometric Survey of India and Nepal. The peak rests in both Tibet and Nepal. Edmund Hillary and Tenzing Norgay first scaled the mountain in 1953. Now, over 5,600 people have completed the trek, about 500 annually, often on the same few days. *Read:* It gets crowded on summit days in May.

Nowadays, you can book a guided trip with basic mountaineering experience so long as you are in primo physical condition. Guides use fixed ropes and ladders, supplemental oxygen, and porters to haul gear, lessening the burden for climbers and increasing likelihood of guided clients reaching the top. The downside: It's not cheap and you're climbing as a paid client, expedition style—fully assisted.

Don't Miss. Kathmandu, a bustling cultural city, and Namche Bazaar, gateway to the big mountains, are meeting centers for Sherpas, Tibetans, and Nepalese buying and selling goods. Check out the bakeries, tea shops, museums, and monasteries. Visit Tengboche, the largest Sherpa monastery on the trek. Bunk at the Hotel Yak & Yeti (www.yakandyeti.com).

Logistics. Time and cost are major considerations for this trip. You'll need 2 months (not to mention scads of time training and preparing). Fly into Kathmandu through Bangkok. Then hop a commuter flight to Lukla and begin the trek to base camp up the Dudh Kosi River, passing through Namche Bazaar, Tengboche, and Pheriche to Everest Base Camp at 17,575 feet (5,357 m). Here, you'll need multiple days up and down the mountain to acclimatize, depending on weather and fitness level. Check out Alpine Ascents International (www.alpineascents.com), International Mountain Guides (www.mountainguides.com), and Mountain Madness (www.mountainmadness.com) for guided trips.

Best Time. Typical climbing season is March through May before summer monsoons hit.

Pit Stop. You can climb the "express," in only 6 weeks through International Mountain Guides. That's if you're strong and experienced. Or try one of the non-summit trips, like the climbs to Camp 2 or Camp 3 past the Khumbu Icefall. You can also just trek to Everest Base Camp, a trip of a lifetime in itself (Trip #60); that's still a 3-week endeavor. Then again, Reinhold Messner, the first to climb all fourteen peaks over 26,000 feet, climbed the North Col in 3 days from Base Camp in 1980. And he did it alone. Without supplemental oxygen.

Extended Play. Want to extend your Everest trip? Climb all Seven Summits (Trips #29, #47, #59, #66, #73, #81, #82, and #84), or try climbing the Second Summits, the second highest peaks in each continent, some of which are more difficult!

Travel Smart. Altitude illness, hypothermia, frostbite, and injury are very prevalent. This is a dangerous trip. Fortunately you can get help. There's a travelers' clinic in Kathmandu, CIWEC (ciwec clinic.com). The Himalayan Rescue Association also operates Everest ER, a clinic at Everest Base Camp (www.himalayanrescue .org).

Atlantic Ocean

EUROPE

Casablanca ■ ■ **Fez**
MOROCCO

TUNISIA   Mediterranean Sea

MIDDLE EAST

WESTERN SAHARA

ALGERIA

LIBYA

EGYPT

Marsa Alam ■

Red Sea

MAURITANIA

MALI

NIGER

CHAD

SUDAN

ERITREA

DJIBOUTI

SENEGAL
GAMBIA
GUINEA-BISSAU
GUINEA
SIERRA LEONE
LIBERIA
CÔTE D'IVOIRE
BURKINA FASO
GHANA
TOGO
BENIN

NIGERIA

CENTRAL AFRICAN REPUBLIC

ETHIOPIA

SOMALIA

CAMEROON

EQUATORIAL GUINEA

GABON   CONGO

ZAIRE

UGANDA

KENYA

■ **Mount Kenya National Park**

Serengeti National Park

■ ■ **Mount Kilimanjaro**

Ngorongoro

TANZANIA

ANGOLA

ZAMBIA

MALAWI

MOZAMBIQUE

Zambezi River ■

ZIMBABWE

NAMIBIA

BOTSWANA

MADAGASCAR

SWAZILAND

SOUTH AFRICA   LESOTHO

Atlantic Ocean

Indian Ocean

■ **Jeffreys Bay**

0   400   800 miles

0   800 kilometers

AFRICA IS vast, vivid, and exciting. You'll find ancient cultures steeped in ancient traditions. Snowcapped volcanoes tower over savannas and valleys. Raging, unexplored rivers pierce the hillsides.

When you think of Africa, and you might think about the scorching heat of the Sahara Desert or the lush equatorial rainforests. But the continent actually stretches between 2 temperate zones, from the Mediterranean Sea to Cape Horn. There you'll find abundant wildlife, rich cultural tradition, circuitous trails, and at least 1 perfect wave.

Few adventures take priority over others on the adrenaline junkie's bucket list. There are definitely some standouts, like climbing in Patagonia, skiing the Haute Route, running a marathon, and rafting the Grand Canyon. Visiting Africa should go darn near the apex of the list.

Climb Kilimanjaro, surf Jeffreys Bay, and jump on a wildlife safari. If you're looking for something more exotic, ski, surf, or bike Morocco and dive the Red Sea. If you're a whitewater junkie, run the Zambezi River.

Whatever you choose, buckle your seat belt, bring a camera with an elephant-sized memory card, and prepare for a rhino-size epic adventure.

Don't hesitate. Book your ticket now.

67. WHITEWATER RAFT THE ZAMBEZI RIVER (ZAMBIA AND ZIMBABWE)

The Zambezi, one of the great whitewater rivers in the world, boils and churns its way through the legendary Batoka Gorge, bisecting Zambia and Zimbabwe. It drops through 2-dozen rapids into the remote land of East Africa. It meanders through savannas and woodlands, drops over Victoria Falls, and then rips through the sandstones of the Batoka Gorge.

Begin your adventure at the famed Victoria Falls and Victoria Falls National Park, which hosts humongous megafauna: elephant, buffalo, giraffe, zebra, lions, leopards, vervet monkeys, and antelope. Beachside camping coupled with raging whitewater is the prime way to experience this river.

Run a range of rapids, like Star Trek, Devil's Toilet Bowl, Oblivion, and Moemba. You may have to portage a few of the big ones.

Don't Miss. Canoe Victoria Lake above massive Victoria Falls, named after England's Queen Victoria. Its native name, *Mosi-oa-Tunya*, means the "Cloud that Thunders." Look down as the falls plunge a whopping 355 feet (108 m).

Logistics. Book a trip with Bio Bio Rafting (www.bbxrafting .com). Fly into Livingstone Airport in Zambia or Victoria Falls Airport in Zimbabwe.

Best Time. River-running season is August to October when rainfall is light.

Pit Stop. You can run the river in as few as 3 days and catch a helicopter ride back up to Victoria Falls. If you're short on time, canoe the tranquil upper Zambezi, tour Victoria Falls, and camp near Victoria Falls National park in just a few days.

Extended Play. You've made it all the way to Africa so take advantage. Check out the wildlife game preserves and national parks, particularly Chobe National Park in Botswana and Hwnage National Park in Zimbabwe. Climb Kilimanjaro, the highest peak in Africa (Trip #73), and tour the East Africa Game Parks (Trip #68).

Travel Smart. Africa is big, dangerous, and wild. Make sure to visit a travel clinic and get all necessary shots prior to leaving. Bring emergency antibiotics for travelers' diarrhea, and prophylactic meds and insect repellant to ward off malaria. And watch for sun exposure. In motor vehicles, buckle up. Always wear helmets and personal-flotation devices on the rafts.

68. TREK THE GREAT GAME PARKS (KENYA AND TANZANIA)

The famous East African national parks of Kenya and Tanzania, the Serengeti, Amboseli, Masai Mara, and Ngorongoro Crater national parks, are perhaps the last great wildlife lands in the world. You'll find expansive plains and grasslands, verdant wetlands, huge craters, zebra, wildebeest, elephants, lions, leopards, buffalo, rhinos, and thousands of birds. You may even spy the elusive Grevy's zebra.

There are a variety of accommodations, from high-end luxury camps to more rudimentary budget accommodations. You don't want to be stuck in a 4 x 4 the whole trip, so pick a trekking tour where you can hike as much as possible.

Don't Miss. Ngorongoro Crater is the largest unbroken caldera in the world with some 30,000 wild animals roaming the grasslands. Keep your eyes peeled for black rhinos. Visit the Olduvai Gorge archaeological dig.

Logistics. Fly into Arusha, Tanzania, direct from Europe, where you'll meet a guide. Book through Wilderness Travel (www

.wildernesstravel.com), Mountain Travel Sobek (www.mtsobek .com), or Bio Bio Expeditions (www.bbxrafting.com).

Best Time. To avoid the wet season, go in July through February.

Pit Stop. Visit Chobe National Park in Botswana with a short visit to Victoria Falls (Trip #67).

Extended Play. Check out the national parks in Uganda and Rwanda with their famous mountain gorillas. Explore the Kalahari Desert and the Okavango River Delta in Botswana. Tsavo National Park in Kenya is famous for its man-eating lions. And climb Kilimanjaro: It's right around the corner (Trip #73). If you are a surfer, windsurfer, or kitesurfer, zip over to exotic Zanzibar.

Travel Smart. Prior to travel, get all necessary shots, bring emergency antibiotics for travelers' diarrhea, and bring prophylactic meds for malaria prevention. And always buckle up.

☑ 69. *SURF AND SKI AFRICA (MOROCCO)*

This may be one of the most dichotomous countries in Africa. You'll find some of the best skiing on the continent as well as spectacular surfing waves. Throw in a few romantic towns like Casablanca, the mountain villages of Marrakesh and Fez, and the dramatic High Atlas mountains, and you've got a majestic playground for all kinds of adventure sports.

The nomadic tribes of Ait Atta and Berber have long lived in the Central High Atlas Mountains. These mountains include Jbel M'goun (13,356 ft/ 4,071 m). You'll be skiing among nomads, snake charmers, artisans, and cooks. Make sure to try the delicious traditional cuisine of couscous, lamb, curry, and raisins.

When you're finished skiing, head to the coast. The best surf breaks lie between the city of Agadir and Cape Ghir. You can rent gear in towns near the cape and book a bungalow.

Don't Miss. Experience the fusion of Berber and Arab culture at the medina in Marrakesh. Check out the colorful, narrow-street casbah in the village of Fez where hill tribesman tan leather on rooftops. And cruise the magical, romantic coastal city of Casablanca.

Logistics. To shred the Atlas, fly into Casablanca, take local transport to Marrakesh, and head up the Ait Bouguemez Valley. Ice Axe Expeditions runs guided ski trips (www.iceaxe.tv) out of the Tarkedit Refuge where they use mules for support and provide traditional Berber meals. For surfing, head to the coastal city of Agadir. There you'll find gear rentals and lodging.

Best Time. February or March are the best times if you want to ski and surf.

Pit Stop. Ski Jebel Toubkal 13,671 ft (4,167 m.), the highest peak in the country, is 2 days from Marrakesh.

Extended Play. Morocco is a fabulous country with friendly people and zesty meals. If you're itching for more play, consider a whitewater raft trip with Water By Nature (www.waterbynature

.com). Go windsurfing in the Canary Islands or Tarifa, Spain. Still need a workout? Book a fat tire tour: mountain bike the town of Ait Ourir, Tichka Pass, and the Oruika Valley in the Atlas Mountains with Big Mountain Adventures (www.ridebig.com).

Travel Smart. Skiing and surfing in any remote land is a bit risky. Use caution. Make sure conditions are commensurate with your skill level. Remember, on a trip like this, the thrill is in the expedition, the culture, the landscape, and the adventure. Save the big hucks and all-out tricky moves for mountains and waves back home. Watch out for mosquitoes and use typical water and food precautions so you don't get stuck with gastroenteritis (as in diar-rhea!).

 ## 70. DIVE THE RED SEA (EGYPT)

Egypt is a land of ancient temples and pyramids and a political and cultural melting pot. It also has a natural marvel as rich in marine life as its history: the Red Sea.

The Red Sea is replete with coral reefs and abundant underwater life. Very few rivers feed into it, and it's also a limited outlet (the Bab-el-Mandeb is a narrow connection to the Indian Ocean). There is also a high evaporation rate in the scorching Sinai desert climate. All these factors lead to increased salinity in the Red Sea. At 41 percent, it's one the saltiest bodies of water on the planet.

You'll find many great dive sites here. One key spot is Marsa Alam, where you can dive among coral gardens, sea grass fields, whitetip and reef sharks, barracuda, blue-spotted stingrays, morays, octopus, and sea dugong (aka sea cow). Fortunately, there are beginner sites, boat dives, and great snorkeling, so this a great trip for water junkies of any level.

Don't Miss. In Cairo, don't miss the Sphinx and the Great Pyramid of Giza right outside of the city.

Logistics. Fly into Cairo. Most dives are near there. Check out Dive in Egypt (www.diveinegypt.net). They have a dive center in the Sentido Hotel in the Marsa Alam resort.

Best Time. You can dive here year-round so pick the best time for you.

Pit Stop. You can zip out to the Red Sea for a 1 or 2 days of diving.

Extended Play. Cruise the Nile and see the Aswan Dam, the Abu Simbel temples, King Tut's tomb, and the Valley of the Kings in Luxor. If you're a wind junkie, windsurf and kite the Red Sea at Hurghada (www.redsea-windsurfing.com).

Travel Smart. Get sturdy dive gear and rent from a nationally certified resort. Book a diving guide. Make sure you pay attention to dive recommendations before you fly. For help with a medical conditions or pre-trip advice, consult Divers Alert Network (www .diversalertnetwork.org). They offer travel and accident insurance with membership.

Do you recall Bruce Brown's epic 1966 film, *Endless Summer*? Mike Hynson and Robert August traipse the globe in search of the best waves. The 2 surfers found the perfect wave, at Jeffreys Bay, or J-Bay, in South Africa.

Named for Jeffrey & Glendinnings, the famous mercantile in town, this is primo wave central. The town of Jeffreys Bay is part of the surrounding St. Francis Bay area. Catch a ride at one of the local breaks: Magna Tubes, Boneyards, Supertubes, Impossibles, the Point, or Albatross. They are long, clean waves formed by underwater lava beds. Although there's been massive development since Brown's film first put J-Bay on the map, it is still a destination worthy of the list.

Don't Miss. Grab a stand-up paddleboard, and cruise the Kabeljous, Seekoei, and Krom river lagoons nearby. Keep watch for migrating whales, or take a hike in the Drakensberg Mountains.

Logistics. Fly into Cape Town, South Africa, and then head up the Indian Ocean coast past Port Elizabeth. You'll want a southeast or southwest swell to make J-Bay happen big. You'll find plenty of lodging, rental shops, and hangouts in J-Bay. Check out J-Bay Getaways for info (www.jbaygetaways.co.za).

Best Time. The waves come in year-round, but they are best in May through June.

Pit Stop. You'll find tons of breaks for board, wind, or kite surfing on the west and east of South Africa. You won't need to go far from Cape Town.

Extended Play. North of J-Bay, visit the Kabeljous and Seekoei river nature reserves. Spend a few days in Cape Town and windsurf or kitesurf the West Coast. Trail run among 120 different bird species. And don't miss a safari at one of the South African game parks if you can't make it up to Kenya or Tanzania.

Travel Smart. This is advanced surfing so be realistic. If you're a novice, you may want to hang back and watch the pros. Sharks do make an appearance here from time to time. Avoid dawn and dusk sessions and after rainfall when sharks like to nibble.

72. CYCLE THE CONTINENT: TOUR D'AFRIQUE

You probably have to be crazy to ride across the African continent. It's right up there with hiking the Pacific Crest Trail (Trip #22) or riding across America (Trip #23). Only this is Africa—dry, hot, and dusty—and there are big, dangerous animals. Really big ones. You can do it.

If you have a few months, what better way to explore the continent than on 2 human-powered wheels instead of a motorized gas-guzzling Land Rover.

The Tour of Africa peddle is a Cairo to Cape Town endurance ride that covers more than 7,281 miles (11,718 km) through 10 countries. It's the equivalent of riding across the United States *and back*. You can complete the route in about 4 months, with about 30 rest days.

Don't Miss. Make sure you check out the Great Pyramid of Giza in Cairo, and at least 1 of the game parks (Trip #68) when you stop in Arusha, Tanzania, or Fish River Canyon in Namibia.

Logistics. Explore the official site (www.tourdafrique.com) for the full race program. You'll need to fly into Cairo and home from Cape Town.

Best Time. The tour begins in January and ends in May.

Pit Stop. If you don't have time or energy or will power for the full shebang, the Tour d'Afrique has several stages you can ride in 1 to 3 weeks. Alternatively, book a trip with Big Mountain Bike Adventures and bike over Olifant's Neck to Pilgrim's Rest, down Mount Anderson, and through the Limpopo Valley (www.ridebig.com).

Extended Play. If you're really ambitious and have loads of time (and no responsibilities), try several of the classic cross-continent treks, like the Silk Road from Istanbul to Shanghai, the Orient Express from Paris to Istanbul, the Vuelta Sudamericana from Buenos Aires through Argentina to Lima, or the Trans-Indian ride from Taj Mahal in Agra to Kanyakumari in the southern tip. Or just cycle across Europe (Trip #54).

Travel Smart. Biking through the Africa is no easy feat, even on a supported trip. Make sure your mountain or cyclo-cross bike is in excellent working condition and that you know how to fix the basics. Wear a helmet, carry lots of water, and keep your eye out for cars, rickshaws, other bikes, carts, and wildlife, all of which can block your path. Keep your guard up at all times —this ain't Kansas.

73. CLIMB KILIMANJARO: THE SEVEN SUMMITS, AFRICA (TANZANIA)

If you're going to climb only one of the Seven Summits and you are not a hard-core, freezing-cold, snow-climbing junkie do this one. No question. You can experience this high-altitude mountaineering expedition without blocking off a big chunk of time. You also don't need extensive mountaineering skills and you won't subject yourself to bitter cold, unlike the wild, frigid, technical Everest, Vinson, and Denali climbs. Kilimanjaro is also one of the most rewarding from a cultural and scenic standpoint.

Uhuru Peak, aka Freedom Peak, at 19,340 feet (5,895 meters) is still a pretty grand undertaking. A giant stratovolcano with 3 distinct cinder cones, lies above the Rift Valley in Tanzania. It was first summitted in 1889 by 2 professors, German Hans Meyer and Austrian Ludwig Purtscheller. There are 6 official trekking routes, but the Machame is most common because it's scenic, steep, and can be completed in a week.

Called an Afromontane sky island because it singularly rises above the lowlands, Kilimanjaro has a distinctly diverse environment from the hillsides and savannas below. Your climb will take you through multiple biotic zones. First, hike through the Ocotea Forest, replete with sweetwood, camphorwood, rosewood, and stinkwood shrubs. Then traverse through grasslands, volcanic rock, and subalpine forests. Finally, climb along glacier-fed streams and high deserts to the barren ice and volcanic rock of the summit.

At last, you'll be atop Kilimanjaro.

Don't Miss. Really, if you've come this far, add in a safari. In 2 weeks, you can summit Uhuru Peak and tour a game reserve.

Logistics. Most trips start in Arusha, Tanzania, at Kilimanjaro International Airport. You can connect directly from Amsterdam. From there, your guide will meet you. Check out Wilderness Travel (www.wildernesstravel.com), Mountain Travel Sobek (www.mtsobek.com), or Bio Bio Expeditions (www.bbxrafting.com). Arusha is also a central point for game reserve safaris.

Best Time. October is the best month for clear weather. April to May is the rainy season. January is a good time too.

Pit Stop. It's hard to shorten the trip to Kilimanjaro. But if you just opt for the climb, you can fly down from Europe, and complete it in a week. Otherwise, tackle Mount Kenya, Africa's second highest peak. At 17,058 feet (5,199 m) Mount Kenya can be ascended in just 4 days.

Extended Play. If you have more time, combine a Kili summit with a week safari (Trip #68). The most convenient parks are Arusha,

Tarangire, and Ngorongoro Crater in Tanzania. Ngorongoro is the world's largest intact volcanic caldera with grassy plains, swamps, bubbling creeks, and abundant wildlife. There are 25,000 large animals per 100 square miles (160 km^2). You can also visit Lake Manyara, which overlooks the Great Rift Valley. And, surf, windsurf, or kitesurf the exotic Spice Island of Zanzibar!

Travel Smart. Acute mountain sickness is a danger if you don't give yourself time to acclimatize. Most guides carry a portable hyperbaric chamber and medicines to treat altitude illness. Otherwise, consider taking acetazolamide and ibuprofen to help prevent AMS. Also, hydration is extremely important when trekking at this altitude.

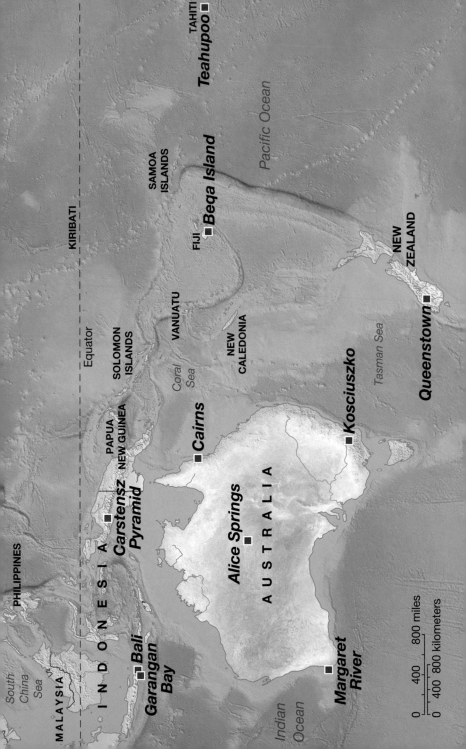

PHILIPPINES

South
China
Sea

MALAYSIA

I N D O N E S I A

Bali
Garangan
Bay

Carstensz
Pyramid

PAPUA
NEW GUINEA

Equator

KIRIBATI

SOLOMON
ISLANDS

Cairns

Coral
Sea

VANUATU

NEW
CALEDONIA

SAMOA
ISLANDS

FIJI
Beqa Island

TAHITI
Teahupoo

Pacific Ocean

A U S T R A L I A

Alice Springs

Kosciuszko

Tasman Sea

NEW
ZEALAND

Queenstown

Margaret
River

Indian
Ocean

0   400   800 miles

0   400   800 kilometers

AUSTRALASIA AND OCEANIA

BLUE WATER, warm, sandy beaches, rich coral, and gentle sea breeze. Paradise. Geographer Conrad Malte-Brun named the continent, Oceania, in 1812 after the Greek god of fresh water, Okeanos.

Where exactly is Oceania? It's a collection of islands that makes up the South Pacific, one of the most romantic places on Earth. It's also got some of the gnarliest waves, the best dives, smoothest sailing, and sickest saltwater kayak tours out there. Not to mention a few jungles. Oceania is comprised of Australia and New Zealand, the South Pacific islands of Melanesia (aka Australasia), Micronesia, Polynesia, and Malaysia (aka Malay Archipelago). You can spend a lifetime exploring these islands … or at least a year.

I have a friend who traveled the entire South Pacific on a sailboat with her husband and 2 kids in the course of 3 years. If you can't afford to take 1 year or 3, think about heading to adventure central New Zealand. It's often referred to as the birthplace of adventure sports. Go on a multisport binge on the South Island. If surfing, diving, or sailing is more your flavor, you can have it all in Fiji, one of the best water sport sites in the world. A pure surfer? Go to Indonesia. No question.

Get after it!

74. TRAVERSE THE MILFORD TRACK: THE FINEST WALK IN THE WORLD (NEW ZEALAND)

Heralded as the "Finest Walk in the World," the Milford Track winds through New Zealand's Fiordland National Park. The biodiverse fjords of the Milford Sound are punctuated by huge glacier-carved valleys, 5,000-foot (1,500 m) mountains, roaring waterfalls, and 1 rugged Alpine pass.

The Maori people hiked this route long ago to collect *pounamu*, a nephrite jade called "greenstone" used for tools, ornaments, and weapons. In 1888, explorer Donald Sutherland cut the track to what is now called Sutherland Falls, the highest waterfall in New Zealand at 1,903-feet high (530 m). Legend has it that Sutherland and his wife are buried under the falls and washed into the deep Milford Sound after a giant rainstorm. They forever protect the famed route.

Now 14,000 people every year make the 33-mile (54 km) trek from Glade Wharf on Lake Te Anau to the spectacular cliffs and blue waters of Milford Sound.

Don't Miss. Book a boat tour of the Te Anau Glowworm Caves. Using clues from Maori legends, explorer Lawson Burrows found these water-filled caverns in 1948. Travel by boat to spy thousands of shimmering bioluminescent flies.

Logistics. Fly into Queenstown, make the 2-hour drive to Te Anau, and then catch a boat to the trailhead at Glade Wharf. During the summer-trekking season there are many guide and transportation options. Most people hike the Milford Track in 4 days/3 nights, but fastpackers and trail runners may only need 2 days. During the summer-trekking season, October to April, only 40 independent and 50-guided northbound starts are allowed per day. At the trail head, crash at Glade House or Te Anau Lakefront Backpackers hostel (www.teanaubackpackers.co.nz). On the trail, independent trekkers can book one of 40 bunks at rustic Clinton, Mintaro, or Dumpling huts operated by the Department of Conservation. They are stocked with sleeping pads, restrooms, and cook stoves (www.doc.govt.nz).

Best Time. Make the trek in the summer down under—November to January.

Pit Stop. If you don't have time or energy for the 4-day trek, consider a boat ride across the lake, a night in the Glade House, and a day hike on part of the trail. If you can't get south from Queenstown, climb Ben Lomond Peak (5,735 ft/1,748 m).

Extended Play. If you're a hiker, consider doing several—or all 9—of New Zealand's Great Walks, also called Tramping Tracks. They're sprinkled across the North and South Island mountains and fjords. Try the Routeburn Track to Key Summit in Fiordland National Park or the Rob Roy Glacier Track into Mount Aspiring National Park.

Travel Smart. You'll need wet-weather gear, it rains 200 days per year in Fiordland National Park. Bring cold-weather clothes, too. You'll be tramping through rainforests as well as over mountain passes. The track is well maintained during the summer, but in off-season be careful on stream crossings as bridges may be out, cooking fuel and wood may be removed from huts, and avalanches are prevalent. Guard against hypothermia, frostbite, and trench foot—a result of walking on cold, wet feet for several days. Essentials include sunscreen, insect repellent, earplugs for the bunkrooms, and a water purifier or purification tablets.

Queenstown is arguably the birthplace of adventure sports. It's one of the best spots in the world for a multisport binge. You'll be surrounded by stunning landscape, made famous by The Lord of the Rings films. There are spectacular mountains, deep fjords, bubbling creeks, grassy plains, and emerald lakes.

Interested in world-class whitewater, canyoneering, and glacier skiing? How about hiking or trail runs? Surfing or kayaking your thing? And what about skiing and scaling mountains? The only problem is figuring out how to fit everything in!

Here's a South Island sampler to start:

- The tracks are among the most famous in the world for trekking and trail running. Try the Milford (Trip #74), Routeburn, and Hollyford tracks.
- Ski or snowboard The Remarkables, Coronet Peak, and Treble Cone, the world-famous winter resorts near Queenstown (www.nzski.com). Head here for summer hiking and mountain biking, too.
- Climb, ski mountaineer, or ice climb the Tasman Glacier on Mount Cook with Alpine Guides (www.alpineguides.co.nz).

They also guide at Mount Aspiring Fiordlands National Park and at The Remarkables, the latter is closer to Queenstown. Hang out in quaint Mount Cook Village for a few days.

- Tandem hang glide, skydive, paraglide, or, *gulp,* BASE jump with Pure Adventure (www.pureadventure.co.nz) or Nzone Skydive (www.nzone.biz).
- Whitewater raft or kayak the Shotover and Kawarau rivers with Challenge Rafting (www.raft.co.nz).
- Go river boarding (aka river surfing) on the standing waves, whirlpools, and rapids of the Kawarau with Serious Fun River Surfing (www.riversurfing.co.nz).
- Surf at Taranaki or the Mahia Peninsula on the North Island.
- Windsurf, kitesurf, or stand-up paddleboard the east coast near Christchurch with Canterbury Windsports Association (www.cwa.org.nz) or Kite Sports (www.kitesports.co.nz).

Are you tired yet?

Don't Miss. For a quick thrill, go bungee jumping at the 140 feet (43 m) Kawarau Bridge. Bungee jumping started in 1988 when inventors AJ Hackett and Henry van Asch built a rubber cord after observing Papua New Guinea natives leaping from vines. Check AJ Hackett Bungy (www.bungy.co.nz).

Logistics. Fly into Queenstown, rent a car, book a flat, and find rental gear. Start with Queenstown Adventure (www.queenstownadventure.com). In Queenstown, crash in budget-friendly Hippo Lodge (www.hippolodge.co.nz) or The Black Sheep (www.blacksheepbackpackers.co.nz) hostels; either place can also book day excursions.

Best Time. Spring is a good time to get on the snow and water, but you may want to book a winter or summer trip and focus on seasonal sports.

Pit Stop. Try ski mountaineering on the Tasman Glacier on Mount Cook. If you have more time, kitesurf Canterbury and fastpack the Milford Track (Trip #74).

Extended Play. It's a long way to travel, so do it all. Take a month, or just get a job in New Zealand (Trip #100).

Travel Smart. Unless you're very skilled, it's smart to use a guide for most of these adventures. Be careful and don't try to keep up with the locals.

76. TOUR THE GREAT BARRIER REEF: THE LARGEST LIVING STRUCTURE IN THE WORLD (AUSTRALIA)

Dive, snorkel, and sail in the largest coral reef in the world. The Great Barrier Reef spreads over 133,000 square miles (344,400 km). The massive living structure is comprised of 2,900 individual components, with some 600 islands, and 300 coral-encrusted cays.

There are many ways to explore this place. Rent a sailboat, kayak, dive, or snorkel.

For diving, snorkeling, and kayaking, check out the remote Coral Sea atoll Osprey Reef, where sharks feed. Ribbon Reef has many buttresses, walls, and pinnacles home to bigeye trevally, anthias, yellow goatfish, lionfish, and stonefish. The more remote Detached Reef houses sharks, tuna, barracuda, sweetlips, pufferfish, and other such underwater beauties. Explore the underwater wreck the SS *Yongala,* a ship that sank in a 1911 storm, which is buried in the ocean grave just off Townsville, Queensland.

For sailing, tour the Whitsundays, a collection of 74 islands including Whitehaven Beach and Heart Reef.

Don't Miss. Climb Uluru, aka Ayers Rock, near Alice Springs. If you've come this far, you'll want a taste of the famed Australian Outback, Uluru-Kata Tjuta National Park, and the culture of the Aboriginal Anangu.

Logistics. Fly into Cairns, Queensland, and you'll find an abundance of resorts. Make sure to book one that's internationally certified. They'll have professional instructors and gear.

Best Time. This is a trip you can do almost year-round. Pick June through November for minke and humpback whale sightings and coral spawning. December through February yields warm, clear waters.

Pit Stop. In less than a week you can see tons from a live-aboard boat. Or just plop down in Cairns and see as much as you can from day excursions.

Extended Play. Surf, kitesurf, and windsurf Down Under (Trip #77). Rent a pop-top camper and see the whole country the way the Aussies do.

Travel Smart. Touring the reef requires basic water sports precautions. Wear a personal-flotation device. Go with a guide or make sure you get accurate information on weather, water currents, and tides.

77. SURF, WINDSURF, AND KITESURF MARGARET RIVER (AUSTRALIA)

Open beaches, brisk wind, steady waves, and pure Down Under surf culture.

To avoid the skyscrapers and crowds of the Gold Coast and the Great Ocean Road in the southeast, head west, grommet. The Western Australia sports scene pivots around the city of Perth. It's more properly a board sport scene: surfing, windsurfing, kitesurfing, and stand-up paddleboarding abound.

There's a great surf vibe here and lots of room to spread out. The best way to see this region is from a camper van. You can carry all of your gear with you and camp along the coast.

Don't Miss. Find a way to make it to the famed Outback. If you can, visit Uluru, or Ayers Rock, and Uluru-Kata Tjuta National Park.

Logistics. Fly into Perth and rent a car or camper van. For extended stays, consider buying a van. You can sell it when you leave.

The famed Margaret River is 168 miles (270 km) south of Perth where you'll find lots of breaks and beaches north and south. Lancelin and Geraldton have great windsurfing. Definitely check out Coronation Beach in Geraldton. Swan River, Pinnaroo Point, and Cervantes are excellent launches for kitesurfing. For gear, lessons, and other info look into Surf Schools of Australia (www.sasurfschools.com.au).

Best Time. December through February are hot and dry with great surf and wind.

Pit Stop. If you can't make the trek to Western Australia, then grab a rental board and surf near Sydney or the famed Surfer's Paradise on the Gold Coast near Brisbane.

Extended Play. Rent a pop-top camper van and spend a few months in Western Australia. If you spend time in the Outback, consider a 4 x 4 with a rooftop tent and a few cases of lager. Visit the Great Barrier Reef (Trip #76) or Narawntapu National Park on Tasmania, abundant with wildlife. I have a friend who bought a van, toured the West Coast for a few months, then sold the van for what he bought it for!

Travel Smart. Be careful in the wind and waves of Margaret River. You can get information about weather and ocean conditions from local shops. Watch for sharks!

Indonesia is one of the most mystic, remote surf zones in the world. And you'll find some of the best waves.

G-Land is a lava reef encrusted with coral that pokes up from a 10,000-foot (3,000 m) trench just 3 miles (5 km) offshore in Grajagan Bay. It rests on the Blambangan Peninsula in Java, Indonesia. The swells that move in from the south put out some of the best waves in the world.

G-Land Surf Camp was founded by Mike Boyum and made popular by surf legend Gerry Lopez. There you can ride any number of reef breaks. Speedies is the crown jewel, the big honking barrel. You can ride Money Trees on almost every tide, as well as waves like Kongs, 20/20's, and Tiger Tracks.

It's about a ½-day bus or boat ride from Bali to Grajagan Bay and Plengkung Point in East Java.

Don't Miss. Spend 1 night or 2 in Bali, the hub of Indonesia.

Logistics. G-Land is accessible by boat and bus. A surf camp can help arrange logistics. Pick from several camps like G-Land

Bobby's Surf Camp (grajagan.com) or G-Land Surf Camp (www
.g-landsurfcamp.com).

Best Time. The surf season here is March through October.

Pit Stop. Come out for a couple days to surf if you're cruising
around Indo. Otherwise, if short on time, fly to Denpasar, Bali, rent
gear from one of many surf shops, and surf one of the numerous
breaks near the city in Jimbaran Bay and around the Bukit Peninsula.

Extended Play. There are many uncrowded breaks in Indo.
Beyond Bali and G-Land, you can surf West Java, the Mentawai
Islands, and West Sumbawa in Indonesia. Or check out breaks on
the east coast of the Philippines.

Travel Smart. Watch out for monkeys and rodents who live off
of garbage and carry disease. Talk with your doctor about getting a
rabies immunization series before you go. Bring a spring wetsuit;
July and August can bring cool currents. Consider booties for long
walks across the reefs. Cuts can easily lead to infection. Bring a surf
helmet for wipeouts on the reef. Remember sunscreen, bug juice,
and a pre-trip visit to a travel clinic for malaria pills. Check to see if
the room you booked has a mosquito net over the bed.

79. SURF THE WORLD'S HEAVIEST WAVE: TEAHUPOO (TAHITI)

When swells rip across the South Pacific, surfers gravitate to a few places known for huge waves, the burliest of which breaks on the shores of the town of Teahupoo (spoken "cho-po") in Tahiti. In fact, it's so deadly you might want to stop reading.

Teahupoo is a close out wave like Pipeline on the North Shore of Oahu. But if you catch it right, it is a flawless, smooth, bad barrel rivaling no other spot on the world.

Ripping into the Tahiti Iti, Teahupoo means "the hot head." Legend has it that King Teahupoo's son avenged his father's demise by feasting on the brain of the murderer's son. The real Teahupoo is a coral atoll formed around an extinct volcano. Its break is at the "End of the Road," a 15-minute paddle into the ocean. Thierry Vernaudon, was likely the first to ride this monster in 1985. Surfriders Mike Stewart and Ben Severson rode it in 1986 on bodyboards. It broke into mainstream media with Laird Hamilton's ride in the film *Riding Giants*. Now surfers flock to tackle this monster.

Don't Miss. If you have the chance to tow-in surf, you may have a better chance of riding this wave. Or just watch the pros from shore.

Logistics. Fly into Tahiti and take local transport to the lovely town of Teahupoo on the southwest of the island.

Best Time. The best swells come in July and August.

Pit Stop. Looking for something a bit tamer? Check out Cloudbreak in Tavarua, Fiji, (Trip #80), or rent a paddleboard and cruise flat water or catch the gentle waves along the Tahitian beaches.

Extended Play. For calmer waves, surf Indo (Trip #78) or Cloudbreak (Trip #80).

Travel Smart. The wave breaks on a dangerous, deadly, shallow coral reef and can result in death. It's for experienced surfers in peak physical condition. Be careful.

✅ 80. *SURF, DIVE, AND SAIL THE SOUTH PACIFIC (FIJI)*

The South Pacific can take years to explore, but your first stop needs to be Fiji, the "Soft Coral Capital of the World."

If you're looking to dive or snorkel, head to the Beqa Lagoon. It's an extinct volcanic crater with a 40-mile (64 km) reef clustered with coral and sea fans. Its clear, temperate water and mild currents make this the premier dive spot in the world and a perfect snorkel spot, too. If you're a surfer, check out the Fiji Pipeline at the Frigate Passage or the Tavarua Island where you'll find the famed surf spot, Cloudbreak. Tavarua also has fabulous diving, snorkeling, kayaking, and fishing.

Have more time? Rent a boat and go island hopping.

Don't Miss. Snorkel Beqa Island's 40-mile reef, the largest collection of soft coral and sea fans around the globe.

Logistics. Fly into Nadi, Fiji, and stay at Beqa Lagoon Resort (www.beqalagoonresort.com). It's chock-full of amenities, including internationally certified dive instructors and gear, plus kayak, surf, and snorkel equipment. If you want to surf Cloudbreak, check Tavarua Island Resort (www.tavarua.com).

Best Time. Get out of town when the rains hit at home: this is a year-round destination. Or be a Web monkey and watch for a good swell.

Pit Stop. Many flights to New Zealand and Australia stop in Fiji for refueling. Check if you can spend a few days here when you are taking a trip down under; some airlines won't charge you for the stopover.

Extended Play. Island hop the South Pacific on a sailboat. You can rent a boat through The Moorings (www.moorings.com) with the option of hiring a skipper. Sail to Bora Bora and French Polynesia, a collection of over 100 islands including Austral, Gambier, Marquesas, Tuamotu, and the Society Islands. They are spackled with beautiful beaches, spectacular snorkeling spots, volcanic remnants, lush foliage, and reefs replete with sea turtles, sharks, dolphins, and endless varieties of fish. Toss kiteboard gear or kayak on the boat for maximum fun.

Travel Smart. Water sports come with the usual precautions. Although the water is warm, currents mild, and wind light, you still need to remain aware. Go with an internationally certified outfitter. If you have dive issues, contact Divers Alert Network (www.diver salertnetwork.org).

81. CLIMB CARSTENSZ PYRAMID: THE SEVEN SUMMITS, OCEANIA (MALAYSIA)

Tell people you're climbing Carstensz Pyramid, or more properly Puncak Jaya (Victory Peak), and you'll get raised eyebrows and quixotic stares. *What? Where?* Little do they know that this is one of the most breathtaking peaks on the list. Travel to the beaches of Bali, trek through the Papua jungles, scramble up rocky crags, traipse through tropical rainforests, ford bridges, and top out on equatorial glaciers in a world rarely seen by mountaineers.

Logistically, Carstensz can be a challenge. It's both technical and remote. Lodged in the Sudirman Range in the jungles of Western Papua, this mountain takes some work just to reach base camp. Once there, you'll need to conjure all your mountain toughness for the climb.

Carstensz Pyramid rises 16,023 feet (4,884 m) up from the jungle in the Indonesian province of Western Papua (aka Irian Jaya), New Guinea. Of the Seven Summits, this is the shortest and the only peak without snow (well, mostly). But because of the region's political instability and dense jungle, this may be the biggest prize. The peak was first scaled in 1962 by Philip Temple, Heinrich Harrer, Russell Kippax, and Albert Huizenga.

There's a bit of controversy surrounding Carstensz. Some say that New Guinea is actually part of Asia, making the highest mountain in Oceania Australia's Mount Kosciuszko at 7,310 feet (2,228 m)

(Trip #82). Others argue, the National Geographic Society for instance, that Carstensz falls in the Oceania region, part of no continent. Regardless, you'll enjoy traipsing through its lush jungles and surmounting this rugged peak.

Don't Miss. Go surfing in Bali. You'll be close to the ripping waves of G-Land (Trip #78).

Logistics. Fly into Denpasar, Bali. Take a commuter flight to Timika, and then hop another to Ilaga You'll then trek through thick rainforest canopy to Carstensz Base Camp. Dani tribesman often work as porters and will help you on the trek. Alternatively, jump on a helicopter and save your legs. Continue through equatorial tundra, glaciers, limestone crags, and alpine lakes to the summit. There is 5.8 class rock climbing, fixed lines, and Tyrolean traverses. This is not your mother's mountain. Find a guide with Alpine Ascents International (www.alpineascents.com) or International Mountain Guides (www.mountainguides.com).

Best Time. Weather is temperate year-round, but most guided climbs take place in May and June.

Pit Stop. Why not go for for the easier of the 2 peaks ? Try climbing Kosciuszko (Trip #82).

Extended Play. If you're going to travel all that way, certainly don't miss out on surfing in Indonesia (Trip#78). Even better—try knocking off all Seven Summits.

Travel Smart. The biggest concerns are political and bureaucratic. Make sure you go with a reputable guide who will cover permits and work with locals. You'll need to be flexible about your plans. Travel inconspicuously and set an emergency evacuation plan. It's not a bad idea to secure illness, injury, and trip insurance. Remember that you'll be traveling in the jungle. Use precautions against fungal and parasitic infections, and malaria. There will also likely be high altitude to contend with. Give yourself time to acclimatize.

82. CLIMB KOSCIUSZKO: THE SEVEN SUMMITS, AUSTRALASIA (AUSTRALIA)

As noted in Trip #81 there's some controversy surrounding the Seven Summits. Mount Kosciuszko is the wild card. Some consider it one of the Seven (or Eight) Summits, and others don't. Regardless, it's the highest peak in Australasia at 7,310 feet (2,228 m), and certainly worthy of a visit. This climb, or trek, may be better for budding Seven Summits mountaineers as it's not nearly as physically demanding.

"Kozzie" rests in the snowy mountains of New South Wales, Australia.

Don't Miss. If you're going to Aussie land, don't miss the Great Barrier Reef (Trip #76).

Logistics. Fly to Sydney or Melbourne. Drive to Kosciuszko National Park or fly to Canberra. Start at 1 of 2 trailheads: Charlotte's Pass, near Perisher Valley ski area, or Thredbo ski resort. If you want to shorten the climb, hop on one of the chairlifts for a little help up the mountain.

Best Time. Climb in the clear summer days of November to February.

Pit Stop. If you don't have time for the climb, ski Perisher Valley or kayak Lake Jindabyne.

Extended Play. Surf the coastal beaches, tour the Outback, dive the Great Barrier Reef, and tour the South Island of New Zealand. Climbing "Kozzie" only takes 1 day, so you'll have plenty of time to enjoy the region.

Travel Smart. You may run into snow and ice. Hypothermia, frostbite, and acute mountain sickness are real dangers. Take proper precautions.

CHILE **ARGENTINA**

South Atlantic Ocean

South Pacific Ocean

Antarctic Peninsula

Weddell Sea

■ **Mount Vinson**

ANTARCTICA

Ross Sea

Antarctic Circle

Indian Ocean

NEW ZEALAND

| 0 | 400 | 800 miles |
| 0 | 400 | 800 kilometers |

AUSTRALIA

BITTER COLD. Raging wind. Harsh wasteland. Maybe "wasteland" is a rough assessment, but this region comes close to that description on many days.

The Antarctic is probably the coldest and windiest continent. But few know that it also has the driest desert region with only 8 inches (20 cm) of precipitation annually. So it is indeed often sunny. Then again, it does span 5.5 million square miles (14 million sq km) of ice. Oh, and it's cold. Really cold. In 1983, temperatures reached a whopping low of -128 degrees Fahrenheit (-89 degrees C) according to the Russian Vostok Station.

With no permanent residents, no formal government, and no indigenous people, the only human civilization you'll find is the smattering of research stations littered among the ice-encrusted islands. The flora and fauna have adapted to the harsh, bitter cold; mites, penguins, seals, and tardigrades survive in the tundra.

But don't be fooled. Antarctica is just for ascetics. There's no better place to explore the extremes of wild nature: the cold, windy, desert; the tundra biome; epic ski lines; and one cold, white summit.

It used to be difficult to get to the Antarctic unless you were on official business. In recent years, several guide companies have launched wildlife exploration via boat or plane from South America. Now you can head to the South Pole to ski and climb on one of a number of expeditions. And you don't need a whole month. You can make this trip in just 2 or 3 weeks.

Whether you're a backcountry skier, a climber, or just a wildlife enthusiast, the Antarctic has something for you. Scope it. Book it. Go, do now.

83. BACKCOUNTRY SKI THE BOTTOM OF THE WORLD

In 2009, Chris Davenport, the guy who skied all 54 of Colorado's Fourteeners in 1 year, exposed the world to the wonders of Antarctica. His film, *Australis: An Antarctic Ski Odyssey,* whet the appetites of many an adrenaline junkie. Now you can book a backcountry ski tour of the most austere, remote, and beautiful land on earth.

The trip doesn't have to be extreme. If you're an intermediate backcountry skier or snowboarder (*Read:* expert at the resorts), you can rip many of these cool, chalky-white lines. What's more it's a spectacular place with abundant wildlife and spectacular weather. You'll cruise alongside sperm, fin, and humpback whales; orcas; leopard seals; and Gentoo and Adélie penguins.

Although most boat trips stick to the Antarctic Peninsula, you can also make an excursion to the scientific outposts at Almirante Brown Station, Ukrainian Vernadsky scientific station, and Port Lockroy.

Don't Miss. In Ushuaia, the tiny capital of Tierra del Fuego, check out Tierra del Fuego National Park. You can access it by the End of the World Train. There are a couple of ski areas in the region to test your legs—Cerro Castor and Glaciar Martial.

Logistics. Fly into Ushuaia, Argentina, at the tip of South America. From there, board a boat and head across the Drake Passage—one of the most tempestuous straits in the world's seas. You'll pass through to the fjords and glaciers of the Antarctic Peninsula. Then cruise via Zodiac to the snowfields on Mount Scott, Crystal Sound, and Paradise Bay. Book a small group tour with Ice Axe Expeditions (www.iceax.tv) or Chris Davenport (www.chris davenport.com). Ice Axe also runs bigger trips on the *Clipper Adventurer*; the vessel holds up to 122 people. Andes Cross, based in Bariloche, Argentina, runs trips in the region, too (www.ande scross.com). Adventure Consultants has a rugged trip that includes 3 days of skiing and touring on Wiencke Island using a recondi-tioned Royal Dutch Navy research vessel.

Best Time. November is your best bet for good weather and snow conditions.

Pit Stop. You can do this in as little as 10 days, but if you're go-ing to spend the money, take 3 weeks.

Extended Play. There is fabulous skiing in southern Argentina around Bariloche if you want to combine your trip with a Patagonia tour (Trip #42).

Travel Smart. Antarctica is essentially a frozen desert, with little snowfall; it receives less than 4 inches (10cm) annually. The famous katabatic polar winds create chilling temperatures. Pack warm clothes. Extremely warm clothes. As in Everest warm.

84. *CLIMB MOUNT VINSON: THE SEVEN SUMMITS, ANTARCTICA*

Although Denali is known for its foul weather and Carstensz Pyramid its remote location, Vinson Massif is perhaps the most logistically difficult and most austere.

Vinson Massif reaches 16,067 feet (4,897 m). It rests on Sentinel Ridge in the Ellsworth Mountains, a mere 660 nautical miles (1,200 km) from the South Pole. You'll be literally climbing to the top of the bottom of the world. The peak was named for Carl Vinson, a congressman from Georgia who was instrumental in exploring this vast continent. Until spotted from a U.S. Navy plane in 1957, no one knew that Vinson Massif existed. In 1966, Barry Corbet, John Evans, William Long, and Pete Schoening first scaled the mountain.

Don't Miss. Make sure to scope out the exotic wildlife.

Logistics. You can only access the mount via a guided commercial trip. And it's necessary. You would not want to try this on your own. Fly across the Drake Passage from Punta Arenas, Chile. Once you touch down in Antarctica on the blue-ice landing strip on Union Glacier, you'll take a second flight to Vinson Base Camp at 7,500 feet (2,286 m) in the Ellsworth Mountains. From there, you'll trek up the massive, endless ice fields to the top of the mountain at the bottom of the world.

Best Time. Go in November through January, which is "summer" in Antarctica. Hopefully the temperature will reach above 0 degrees Fahrenheit.

Pit Stop. There's no short way up Vinson Massif. If you don't have 3 weeks, book a 10-day wildlife viewing hike or backcountry ski tour through a number of outfitters, like Mountain Travel Sobek (www.mtsobek.com), Wilderness Travel (www.wildernesstravel .com), or Quark Expeditions (www.quarkexpeditions.com).

Extended Play. Take a boat and take your time. Several outfitters access Antarctica by taking a boat from Ushuaia. You can camp and kayak at the wildlife colonies of King George and South Georgia Islands. Check Mountain Travel Sobek (www.mtsobek.com), Wilderness Travel (www.wildernesstravel.com), or Quark Expeditions (www.quarkexpeditions.com) for ideas on combining island tour with a Vinson Massif summit. Quark does have a fly-in option with a local weeklong cruise. They also offer multisport trips.

Travel Smart. Ernest Shackleton's ill-fated voyage was advertised as "Men wanted for hazardous journey. Small wages, bitter cold, long months of complete darkness, constant danger, safe return doubtful." The 1914 shipwreck stranded his crew on the ice for over 2 years as recounted in Alfred Lansing's *Endurance: Shackleton's Incredible Voyage*. Thankfully, you'll be going with an outfitter, but it's important to remain cognizant of the altitude and cold. Dress appropriately. Keep hydrated and nourished. And watch out for frostbite and hypothermia.

SOMETIMES JUMPING into a new sport is easy. Join some buddies who are already well-versed or learn on your own. You may want some help, however, with more complex sports such as ski mountaineering or kitesurfing. So, before paddling into head-high waves or Class 3 rapids, get some training. Sometimes getting worked in the water, winds, rapids, or mountains as a novice is pure joy. (Okay, sometimes it's miserable, but it makes for a great story.) But let's admit it. Most adrenaline junkies are methodical and competitive. We want to conquer, not be conquered. So get some training and prepare appropriately.

Peruse the candy store at your local gear shop. Grab a guide and how-to books. Grill your buddies who are ripping up the mountains, rivers, trails, and oceans of the world. Maybe take a course or even, *gulp*, lessons. Sometimes going guided is a great introduction to a strange land and a new sport.

That said, a few things in the adrenaline junkie arsenal require formal, certified instruction, and *mucho* practice. You'll want to make sure your partners have their skills down, too; you will be trusting them with your life.

So herein lies the course list, the Toolbox, for the education of an outdoor thrill seeker. These are the basics. And if you really groove on a sport, you may want to further your knowledge with more advanced classes. You may not decide to do them all. But if you do, you'll be a well-rounded athlete who can dominate the world in almost any situation.

85. TAKE A LEVEL 1 AVALANCHE COURSE

You're in the mountains. Sometimes just for a week. Sometimes all winter. Where I live in the Pacific Northwest's Cascades, we ski and snowboard year-round. We ride powder and tracked up powder, or *chunder,* all winter, corn snow in the spring, glacier hardpack in the summer, and whatever we can get in the fall.

Avalanche Awareness presentations are usually 1 or 2 hours, and provide just enough information to scare you out of your wits. For solid backcountry foundation, take a 3-day Level 1 avalanche course called "Decision Making in Avalanche Terrain." It will be the most fun you've ever had digging around in the snow. The course is geared toward recreational backcountry skiing and snowboarding.

You can find courses all over the United States through the American Institute for Avalanche Research and Education (avtraining.org). Pick up information from the American Avalanche Association is (www.americanavaalncheassociation.org), or the Canadian Avalanche Association (www.avalanche.ca) for the Great White North.

Don't Miss. Take an avalanche course coupled with a backcountry hut tour like Three Sisters Backcountry (threesistersbackcountry.com) in Oregon, or Eastern Mountain Sports Schools who operate in the famed White Mountain of New Hampshire (www.emsexploration.com).

Logistics. Grab gear, block out a weekend, and sign up. You'll need an avalanche beacon (aka transceiver, beacons transmit rescue signals if you're buried), shovel, probe, and, if you can afford it, an avalanche-specific safety backpack.

Best Time. For training, you'll find the best (and usually the safest) snow and weather conditions in the spring.

Pit Stop. You only need a weekend. If you can find a local class, you'll get to know the guides and other backcountry enthusiasts.

Extended Play. Further your knowledge with a Level 2 class— "Analyzing Snow Stability and Avalanche Hazard." You can take a Level 3, too, which is geared for professional ski patrollers, guides, and avalanche forecasters.

If you want the cadre of adrenaline junkie courses for other sports, these are the ones I think are the most important:

- Kayakers and rafters should consider Swiftwater Rescue from one of many companies like Rescue 3 International (www.rescue3international.com).
- Climbers, cavers, and canyoneers should take Rope Rescue to prepare for crevasse, cave, canyon, or any other type of confined-space rescue. Check out the ones offered by Rainier Mountaineering (www.rmiguides.com) or Eastern Mountain Sports Schools (www.emsexploration.com).

Travel Smart. Just because you take the course doesn't mean you're invincible. Remember, you can almost always find safe snow, safe terrain (low angle), and safe weather. If not, stay off the mountain and ride your bike.

86. COMPLETE OPEN WATER DIVE CERTIFICATION

Diving opens the world of Neptune and Poseidon, the under-seascape that Jacques Cousteau made famous on film. You may not use diving skills all the time, but they're important for safety, and necessary to rent gear.

Diving certification usually takes a few weeks or a long weekend. Even if you don't live near the ocean, you can take a course in open water, like a lake. There are 2 main national organizations that certify instructors and dive schools—PADI is the Professional Association of Diving Instructors (www.padi.com) and NAUI is the National Association of Underwater Instructors (www.naui.org).

Don't Miss. Couple a dive course with a vacation so you can immediately tour the underwater realm.

Logistics. Head to the PADI or NAUI Web sites, find a local dive shop, and book it. Or plan a vacation around your diving certification and go a few days early to complete the open-water dives.

Best Time. Try to do this well before your trip so you're familiar with the gear and have an opportunity to practice.

Pit Stop. Don't have much time? Cover the basics online and then book the swimming pool and open-water portions through a local dive shop. Alternatively, take a resort course instead of an open-water course; the former allows you to go down 40 feet (12 m) with minimal instruction, a few hours, and a guide.

Extended Play. Already certified? Add to your credential by mixed-air (nitrogen and oxygen), diving below 100 feet (30 m). You can also try diving at night, or using a rebreather (a special device which recirculates air to minimize expired bubbles).

Travel Smart. If you have a dive emergency or a question about anything related to dive medicine, check out Divers Alert Network (www.diversalertnetwork.org). It's a nonprofit safety association with a team of doctors and dive professionals based at Duke University. They give medical advice on any type of dive-medicine issue. Diving has a whole slew of medical risks that result from the pressure differences between the deep ocean and sea levels. There are also risks involved with flying right after diving so consult your local dive doc or dive textbook.

87. BUILD A BIKE

If you try cyclo-cross racing (Trip #7), learning to build or repair a bike is mandatory. You'll spend hours repairing your components after a race in the mud. Likewise, whether you're a freeride, downhill, or cross-country mountain bike rider, routine maintenance is cheaper and easier than lugging your bike to a local shop. Plus it's an essential skill to have when you hit a tree branch and it tears your derailer off a 3-hour hike from your car. (Yup, been there.)

The best place to start is learning how to put on a new chain. Changing the chain regularly allows your bike gears to last longer and operate smoother. As the chain wears, it can eat at the cogs on your rear cassette and front chain rings. The rough rule is to change the chain every year.

A few other key maintenance items are also essential and easy to learn:

- Change the brake pads for your disc or caliper brakes.
- Do a basic derailleur adjustment. As the cables stretch or get dirty, minor adjustments keep the bike shifting smoothly.
- Learn to swap out cables and housing. If you ride in the mud, you'll likely have to do this once or twice a season. If you're a cyclo-cross racer, you may have to do this every weekend!
- Change the bearings in your headset if they aren't rotating smoothly.
- Check the air pressure in your mountain bike shock.

Don't Miss. Take a class to learn the skills. And befriend your local wrench (aka bike mechanic) to get guidance and a helpful hand when you screw up your adjustments. (Done that, too.)

Logistics. You'll need some tools that are particular to bike repair. Owning a complete kit and a bike stand can make life way easier. If you don't want to buy the whole shebang, purchase the basics: a chain-link tool, cutters for cables and cable housing, a set of Allen wrenches, screwdrivers, and pliers.

Best Time. I work over my bikes every spring, replacing brake pads and chains, checking the bearings, adjusting the derailers, and replacing cables and housing if needed. For cyclo-cross, it's a good idea to tear down your bike after the season, clean the components thoroughly, and then rebuild it—the dirt gets everywhere. It's a good rainy day (or week) project .

Extended Play. Build a bike from scratch. You can order a frame and gruppo online or from your local shop. If you go through a shop, they may be willing to help you.

Here are a few other basic gear-maintenance functions you may want to learn:

- Basic tuning and waxing for your skis and snowboard
- Ding repair for your surf, windsurf, kite, and SUP boards
- Basic field repair for your raft and kayak

Travel Smart. Building a bike requires skill. If you're a newbie, have a pro wrench (aka bike mechanic) help you. It may cost a bit, but it can be a worthwhile accomplishment.

88. *LEARN A LANGUAGE*

As adventure seekers we are constantly in motion, traveling from country to country. Learning a foreign language is not necessarily vital, but having knowledge of the language, customs, and history of wherever you visit can definitely help you across borders, order a *cerveza* and *pollo*, blend in, and have a richer experience. Many locals appreciate when travelers try to communicate (however poorly), and may be more willing to help if you do.

It does take some effort, and, of course, the nature of an adrenaline junkie is not to sit still in a classroom, but rather wander around the *mercado* or *zocolo*. You may find a computer-based course, such as Rosetta Stone (www.rosettastone.com), more flexible. Many community colleges also offer courses, or you may incorporate language learning into your travel experience and take an immersion course.

Spanish is probably one of the more useful languages, especially when exploring Central and South America.

Don't Miss. Take a Spanish immersion course in Panama, Mexico, or Belize. Don't forget you're going surfing, sailing, and diving there, too!

Logistics. A quick Google search will identify hundreds of language programs in Central America and beyond. In Panama, Habla Ya (www.hablayapanama.com) hosts a Spanish course coupled with surfing the gentle breaks of Bocas del Toro. You'll also get to live with a local host family, which is a great way to practice the language and get to know the culture. You can also stay at a budget hostel, boutique hotel, bed-and-breakfast, or full-deluxe hotel.

Best Time. If you're combining a language course with a sport, the latter will dictate the season.

Pit Stop. Take a week for a Spanish-immersion course, and then once home, you can use it if you have the opportunity.

Extended Play. Learn a language and a new sport. Check out Panama, Costa Rica, or Belize for language immersion paired dive, surf, or kayak camps. Central America has an abundance of language schools and sports camps. Think about taking a course specific to your profession: health care workers can take medical Spanish, for example.

Travel Smart. Learning something new can be daunting. But buckle your bootstraps (or bike shoes or surf booties) and set your mind to it. Make sure you choose a reputable school. You can ask for references from a past students.

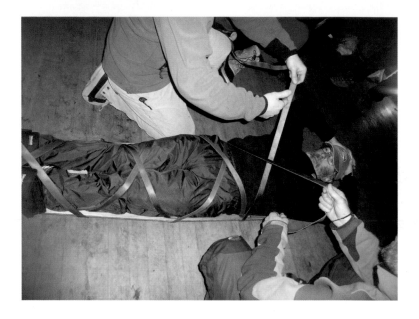

Accidents occur even when you're doing everything right. You can slip on a rock and fall, or be in the wrong place when an ice serac collapses or a rock peels off a cliff. So if you spend time in the backcountry, it's smart to be armed with basic medical skills.

For the bare basics, you can take "Wilderness First Aid," a 1- or 2-day course that covers splinting and wound care basics. For those with time, "Advanced Wilderness First Aid" is a robust course that usually lasts a weekend.

Either class should cover basic life support, which includes CPR and use of a defibrilator. Depending on which class you take, certification needs to be renewed every year or 2.

Wilderness First Responder (WFR), or "woofer" is a 70-hour course geared primarily for guides, rangers, search-and-rescue folks, and travelers to remote areas. In addition to basic life support (CPR and AED use), wound care, and splinting, the class teaches avoidance and field treatment of hypothermia, frostbite, heat exhaustion, and acute mountain sickness. The WFR course also includes instruction on emergency improvised splints made from ski poles, tree branches, and tent stakes—extremely valuable skills for the adrenaline junkie. You'll also learn how to build improvised stretchers.

Don't Miss. Take a course in your area if it's offered. They don't come around that often.

Logistics. Many of the national schools have classes all over the country. Check out Wilderness Medicine Institute (www.nols.edu/wmi), Wilderness Medicine Associates (www.wildmed.com), Remote Medical International (www.remotemedical.com), and Wilderness Medicine Outfitters (wildernessmedicine.com).

Best time. Take a course now, before you need the skills. Hopefully, you'll never need to use them.

Extended Play. If you're interested in a career in wilderness medicine, you can check out Wilderness Emergency Medicine Technician (WEMT): 180-hours of field practicum and coursework prepares you for a professional career in firefighting, ambulance response, and backcountry rescue. You may also want to consider these courses:

- Wilderness Survival: in case you need to spend the unexpected night in the outdoors
- Navigation: GPS, map, and compass skills will help you find your way in a whiteout

Travel Smart. Take a course, keep certifications current, and practice often. You may never need to use any of the skills. Also, make sure to carry first aid, survival, and repair kits with you on all expeditions.

The open ocean is a wilderness unto itself. Sailors earn special respect for navigating the sea.

You don't necessarily have to own a boat to become a sailor. The world's seas are open if you rent a boat. You can also just cruise in your local lake!

Don't Miss. Take a class as soon as you can. You'll learn lifelong adventuring skills.

Logistics. Take a course through a local sailing club, community college, or community education program. You can search U.S. Sailing (home.ussailing.org) for opportunities in your area.

Best Time. Pick a summer class when wind is light and the water is warm . . . in case you capsize! If you can, learn in the confines of a lake or bay.

Pit Stop. To learn the basics on a small dinghy, you'll only need a week.

Extended Play. Once you learn to sail a bigger boat, the world is open to you. Once you've built up a sailing résumé, you can charter boats from yacht clubs around the world. Multihull catamarans and trimarans are stable and spacious; they're especially popular in the Caribbean. Check out The Moorings (www.moorings.com), a company that allows you to buy shares in a yacht, charter a bareboat, or book a skippered sailboat if you want some support. You'll have to develop a sailing résumé if you want to rent a bareboat (one without a skipper or crew).

Travel Smart. Whether you're in the open ocean or inland lakes, be careful. Carry a personal-flotation device, make sure you have basic knowledge of water rescue, and carry emergency gear (raft, marine-frequency radio, and spare food and water). Stay within your sailing skills and don't be afraid to seek safe harbor if the wind and water become rough. It's good to have a backup motor or paddle if the wind dies down.

91. LEARN TO FLY

Flight is one of the most valuable and unique inventions of the modern world. Ever since Orville and Wilbur Wright successfully sustained flight for 12 seconds in 1903, air travel has been part of our reality. This 12-second flight launched us into the stratosphere.

If you get thrills from the air, a great place to start is with hang gliding or paragliding. A paraglide can pack into a 30-pound kit, easy to store in a trunk or check on an airplane so you can soar among the mountains and deserts.

Don't Miss. If you live near a flight school, which most people do, book a class.

Logistics. Start with the United States Hang Gliding Association, sanctioned by the Federal Aviation Administration to regulate hang gliding and paragliding. It takes about 7 to 10 days or 25 flights to become a proficient novice.

Best Time. It's best to schedule flights during clear weather. Although some stretch their 10 hours out over several months, it's best to block off a few weeks in the summer or fall and get 'er done.

Pit Stop. If you don't have time for a course, go tandem. Try a tandem jump while you're in Chamonix or Queenstown.

Extended Play. Why stop at small crafts? Learn to fly a plane. You can take a course sanctioned by the Federal Aviation Administration or an equivalent. It takes at least 40 hours of flight time plus classroom time, which covers aviation law, meteorology, and flight rules, to get certified pilot license in the United States. Then the skies are open to you. You don't have to own a plane. Many local airports rent out small planes.

Travel Smart. Find a reputable school. Go in good weather. Take your time. If you're paragliding or hang gliding, carry a parachute for backup.

VOLUNTEER

EVERY ONE of us has needed help at one point or another in our travels. Maybe you've gotten advice from a climbing ranger or avalanche forecaster before a ski tour or mountain climb. Perhaps you've needed medical assistance or evacuation from a ski patrol or search and rescue team.

So, why volunteer? Sometimes it's good to pay back karma. It also gives back to the community, be that regional or global, and helps those in need. And, volunteering is a great way to explore a country, meet new people, and combine your passion for sports with good deeds.

Whether you have expertise in medicine, engineering, meteorology, or trail building … or you're just good at rolling up your sleeves, here are the best ways to help. Get dirty.

We all use trails, but someone has to maintain them. Many trail routes are maintained by volunteers, even some of the state, provincial, and national park trails.

Every year, trails need to be refurbished, stray logs removed, switchbacks rebuilt, water damage repaired, and signs reposted. There is actually a science to properly building and repairing trails. Many of us have dropped into a descent on a mountain bike and experienced what a good trail can yield—those smooth, swooping high-speed turns. If they're done properly, they can be magical.

Don't Miss. If you get a chance to volunteer for a few hours, do it.

Logistics. Find a trail crew through your local hiking, running, or biking club. Rails-to-Trails is an organization that builds trails on old railroad tracks (www.railstotrails.org). Check out the International Mountain Bicycling Association for trail-building advice (www.imba.com/resources/trail-building).

Best time. Spring through fall is prime building and reparation time.

Pit Stop. If you don't have time to volunteer, float some cash to your local group.

Extended Play. Build a trail from scratch. It's a big undertaking. so make sure you coordinate with local trail builders, clubs, and the public agency that owns the land.

Travel Smart. Do your homework. Get permission from the landowner, and build the trail correctly.

 ## 93. *JOIN SEARCH AND RESCUE*

Getting hurt is every adrenaline junkie's nightmare. But it happens. It's inevitable. And who comes to help? Volunteers. My group, the Hood River Crag Rats, in Oregon is the oldest mountain rescue group in the country.

Nearly every community in an outdoor recreation area has need for volunteers.

Search-and-rescue (SAR) teams are usually made up of climbers, bikers, ski patrollers, ski instructors, guides, and other adrenaline junkies. Who else is willing to get out of bed at 2 a.m., climb into ski gear, and head into a midwinter mountain storm? Who has the expertise to set up a swiftwater rescue? We are the ones who want to help our friends and colleagues when they get hurt or lost. Who better to make up a SAR team than those of us living and breathing the outdoors? We climb, ski, hike, paddle, mountain bike, road bike, and trail run all the time.

So what does it take? Nearly every state has volunteer search-and-rescue groups. Most run through county sheriff's offices.

The requirements for every team are different; many just require CPR training, a first-aid course, a background check, and a desire to help. Some have specialty requirements like high angle, avalanche, crevasse, swiftwater, and dive rescue. Just know that you'll be on call 24/7.

Don't Miss. If you have the skills, help in swiftwater, dive, crevasse, cave, avalanche, or rope rescue. No medical or technical outdoor skills? No problem. Work as a telecommunication volunteer. You'll serve as a radio relay in emergency situations. Or just schlep gear up the trail (done it, many times). In whatever capacity you decide to volunteer, your work will be necessary and appreciated.

Logistics. Find a team in your region and ask about volunteering, or check out one of the national groups. The 2 primary organizations for volunteering are the Mountain Rescue Association (www.mra.org) and National Association for Search and Rescue (www.nasar.org). You can also contact your county sheriff's office or local fire rescue team.

Best Time. The mountains don't care. Neither do the rivers, forests, and oceans of the world. You'll be on call 24/7. Be prepared in all seasons, any terrain, and any weather.

Pit Stop. If you don't have time for a full commitment, consider volunteering with adjunct tasks. Or just donate some cash.

Extended Play. If you really get into it, you can get certified for special teams: Technical High Angle, Dive, Swiftwater, Avalanche, and Crevasse. There are many companies that provide training.

- For rope rescue, check out Rescue 3 International (www.rescue3international.com) or CMC rescue (www.cmcrescue.com).
- For swiftwater rescue, look into PRI Rescue Specialists (www.swiftwater-rescue.com), American Canoe Association (www.americancanoe.org), and U.S. National Whitewater Center (usnwc.org).
- For avalanche rescue, see the American Institute for Avalanche Research and Education (avtraining.org), Canadian Avalanche Centre (www.avalanche.ca), or All Over Europe (www.chamex.com).
- For crevasse rescue, look at Rainier Mountaineering (www.rmiguides.com), Revelstoke Ski Touring in Canada (revelstokeskitouring.com), or Chamonix, France (www.chamex.com).,

Travel Smart. If you join a team, it doesn't mean you have to do every rescue or jump into a dangerous technical situation if you aren't trained. Stay within your skill level and follow the mantra of search and rescue: self first, team second, patients third.

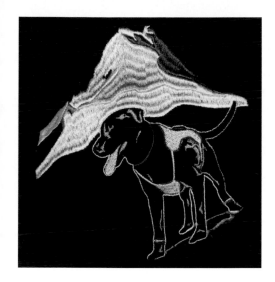

94. TRAIN A SEARCH DOG

They are so cute as puppies, but training a search dog is a commitment. It is time-consuming, costly, and takes discipline. Very few have the patience for this rare and indispensible service. Canines are some of the most valuable rescuers for wilderness, avalanche, and disaster searches. So good trainers are needed! A good dog can save hundreds of searching hours.

Saint Bernards have long been SAR dogs. The Italian and Swiss work dogs were bred for pulling dairy carts as well as injured travelers. In 1707 the monks of the Great St. Bernard Pass were the first to use these dogs for mountain rescue of travelers who got lost. Now herding dogs like German Shepherds and Border Collies, and as well as sporting dogs like Golden and Labrador Retrievers join the ranks with Saint Bernards. These dogs must be even-tempered, trainable, intelligent, agile, and fit.

Keep in mind you will spend a year or more training a dog. You must bond!

Don't Miss. Check in with your local ski resort, avalanche forecast center, or search-and-rescue group to see if there is need for search dogs in your area.

Logistics. Join a local dog group. Find complete lists of search-and-rescue teams at the National Association of Search and Rescue (www.nasar.org) and the Mountain Rescue Association (www.mra .org), the former has a canine-tracking division, which also provides certification. The American Rescue Dog Association (ardainc. org) has complete information on standards and training.

Best Time. Pick 1 year, or 3.

Pit Stop. Don't have time, temperament, or funds? Donate to your local search-dog group.

Extended Play. Start with a puppy, and go from there. They can start searching at 1 year, but will take several to train fully. Teach them avalanche rescue if you live near the mountains.

Travel Smart. Get professional help training your dog. Not all dogs are fit for SAR training so pay attention to how training progresses. You may just have to adopt a snuggly new family member.

95. *SKI PATROL FOR A SEASON*

Ski patrol. Try it for a season, a month, or just a few days. Maybe you'll find a career.

You don't have to patrol at a big mountain. There are over 400 winter resorts in the United States and another 100 in Canada. In the United States, many small winter resorts use volunteers from the National Ski Patrol (www.nsp.org). The organization educates and certifies many of those responsible for safety on the slopes. National Ski Patrol formed in 1938, after Roger Langley organized a team at Mt. Mansfield in Stowe, Vermont. It's now 26,000 members strong.

Don't Miss. If you have a chance, volunteer for a season at your local hill. Sure, you'll be lugging toboggans instead of making turns on some days, but you'll become embedded in local ski culture, meet lifelong friends, and become part of an elite tribe. Who knows . . . you may quit your job and join the ranks of big mountain pro patrollers?

Logistics. If you don't have an advanced degree in medicine, you can take Outdoor Emergency Care, which preps you for first aid on the mountain. Then you'll need to do a practicum, learning how to evacuate chairlifts and bring injured skiers and snowboarders down the mountain in a toboggan.

Best Time. Ski patrollers start training early so look for a job in the spring. The real work is done during the winter season.

Pit Stop. Short on time or no stomach for ER on the slopes? You can still volunteer. You can be a mountain host and provide tours or help out without providing medical care. Try Nordic Patrol, which covers cross-country skiing. It's a great way to help out on weekends and cross-country skiers usually have more minor injuries. You can also become a ski instructor, work at mountain clinic if you're a doc or nurse, or even drive a Pisten Bully snowcat groomer.

Extended Play. Quit your job. Sell the house, boat, and RV, and move to a mountain town. Go first, then find a way to make a living—it's a big risk, but it worked for me.

Travel Smart. Take a course in Outdoor Emergency Care, and always know your limits. Remember, it's okay to ask for help. And take care of yourself first. An injured rescuer can't rescue an injured person.

Roll up your sleeves and get dirty. Go work in a park.

With hundreds of national, state, county, and provincial parks, there's abundant opportunity to help for a few weeks or a whole season. If you have particular skills, you may get a job teaching or working as a naturalist in a visitor center. If you're strong, you may be out hammering a trail. Got a good smile and *mucho* patience with tourist types, work as a campground host. If you're more bookish, consider a resource management position, like removing invasive species, monitoring water quality, or replanting native plants.

You don't have to make a full summer commitment. Sign up for 1 week or 2 at your local park. Go for a month and live in the park if you can swing it.

Want to go all the way? Check out the adrenaline junkie's dream job: backcountry patrol. Sign up for Denali National Park Volunteer Ranger Patrol to assist the Denali Mountaineering Rangers and the medical camp at 14,000 feet (4,300 m) (www.nps.gov/dena).

Don't Miss. Book a week at a park you've never been to.

Logistics. Start your search with the National Park Service (www.nps.gov/getinvolved/volunteer.htm) or Parks Canada (www

.pc.gc.ca/eng/agen/vol-ben/index.aspx) You can also look for a state or provincial park opportunity. There's a good chance a county park near your home needs volunteers.

Best Time. Most parks need help year-round. Summer is visitor season and much of the maintenance takes place during spring and fall.

Pit Stop. Go for 1 week or 2 and stay close to home.

Extended Play. Take a sabbatical and go all summer!

Travel Smart. Know exactly what you're signing up for. Your expectations may be different from reality. Make sure you know the emergency procedures including emergency medical systems and law enforcement protocol. Hopefully, you won't need, either. And remember to be patient with visitors!

☑ 97. *JOIN A MEDICAL RELIEF TEAM*

Adrenaline junkies are always seeking out new challenges. We usually happen to be organized pros at maintaining gear and experts at logistical planning. We are a great blend of organized Type A behavior and thrill-seeking personality. It's in our nature to push out of the comfort zone and buckle down and help. So why not head to an adventure-filled country . . . and help!

I spent a few weeks volunteering with Medical Student Missions (medicalstudentmissions.org) in Haiti, an organization my friend started that focuses both on helping the people of Haiti and educating those interested in global health careers. Another friend founded Waves of Health (www.thewavesofhealth.org) through which surfers bring medical help to rural underserved countries.

There are many opportunities that combine volunteering and adventure fun. Do your research.

Don't Miss. Ask for help. You may be able to get financial aid from your community, church, or employer to offset the cost of your trip or buy medical supplies, books, educational materials, and clothing. You'll find that many people are willing to donate supplies as well.

Logistics. Many groups have organized trips that include airfare, food, lodging, transportation, and security.

Best Time. Winter usually has the mildest weather and fewest mosquitoes in the tropics. If you're combining relief efforts with a particular sport, check out the best season for the latter.

Pit Stop. You can easily volunteer for just a week.

Extended Play. Spend some time and do some good, whatever your skills. Consider allocating 1 week to work and another to play. If you head to Haiti, you can catch a commuter flight to the Dominican Republic for a kitesurfing expedition. In Central America, combine a week volunteering with some downtime surfing, diving, kayaking, or trekking. If in Africa, bag a trifecta: hit up a safari (Trip #68), climb Kilimanjaro (Trip #73), and raft the Zambezi River (Trip #67).

Travel Smart. Many medical-relief programs are based in politically unstable or impoverished countries. Be prepared to evacuate if necessary. Make sure you have good travel and evacuation insurance. Make a list of emergency contacts that includes in-country medical clinics and information for your nation's embassy. Traveling inconspicuously is vital; this is not the time for flashy sports attire, high-tech sunglasses, or loads of gear. Take your gear in nondescript duffels, especially kitesurfing and dive equipment.

98. BUILD A HOUSE

There are 9 million people in the colorful Andean country of Bolivia, nearly half without adequate water, sewage, or housing. Habitat for Humanity has set out to change the situation in Bolivia and many other developing countries around the world. The organization was founded in 1976 and has since facilitated in the building of 500,000 homes for 2 million people worldwide. Consider volunteering with Habitat for Humanity. You'll get to travel, help others, and work with your hands.

Don't Miss. If you make it to Bolivia, spend a few days in the culturally rich city of La Paz.

Logistics. Habitat for Humanity will help with trip logistics (www.habitat.org).

Best Time. There's no bad time to help build a house.

Pit Stop. If you don't have time to travel abroad, consider helping right in your backyard. The 10th Mountain Division Huts (Trip #18) regularly use volunteers to rebuild and repair their huts.

Extended Play. If you go to Bolivia, climb the volcanoes or zip over to Peru's famous Sacred Valley and hike to Machu Picchu.

Travel Smart. Building a house is hard work, but Habitat for Humanity has it down to a science. Show up, do the work, and don't get injured.

 ## 99. *REMOVE A FENCE*

You've read about Patagonia. It's one of the most beautiful places on Earth. But why go there as a volunteer?

In 2000, Kris Tompkins bought a tract of land in Patagonia and assembled a team of wildlife biologists, animal trackers, species restoration specialists, architects, landscapers, carpenters, teachers, and chefs. She founded Conservacion Patagonica in hopes of creating Patagonia National Park in southern Chile and Argentina. Volunteer there to help restore native species and remove parasites. Plant trees. Teach children. Remove fences. All in one of the most scenic places on Earth.

Be ready to roll up your sleeves and help.

Don't Miss. Hike or run the Lagunas Altas trails, take a dip in one of the alpine lakes, check out the Aviles Valley and Lago Pepa, raft the Baker River, or fly-fish the Aysen River. There's a month's worth of adventure here.

Logistics. Fly to Santiago, Chile. Then take a commuter flight to Balmaceda. From there, catch a bus or drive (if you can deal with the steep cliffs and potholes) to Coyhaique. The park headquarters are located in Valle Chacabuco. You can stay at the ecolodge or camp at Los Alamos where there are bathrooms and a cook shelter. The nearby town of Cochrane has hotels, inns, and cabins.

Best Time. Go during the South American summer—November through January.

Pit Stop. If you don't have time for this kind of trip, you can still help with conservation. Check out the Surfrider Foundation (www .surfrider.org), Leave No Trace (www.lnt.org), or the many other conservation groups you can find on the Web.

Extended Play. Conduct scientific research abroad. The Galápagos (Trip #42) and Antarctica (Trip #84) are prime locations for this kind of study.

Travel Smart. Volunteering can be physically taxing. Try to avoid injury, even minor cuts and scrapes, because they can turn into infections. Ask your doctor about emergency antibiotics before you go. Make sure to clean all cuts, and stay up-to-date on tetanus shots.

100. WORK OVERSEAS

If you've ever had the chance to live and work overseas, you know that it can be transformative. You morph from traveler, guest, or athlete, into an integral part of a community.

Whether you go as a professional—like a teacher, doctor, or nurse—or you get a night job washing dishes, it's well worth it. This is also a great way to test out a career shift, take a sabbatical, or try a professional exchange.

Rent out your house, put your bills on autopay, sell the boat or RV, and perhaps even ditch your car—you can always get another one when you get home.

Don't Miss. If you're young and mobile, try this before you get locked into house payments, a family with kids, or an inflexible career. If you're already entrenched in a career, see if your company has a sabbatical policy or visiting professional program. And take your kids before they are entrenched in high school!

Logistics. Scope out every possible angle. Look for a professional enrichment grant. If you're in the medical field, look at companies such as Global Medical Staffing (www.gmedical.com).

Best Time. It doesn't matter. Whether you are young or mid-career, go now.

Pit Stop. You may be able to work overseas for just a few weeks or a season. My ski patrol friends often do exchanges with patrols abroad to learn how their counterparts around the world function. I have another ski-lift maintenance friend who traveled to Europe for 2 weeks on a program to investigate ski-lift operations. Start digging around for opportunities in your field.

Extended Play. Go for a year and take the whole family.

Travel Smart. Take your time to research a job, arrange housing, and figure out transportation. Many agencies will help with logistics. Before you leave, put all bills on autopay and rent or sublease your house or apartment. If you're worried about renters trashing the fine china, sell it on eBay and use the cash for plane tickets!

A FINAL NOTE

JUST BACK from a surf and stand up paddle trip to Mexico with a great crew of friends, and I am off again as I finish up the last of the copy edit with a great crew of publishing professionals. I'm headed to Kilimanjaro to climb and teach, to France to cycle, to The Netherlands for a meeting of the International Society of Travel Medicine (www.istm.org), and then back to Haiti for another week of medical relief with doctors, medical students, and my daughter. I'm fortunate to have built a life and career around big adventures.

I hope I have inspired and motivated you to tackle a trip. If you are a novice traveler, your first big trip will be fraught with hard work, some unexpectations, and perhaps less than ideal weather or waves. But you're sure to get some thrills, fabulous scenery, and great food! Don't be afraid to book a guide! If you are a seasoned adventurer, then find a new spot or a new sport to explore by reading these pages.

If you find a cool spot I've excluded, and you want to share the beta, let me know. I'm always looking for my next set of 100 adventures.

Safe travels,
Christopher Van Tilburg
Sayulita, Mexico, November 2012
Christophervantilburg.com
www.facebook.com/christophervantilburgmd

APPENDIX A

MY FAVORITE GEAR

I love lists. I have lots of them. They help me avoid forgetting anything crucial. Lists are especially useful for prepping the day before an all-night flight to ski in Chile or climb in Africa. Although I try not to pack the day before I leave.

As a rule, when I return, I unpack promptly. I wash and repair gear and replace anything damaged or worn. That way everything is ready for the next trip. It would be a bummer to pull something out of a bin in the garage only to remember it's broken just a few days before a big trip.

This is a comprehensive packing list. I don't take everything on this list every time I go on a trip, but this is always a helpful reference.

FOOTWEAR
- Travel boots
- Running shoes
- Flip-flops or river sandals
- Hiking shoes or boots
- Mountaineering boots

TRAVEL AND SUN CLOTHING
- Cotton pants for the airplane and urban pit stops
- Cotton shorts
- Cotton button-up shirt, 1 to 3
- Cotton T-shirts, 1 to 3
- Cotton boxers or underwear, 4 to 5
- Synthetic/wool-blend socks, 4 to 5
- Nylon trail pants
- Nylon trail shorts
- Polyester T-shirts, 1 to 3

- Synthetic boxers or underwear
- Nylon long-sleeve insect/sun shirt
- Cap
- Midweight fleece
- Lightweight rain jacket
- Travel sheet
- Small travel towel

MOUNTAIN CLOTHING

- Polyester long underwear tops and bottoms
- Ski socks
- Soft-shell mountain pants
- Midweight full-zip fleece sweaters
- PrimaLoft insulated puffy jacket
- Down parka
- Waterproof, nylon Gore-Tex jacket and pants
- Fleece or wool hat
- Lightweight gloves
- Warm bulky gloves
- Neck gaiter

FIRST AID KIT

- First aid tape
- Self-adhering elastic bandage
- Blister bandage
- Wound closure strips with benzoin glue (aka butterfly bandages)
- Gloves and pocket CPR mask
- Ibuprofen and acetaminophen (Tylenol)
- Loperamide (Imodium)
- Pepto-Bismol
- Diphenhydramine (Benadryl)
- Antibiotics such as Ciprofloxacin for travelers' diarrhea and Azithromycin for respiratory, ear, and skin infections and travelers' diarrhea
- Specialty medicines for malaria (Malarone) and altitude illness (Acetazolamide)
- A full medical kit for big trips

PERSONAL GEAR

- Passport, cash, credit card, debit card

- Paperback book
- Small headlight with batteries
- Sunglasses with interchangeable lenses
- Map, compass, and GPS
- Chemical heat packs
- Whistle
- Multi-tool, SwissTool, or a Leatherman Juice
- Small repair kit: duct tape, Perlon cord, safety pins, plastic cable ties, polyurethane straps
- Ziploc bags: lots!
- Large garbage bags to line duffels to prevent gear getting wet
- Hand sanitizer
- Travel wipes
- Sunscreen, at least SPF 25 with lip balm
- Insect repellent
- Water purification tablets
- Water bottle; 1 to 2 bottles, 1 rigid and 1 collapsible
- Small notebook with pen

ELECTRONICS
- Notebook computer and charger
- Phone and charger
- Camera, spare battery, or charger, and memory card
- Plug converter

BACKCOUNTRY GEAR
- Pack, size varies depending on the trip, usually 25 to 50 liters
- Sleeping bag
- Sleeping pad
- Single-person or group tent
- Small Isobutane or propane stove (sometimes propane canisters can be easier to find than Isobutane) with matches and lighter
- Pot, bowl, spoon, pot holder
- Instant coffee

SKI MOUNTAINEERING GEAR
- Avalanche airbag backpack
- Mountaineering (randonee) skis with mountaineering bindings, climbing skins, and ski crampons
- Mountaineering (randonee) ski boots
- Adjustable ski poles

- Avalanche beacon, probe, and shovel
- Full-frame boot crampons
- Ice ax
- Climbing harness
- Ski mountaineering or climbing helmet
- Goggles

BIKES

- Bike, either road, mountain or cyclo-cross, depending on the trip; packed in a cardboard bike box for airline or train travel
- Bike shoes, sunglasses, and helmet
- Clothing kit including gloves, arm warmers, leg warmers, socks, jersey, bibs, hat

WATER GEAR

- Rash guard, short or long sleeve
- Board shorts
- Spring wetsuit, 2 mm short sleeve
- Winter wetsuit, 5mm long sleeve
- Neoprene booties, hood, and gloves
- Personal flotation device
- Water-specific helmet
- River sandals

LUGGAGE

- Hydration pack, depending on a trip this is usually a 10-liter pack with a 3-liter water bladder
- Wheeled carry-on, which gets me around the world without checking a bag unless I need to bring a lot of gear
- Waterproof duffel with backpack straps
- Ski bag with wheels for traipsing through airports

APPENDIX B

MY FAVORITE BOOKS
You can find loads of information on the Internet, but for those who live without power 24/7 or relish the opportunity to page though a collected volume, here are a few comprehensive guidebooks that you may want to peruse.

Guidebooks

Colas, Anthony. *The World Stormrider Guide*. Cornwall, United Kingdom: Low Pressure Ltd., 2001.

Davenport, Chris, Art Burrows, and Penn Newhard. *Fifty Classic Ski Descents of North America*. Aspen, Colorado: Capitol Peak, 2012.

Davenport, Chris, and Art Burrows. *Ski the 14ers*. Aspen, Colorado: Capitol Peak, 2007.

Dawson, Louis W. *Wild Snow: A Historical Guide to North American Ski Mountaineering*. Evergreen, CO: American Alpine Club Press, 1998.

Hamill, Mike. *Climbing the Seven Summits*. Seattle: The Mountaineers Books, 2012.

Hanan, Ali (ed.). *The Snowboard Guide to North America*. Cornwall, United Kingdom: Low Pressure Ltd., 1997.

Potterfield, Peter. *Classic Hikes of the World: 23 Breathtaking Treks*. Seattle: Mountaineers Books, 2005.

Roper, Steve, and Allen Steck. *Fifty Classic Climbs of North America*. Berkeley: Sierra Club Books, 1996.

Sorrell, Rowan, Chris Moran, and Ben Mondy. *Mountain Biking Europe: Tread Your Own Path*. United Kingdom: Footprint Handbooks, 2008.

Adventure Narratives
You can find lists of the classic adventure narratives all over the place.
Here are a few favorites specific to the trips in this book:

Abbey, Edward. *Desert Solitaire: A Season in the Wilderness.* New York: McGraw-Hill, 1968.

Ibid. *The Monkey Wrench Gang.* New York: Harper, 1975.

Barcott, Bruce. *The Measure of a Mountain: Beauty and Terror on Mount Rainier.* Seattle: Sasquatch, 1997.

Bass, Dick, Frank Wells, and Rick Ridgeway. *Seven Summits.* New York: Grand Central, 1988.

Bowers, Vivien. *In the Path of an Avalanche.* Vancouver: Greystone, 2003.

Brown, Dee. Bury *My Heart at Wounded Knee, The Illustrated Edition: An Indian History of the American West.* New York: Pocket, 1983.

Cahill, Tim. *Road Fever.* New York: Vintage, 1992.

Callahan, Steven. *Adrift: Seventy-six Days Lost at Sea.* New York: Haughton Mifflin, 1986.

Clifford, Hal. *The Falling Season: Inside the Life and Death Drama of Aspen's Mountain Rescue Team.* New York: HarperCollins, 1995.

Cody, Robin. *Voyage of a Summer Sun: Canoeing the Columbia River.* New York: Knopf, 1996.

Darwin, Charles. *On the Origin of Species* (1859) and *The Voyage of the Beagle* (1839).

Duane, Daniel. *Caught Inside: A Surfer's Year on the California Coast.* New York: North Point Press, 1996.

Duncan, David James. *The River Why.* San Francisco: Sierra Club, 1983.

Fletcher, Colin: *The Man who Walked Through Time: The Story of the First Trip Afoot Through the Grand Canyon.* New York: Random House, 1959.

Hansen, Eric. *Motoring with Mohammed: Journeys to Yemen and the Red Sea.* New York: Houghton Mifflin, 1991.

Ibid. *Stranger in the Forest: On Foot Across Borneo.* New York: Vintage, 2000.

Harrer, Heinrich. *Seven Years in Tibet.* New York: Book Society, 1954.

Heyerdahl, Thor. *Kon-Tiki: Across the Pacific by Raft.* Cutchogue, NY: Buccaneer Books, 1950.

Hornbein, Thomas. *Everest: The West Ridge.* Seattle: Mountaineers Books, 1980.

Jenkins, McKay. *The White Death: Tragedy and Heroism in an Avalanche Zone*. New York: Random House, 2000.

Jenkins, Mark. *The Hard Way: Stories of Danger, Survival, and the Soul of Adventure*. New York: Simon & Schuster, 2003.

Junger, Sebastian. *The Perfect Storm: A True Story of Men Against the Sea*. New York: Norton, 1997.

Krakauer, Jon. *Eiger Dreams: Ventures Among Men and Mountains*. New York: Lyons & Burford, 1990.

Lansing, Alfred. *Endurance: Shackleton's Incredible Voyage*. New York: Carroll and Graf, 1959.

Maclean, Norman. *A River Runs Though It*. Chicago: University of Chicago Press, 1989.

Matthiessen, Peter. *The Snow Leopard*. New York: Penguin, 1978.

Messner, Reinhold. *The Crystal Horizon: Everest—The First Solo Ascent*. Seattle: Mountaineers Books, 1998.

Muir, John. *My First Summer in the Sierra* (1911).

Raban, Jonathan. *Passage to Juneau: A Sea and Its Meanings*. New York: Pantheon, 1999.

Rawicz, Slavomir. *The Long Walk: The True Story of a Trek to Freedom*. New York: Lyons Press, 2010.

Roberts, David. *The Mountain of My Fear*. New York: Vanguard, 1968.

Roper, Steve, and Allen Steck (eds). *The Best of Ascent: Twenty-Five Years of the Mountaineering Experience*. San Francisco: Sierra Club Books, 1993.

Simpson, Joe. *Touching the Void: The True Story of One Man's Miraculous Survival*. New York: Harper & Row, 1989.

Stegner, Wallace. *Beyond the Hundredth Meridian: John Wesley Powell and the Second Opening of the West*. New York: Penguin, 1992.

Sutherland, Bruce, Drew Kampion, and Michael Kew. *The Stormrider Guide to North America*. Cornwall, United Kingdom: Low Pressure Ltd., 2002.

Todhunter, Andrew. *Fall of the Phantom Lord: Climbing and the Face of Fear*. New York: Anchor, 1998.

Waterman, Jonathan. *Kayaking the Vermilion Sea: Eight Hundred Miles Down the Baja*. New York: Touchstone, 1995.

Weisbecker, Allan. *In Search of Captain Zero: A Surfer's Road Trip Beyond the End of the Road*. New York: Tarcher/Putnam, 2001.

ACKNOWLEDGMENTS

A love of travel and adventure was gifted to me by Wayne and Eleanor Van Tilburg, married for fifty years and still traipsing the globe. My daughters, Skylar and Avrie Van Tilburg, are great travel partners: They've ventured to sunny Baja beaches and the high Chilean Andes, and slept in many campsites in a tent when the skies were pouring rain, puking snow, buffeting the walls with wind, or all 3. For constant support in a myriad of ways, thanks to Jennifer Sato, Peter Van Tilburg, Susan Rylander, and Joanne Van Tilburg.

For photographs, I thank friends, colleagues, and companies who have provided images.

- Ruth Berkowitz
- Jenni Bergemann
- Margie Bolstead
- Clint Bogard
- Kris Tompkins and Devon Jaffe-Urell at Conservacion Patagonicia (www.conservacionpatagonica.org)
- Michael Carnes
- Dana Cohen on behalf of the Costa Rica Tourism Board (www.visitcostarica.com).
- Mike Coo at Tour d'Afrique (www.tourdafrique.com)
- Jennifer Donnelly
- Jason Edwards (www.mountainguides.com)
- Clayton Everline (www.everlinemd.com)
- Mike and Jennifer FitzSimons
- Luanne Freer at Everest ER (www.everestER.com)
- Debbie Fuller at Slingshot Sports (www.slingshotsports.com)
- Marc Goddard at Bio Bio Expeditions (www.bbxrafting.com)
- Kellie Goodwin at Totally Tourism (www.totallytourism.co.nz)
- Michael Hamill (climbingthesevensummits.com)
- Michael Hauty

- Ryan Heath at G-Land Surf Camp (www.g-landsurfcamp
.com)
- Rupert Hill at Surf Simply (www.surfsimply.com)
- Ian Hylands (ianhylands.com)
- John Inglis
- David Mackintosh
- Karen Matthee and Anton Hafele at ExOfficio (www.exofficio
.com)
- Andrew McElderry
- Andrew Nathanson
- Sheryl Olson (www.wildernesswise.com)
- Courtenay Oswin at Quark Expeditions (www
.quarkexpeditions.com)
- Debra Peckrick at Bequ Lagoon Resort (www
.beqalagoonresort.com)
- Greg Soderlund at Western States 100 Endurance Run (www
.ws100.com)
- Doug Stoop and Karyn Stanley at Ice Axe Expeditions (www
.iceax.tv)
- Viki Tracey
- Kevin Trejo and Clark Merritt at SoloSports (www.solosports
.net)
- Patrick Alberts at World Triathlon Corporation (www
.ironman.com)
- Peter Van Tilburg
- Arthur Wayne Van Tilburg
- Chris Winter at Big Mountain Adventures (www.ridebig.com)
- AJ Wheeler
- Caleb Wray (www.calebwrayphotography.com)

My agent, Joelle Delbourgo, deserves a special note for being highly skilled at her craft and endlessly encouraging in the wild world of publishing.

Because I was so busy adventuring or dreaming of adventuring, I owe thanks to the expert crew at St. Martin's Press. I thank my editor, Nichole Argyres, and Assistant Editor Laura Chasen, who did a fabulous job at shaping the text and accommodating my travel schedule; and Production Editor David Stanford Burr, and Designers Patrice Sheridan and Kathryn Parise.

The equipment companies I work with are too numerous to list but I would have been in many a bind without good gear.

796
Va

5067460

Van Tilburg,
Christopher.

The adrenaline
junkie's bucket
list.

SEP 05 2013

$22.99

DATE			